NEVER WITHOUT LOVE

A MEMOIR BY

MEHRNAZ MASSOUDI

INANNA
Memoir Series

To Baba, who in spite of my imperfect body believed that only the Prince of Iran was good enough to be my husband.
To Maman, who made me believe that I, a woman living in Iran's male-dominated society, could be anything that I wanted to be.

1. Fire

IHAVE NEVER FORGOTTEN the magic of a summer evening in Tehran. After a hot day, when the sun went down, the coolness of the evening caressed our souls. Maman would pick jasmine flowers from the thick vines that clung to the walls of our courtyard. She laid them on a pounded tin dish, already laden with Persian tea, white mulberries, plump figs, and Persian melon. The smell of the jasmine, the cool dry air, and the delicious summer fruits fed my body and soul.

On one such evening, Baba and I were alone.

"Mehrnaz jan, there are so many suitors who want to come to ask for your hand. Why don't you allow them to come?"

"Suitors and their families judge women by their hips and the size of their breasts, Baba. I do not want to marry a man who comes here to judge my body. He doesn't know my soul. My chest is covered with scars. My breasts have deep scars. I do not have nipples. How can I allow suitors to come here?"

"You are beautiful. You are Baba's princess. You are smart. You are the dream of every man."

"Yes, until they see my naked chest."

"They don't need to see your naked chest. You can wear a beautiful nightgown and keep your chest covered during lovemaking."

"Baba, don't talk about this stuff. It's embarrassing. You don't understand. I want a man to fall in love with me. I want a man to touch my heart before he touches my body. I believe when a man falls in love with me he will not see my scars. If he loves me, he will love my imperfect breasts."

1

I was sixteen when Baba and I had this conversation. I saw myself then, and for many years afterwards, as a beauty with my clothes on, but as a beast when they were removed.

I had been placed on the dining room table. Looking up, all I could see was a doctor with giant hands talking to Baba. "There is an infection under her nipples. It's better if I cut them off."

I hated the doctor's big hands. They were half the size of my body. At the age of four, I didn't realize the impact this surgery would have on my life. Where did they throw my nipples? I wondered. In the kitchen garbage?

My brother Jamal and my sister Soraya loved to tease me and always ganged up on me. One morning, at breakfast, the two reached over, grabbed the two whole eggs that were in the basket on the table, and left the cracked egg for me. "Hahaha, you get the cracked one," Jamal snorted.

Jamal was ten, Soraya was eight, and I was four years old. I didn't like it when they tormented me.

"Mehrnaz, stop crying," Maman said, exasperated. "Homa, did you get the shoes from Ms. Mohammadi for me?"

Maman had gotten up that morning with swollen feet. Her shoes no longer fit her, so she had sent Homa to get her some shoes from Ms. Mohammadi, Maman's friend who had large feet. Maman was a teacher. She was getting ready to go to school.

"Mehrnaz, please stop crying," Maman said again. "It is only a cracked egg. Homa, make Mehrnaz a boiled egg, then get her ready and take her to school."

I loved going to school so I could stay with Maman in her classroom. And I was proud when a student from another classroom had come to ask Maman if I could be sent to the grade four classroom. The teacher of that classroom wanted me to demonstrate prayers to the class. I was happy to recite the prayers in front of the older children at school. I was very young to have memorized the prayers already, and the teachers and the principal always praised me for it. Muslims pray five times a day, and students are taught the prayers during religious study.

That day, when my brother and sister left for school, I stayed home with Homa and Fati. Fati was the new cook. She was grumpy, and she never left the kitchen. Since my egg was cracked, Homa was going to prepare another one for me—she did not want to ask Fati to cook it—and then she would take me to school afterwards.

Homa had come to our house as a servant to take care of me when I was born. At the time, we lived in Qazvin, an ancient capital of the Persian Empire, where Maman was from. When Maman was young, she had spent the summers with her parents in the mountainous village of Zavardasht in the Province of Qazvin. Zavardasht is located at a high elevation, and summer temperatures are cooler there than in Qazvin City.

The people of Zavardasht respected Maman, and they eagerly sent their children to our house to be our servants. Buses or cars could not reach the village—people travelled only on horses. As a seven-year-old girl, Homa had been tied onto a horse and sent to our house. Maman said that the horses were trained to do this. Homa's parents needed the money.

Homa prepared another egg for me on a heater. After I ate, she showed me how to blow out the fire from the top, instead of turning down the supply of oil to the heater. I tried to blow the fire out, but my face got hot.

Homa left to go and get something. I got a little closer to the heater to try again, but my nightgown caught fire. Homa ran into the room when she heard my screams. She tried to put out the fire, but it only got larger and more ferocious.

Baba's office was down the hall. He could hear me screaming, but at first he thought I was playing. Then he ran into the room and gasped when he saw me. I was a ball of fire. When Baba arrived, Homa ran away and hid. Baba quickly put out the fire. But by then, all the skin on my chest and arms was badly burned.

All my father's employees—my father worked in a government office next to our home—gathered around me. One of them suggested the old remedy of grinding a fresh onion and pouring it over the skin. I screamed even louder. Baba kept calling for Homa. He didn't know what had happened. I kept crying and saying, "It wasn't Homa's fault." I was afraid that my parents would send her back to her village. Homa was hiding in the attic. They found her later that night. I wanted Homa to sit by my side so no one would hit her or send her back.

I suffered third-degree burns all over my chest and arms. The family doctor told my parents that it was not necessary to send me to the hospital. He came to the house daily, placed me on the dining room table, and cut the dead skin off with a knife.

Maman could not bear to watch, but Baba stood next to me, while any men that happened to be visiting in the house held my hands and feet down while the doctor cut off my skin. I screamed.

Finally, after I had suffered from pain and fever for over a month and a half, my parents decided to take me to Tehran, where there were plastic surgeons and more advanced hospitals.

I spent two more months in the hospital in Tehran. My long curly hair had all been burned off, and I didn't like how I looked without it. So Maman knitted me an orange toque and bought me a black braided wig. She sewed the braid to the toque so it looked like I had long hair underneath it. Baba and Maman requested a big room for me, and Maman stayed with me the entire time. She slept in a recliner chair beside my bed, and they put a futon on the floor for Aunt Roohi.

My grandmother, Maman Aterahm, first met Roohi as a young girl. She went to the same school as my Aunt Masi, Maman's younger sister. Aunt Roohi's mother was a Russian immigrant and Roohi had a deformity in one of her legs. Roohi's mother shared her story with Maman Aterahm. She had emigrated from the Soviet Union with her two children. Her husband had sent them to Iran be safe and had planned to join them later, but he couldn't get out of the Soviet Union, and so he never came. Roohi's mother had to face the hardship of taking care of her two children on her own as well as go to work every day. On top of all that, her daughter's leg needed so much care. Maman Aterahm was so moved by the woman's plight that she took the little girl, Roohi, home.

Iran and the Soviet Union share a border. Armenia and Azerbaijan are northern neighbours of Iran. A mass of people had immigrated from the Soviet Union into Iran in the early twentieth century when hundreds of thousands had to flee from the Bolsheviks. Many refugees started their lives in Qazvin as well as in the two provinces in Northern Iran, Mazandaran, and Gilan. Maman Aterahm took the woman's daughter home and raised my Aunt Roohi as if she were her own daughter.

When I was in the hospital, Aunt Roohi was working at a government office in Tehran. Every day after work she came to the hospital, and at night she slept in my room on a futon next to my bed. My parents set up all my toys and tea sets on a Persian rug that they had laid next to her futon. Aunt Roohi read to me and played with me.

Maman was also in pain—her feet and hands were swollen—but she never left my bedside. It took the doctors a few years before they eventually concluded that she had rheumatoid arthritis. She suffered from chronic pain and joint deformation that only worsened as the years passed.

Her illness began the morning she sent Homa to borrow that pair of big shoes, about an hour before my accident. Although Maman and I had begun our journeys on the same day, we soon began to go down separate paths. Her pain seemed to abate in the evening, but it was extreme in the morning, and she suffered constantly. Our house by the Caspian Sea became a place for hosting guests and hosting dinner parties. These parties distracted Maman from her pain as she slowly disengaged emotionally from us children.

Baba's job required us to move every few years. He chose the cities in Northern Iran because they reminded him of growing up in Neshta. Orange groves, rice paddies, mild temperatures, and the beautiful Caspian Sea: this was home for Baba. These cities were a few hours away from my grandparents' house. "I want to stay with Aunt Masi. I don't want to come home," I would cry every time we left my grandparents' house.

Aunt Masi had a big selection of vinyl albums. She played music and taught me all kinds of dance moves, from Persian dance to the Cha Cha and the Twist. But her favourite music was Elvis Presley's. Aunt Masi and her friends looked like those girls in Elvis's movies. Once, she was really excited because she won a competition dancing to Elvis's music at a local club.

In the summertime, we slept in see-through nets on the flat rooftops. The stars were so big. I loved looking at the night sky and listening to Aunt Masi tell me stories. "What story do you want to hear tonight?" Aunt Masi would ask as we slipped under the covers at bedtime.

"The story of your friend. The friend with the burn scars."

"When she was a child, her whole body was covered with burn scars," Aunt Masi began. "Then when she turned eighteen, she went to England for plastic surgery. We didn't see her for a whole year. When she came back, she had a big party. She was wearing a beautiful sleeveless dress. After the party ended, a few of us stayed for a sleepover. We asked to see her body. The room was lit by moonlight. She took off her dress. She was beautiful—her long black hair hung down over her porcelain skin. She had beautiful breasts with no scars. Her body was flawless except for one strand of hair on the side. When I went to remove the hair, I discovered it wasn't a hair at all: it was the only scar left from the plastic surgery. Her other scars were all gone."

2: Baba's Childhood Story, as He Told It

WE SAT UNDER THE PISTACHIO TREES and counted how many pistachios we had picked. I soon stopped counting and started peeling off their smooth velvety pink-and-green skins. After peeling off each skin, I opened the shell, revealing the fresh pistachio inside. The children around me were still counting, but my thoughts began to drift away.

"I will ask my mother to buy me a velvet jacket the same colour as the pistachio skin," I thought to myself. "Every Persian Prince must have a green-red-and-pink velvet jacket."

The children began to play a game: one child would run away and hide a pile of pistachios and the rest of us would have to find it. Aunt Aterahm said that she would hide her wedding ring instead of pistachios. "Hedayat jan," she giggled mischeviously, "will you be able to find it?"

Just then Aunt Aterahm's mother-in-law arrived and asked what the children were looking for. When Aunt Aterahm admitted they were looking for her ring, her mother-in-law slapped her and made her retrieve her wedding ring immediately. She yanked Aunt Aterahm's arm and said, "You are not a child anymore; you are a married woman, and you must socialize only with adults now." Then she dragged her out of the garden.

Last week, Aunt Aterahm had been so pretty in her wedding dress, with her big green eyes and her silky brunette hair. "Hedayat jan, I won't be able to see you and play with you anymore," Aunt Aterahm told me, trying to hide the tears in her eyes. "I am being forced to move to my husband's family's house, so I won't be seeing much of you anymore."

We always played together when our relatives gathered. Aunt Aterahm was the oldest among us. She was my mother's sister. They had the same father, but different mothers. She was nine years old when she got married. I felt sorry that she would have to move away.

I hated my teacher, Abas agha. He taught my brothers and me math, reading, and writing. He was so mean, and he always carried a whip made of cherry wood. I told my mother about his beatings, and I begged her not to send us away with him, but it didn't do any good.

First, Abas agha would take us for a long walk in our orange grove and ask us questions about our previous lessons. He whipped us when we got the answers wrong. Then he would bring us back inside our house to teach us the new lessons he planned for the day.

Our property consisted of three houses: one for the family, one for the servants, and one where my father met and hosted officials. I was not allowed to eat with my father when he was having officials over. I had heard so much about how especially fancy meals were served to the officials, and it became my dream to be part of those dinners. But I had to pass my etiquette course before I would be allowed to participate in these official meals. I liked our etiquette teacher. When I passed, my mother was very proud of me. She fussed over me, calling me her handsome prince. She liked to do my hair after our servants dressed me up for lunch with the officials.

"You inherited my thick curly hair. I will use some water and oil to style your hair so it stays off your face," my mother said as she started running a comb through my tangles.

While Mother did my hair, I stared at her ruby-and-gold glass jewellery dish. She kept her golden crown, which was covered with rubies, emeralds, and diamonds, on the main plate. The smaller jewellery pieces were on smaller plates, and her necklaces hung on each side of the dish.

"Heda jan, I would like this crown to go to your daughter." Mother called me Heda, short for Hedayat. "I always dreamed

My paternal grandparents, Hormat Khalatbari and Masoud Almolk Massoudi.

of having a daughter, but God gave me five sons. You are my son and my daughter."

When it was time for the meal with the officials, I was too nervous to eat in their presence; my etiquette teacher was standing in the corner of the room observing me. We sat on the floor. Servants brought several dishes of fragrant stew and steaming rice and set them on the tablecloth. I had never seen such an arrangement of fancy dishes. I was halfway through my meal when the servants started collecting the plates and bringing water jugs and bins for rinsing our hands. I had left the best part of my meal to eat last.

I started crying silently. The etiquette teacher quickly came and removed me from the room.

Whenever my father was entertaining officials, Mother always watched from the window of a room that overlooked the entrance of the official house. She took me with her and made me promise not to say a word to my father. A group of entertainers came at night to entertain my father's guests. I overheard one of the

9

Sepahsalar Tonekabon Khalatbari, great-great-grandfather of Mehrnaz Massoudi.

servants say, "They are dressed like men, but they are all female dancers and entertainers." My nose and cheeks were plastered against that window. I could not take my eyes off the dancers. My mother was also enchanted.

I was trained to ride horses. On special days, I rode a horse to the village with my father. All the village people came to watch and wave. The Massoudi families were landowners in the Tonekabon Region in Northern Iran. Father was the eldest of his brothers, so he ran the family business.

Father was worried when the Reza Shah, the first king of the Pahlavi Dynasty, came into power in 1925. Father said that the king was a monarchist who would disempower the landowners in order to centralize his own power.

I did not understand what my father meant until one night when we were woken up and forced to leave our home in a hurry. Mother grabbed most of her jewellery, but there wasn't enough time to get much. Reza Shah had expropriated our home and land. We moved to a small rental house in the city of Qazvin, located northwest of Tehran, the capital of Iran.

I missed the orange grove, the cows, the horses, and the smell of the forest of Northern Iran. But I was happy to be in the same city as Aunt Aterahm, who was pregnant with her third child. Mother and Aunt Aterahm were very close. My father started working in an office, and he made a modest salary. Mother sold her golden crown and much of her jewellery. We needed the money.

"Heda, a relative of ours, is coming to visit. Her son is the same age as you. I think you two would get along."

Although Mother was having difficulty dealing with the sudden loss of our fortune, she liked to socialize with her old friends in the city. "Heda, take Farid and go play outside."

Farid and I ran out to the yard. But I was curious about what was going on inside. "Do you want to go back and play behind the door so we can listen in?" I asked Farid. He chuckled and nodded. So, we walked slowly back to the house and sat quietly behind the rug that separated the two rooms. Our mothers were deep in conversation.

"What are you two doing here?" Farid's mother cried out.

The rug had fallen from the ceiling, burying us underneath. Startled, we had both started crying. "Farid must like listening to the gossips too, then, just like Heda," Mother said, smiling.

But they were not gossiping. Mother was crying, and Farid's mother was soothing her. Mother was feeling terrible because my father had been targeted by Reza Shah.

My mother, Hormat Khalatbari, was the granddaughter of Sepahsalar Khalatbari, the leader of the constitutionalist revolutionary forces of Iran's northern provinces of Gilan and Mazandaran. He was one of the wealthiest noblemen in the region. Sepahsalar had fought against the religious clerics' attempts to create a theocracy, as well as the ruling establishment's attempts to continue a monarchy. He had made frequent visits to France to learn the French system of representative democracy. With the arrival of the Pahlavi Dynasty and the Reza Shah, Sepahsalar had come under increased political pressure. He was openly opposed to the Reza Shah dictatorship, which was externally controlled by the British. Consequently, most of his property was seized in order to control his wealth and his power; even worse, his favourite son, Colonel Ali Asghar Khan, was poisoned by the government. On July 16, 1926, at the age of eighty, Sepahsalar committed suicide.

Now my mother, the granddaughter of Sepahsalar, who had always been wealthy, was broke and dying of pneumonia.

I stayed by my mother. Farid also spent a lot of time sitting with me beside my mother's bed.

"Heda, I still have some jewellery that I haven't sold. Your father doesn't know. Your youngest brother is only two. Please take care of your brothers and sell my jewellery whenever you need money. Don't tell your father."

3. Maman Mahin's Story, as She Told It

I WAS PLAYING IN THE YARD with my brothers when I spotted my mother's face peering at us from behind a bush. She signalled for me to be quiet and to go to her. I had missed Mother so much since she had left. I ran to her, and she wrapped her arms around me and cried. Aunt Anise and Naneh JiJi were waiting in a chariot. "Hurry up, Aterahm!" they urged.

Mother carried me to the chariot, and the driver started galloping. I was frightened and started screaming; then I saw my brothers running after the chariot, also screaming, "Mother, please come back!"

The next day Mother told me that my father might send people to steal me. She told me that Sadr would protect me, and that I should always stay by him. Sadr was our butler.

As a four-year-old, I did not understand why either my mother or my father would steal me. It was years later that Naneh JiJi told me the story of my parents' divorce.

"Your mother was only nine years old when your grandfathers made an arranged marriage," she said. "Both your grandfathers were prominent landowners so it made perfect sense for their two families to join through marriage. Your mother had your oldest brother when she was only fourteen."

I was ten years old when Naneh JiJi shared this story with me. I wondered how could Mother be married at the age of nine. I also wondered why she took me away from my father.

"Your mother wanted a divorce from your father," Naneh JiJi explained. "But he loved her, so he was reluctant. She gave him all her belongings that she'd brought with her from her father's house, including ornate furniture, Persian rugs, and her jewellery, so he would agree to divorce her and let her keep you. She even agreed to leave your three brothers with your father. But then your father came and took you back, which was against his agreement with your mother. He really wanted your mother back—he loved her. Now, can you see why I came with your mother and your aunt to take you away?"

Shortly after our escape, Mother and Jafar, the son of a millionaire in Qazvin, fell in love. Jafar was younger than Mother and had never been married. His family was against their marriage because Mother was older than him and had children; but Mother and Jafar got married anyway. After she married Jafar, I became a ghost child for my mother. When visitors came, she left me with the servants. I wasn't even called into the room when aunts and uncles came to visit.

I missed my father and my brothers. My father managed to see me when I was going to school. Sadr would let my father talk to me, but he made me promise not to tell Mother.

"Father, please take me with you. I want to live with you. I miss you and my brothers," I pleaded with my father on one of our secret visits. But he declined. He told me that he had remarried and he had a daughter with his new wife; she was already taking care of my three brothers.

Then my mother gave birth to my baby sister, Masi, and the barrier came down. I loved Masi, and I wanted to carry her in my arms all the time. This also gave me a chance to spend some time with Mother. Mother's love for Masi made me yearn for her affection even more. I thought that if I loved Masi enough and took good care of her, then one day Mother would love me too.

Mother had a summer house in the mountainous village of Zavardasht. We drove part of the way there, but then the terrain became too steep and we had to switch to horses. It took us half a day to get there from Qazvin. This was where I lost myself to the mountain, the lake, and the people of Zavardasht. I had many friends in Zavardasht, but I was closest with Turahn, Sadr's daughter. I also had my own horse. Her name was Tala, which meant "gold."

My friends and I would meet at the lake for a swim in the

afternoon. The lake was the colour of turquoise; we could see our reflections. Everyone brought treats from their yard: sour cherries, hazelnuts, walnuts, and my most favourite, the *naan sarsheer*, cream bread. Turahn's mother's *naan sarsheer* was delicious. She carefully laid a thin layer of cream on a flat round clay dish, covered it with a cheese cloth, and then left it on the rooftop in the sun to dry. When it was ready to eat, it was like a thin flat bread, except it was made out of only cream and a pinch of salt.

The people of Zavardasht had a lot of respect for Mother. I wanted to be out of the house on my horse galloping around all day because that was the only time I was treated like the daughter of the people's beloved lady Aterahm Khalatbari. In the house, I was the unwanted, unloved daughter. Jafar agha, my mother's husband, did not treat me like a daughter. I always referred to him as *agha*, which means "Mister."

When I was fourteen, a friend of Mother's from Tehran opened the first preschool in Qazvin. Feri, the manager of the school, was in her twenties, and we became inseparable. I started working at the school with her and I was always eager to greet the children when they arrived at school. The anticipation of their smiles and hugs woke me up every morning.

Some time later, Jafar agha bought a blue 1944 Pontiac. It was the first car in Qazvin. I was quick to learn how to drive it. Jafar agha was very generous in allowing me to drive his car; very soon driving became my passion.

When I was a teenager, my friends had many *khastegars*, suitors. Traditionally, women would choose their future husband from among their suitors. The man's family would arrange to visit the woman's family to ask her parents for her hand. This is called the *khastegari*, and the suitor is the *khastegar*.

The *khastegars'* families were only interested in beautiful women from highly reputable families who had money. Divorce was rare in Iranian society, and the fact that Mother had left her husband made me less reputable. Further, I was being raised by a stepfather, and that too was frowned upon. There was one man that I was interested in: Mansour. He was handsome and I admired him, but I believe that his mother didn't find me suitable.

Maman asking the Shah of Iran for funding for building an orphanage in Qazvin, 1950s.

I was disappointed that he didn't come for my *khastegari*. After this, I focused all my attention into my public life.

Qazvin did not have an orphanage, and there were many destitute children. I began writing to the Shah, asking him to fund an orphanage; my letters were ignored. The Shah was a good man, but the people around him were corrupt.

When I was eighteen, I found out that the Shah was coming to visit Qazvin, so I wrote to the organizers and asked for a meeting with him. Although my letters still went unanswered, I was invited to his huge Qazvin reception because the organizers respected Mother. She was highly regarded in Qazvin and was involved with many charity organizations.

When the Shah of Iran passed us, I stepped out of the crowd and stood in front of him. Thankfully, he acknowledged me and pushed away the bodyguards as I presented him with a petition and copies of all the letters I had previously submitted to his government asking for funding for an orphanage in Qazvin. That day, the Shah wrote a cheque for me to establish and supervise the building of the orphanage.

My sister Masi's love for me made my life at home bearable. But I started thinking about getting married in order to escape my home.

Aunt Tajmah started visiting us more often with my cousin Hedayat. They usually came to see us on Fridays, which was the only day that government offices were closed. She was trying to find a wife for him. I suggested introducing Hedayat to a few of my friends, but he was too picky and he did not like any of them.

4. Baba's Story Continued

HOW I MISSED THE SMELL of the orange blossoms and the stroll through our orange grove. Neshta was the land of my dreams, the land that I was forced out of by the Reza Shah. Farid and I went to my mother's tomb often. I felt her energy there; when I cried on her tomb I felt her caressing me. Farid never got tired of me telling stories about my mother.

Mother and I used to pick orange blossoms and then sit for hours making orange-blossom necklaces. Carefully, we would put a soft string through the blossoms with a needle. These necklaces would carry the sweet fragrance of the orange blossoms for days. The fragrance of orange blossoms is the smell of love.

After less than a year, my father married a woman named Iran. She was the same age as me. I fought with my father, hoping to change his mind. I couldn't understand why he was marrying such a young woman and starting a family with her while my brothers still needed to be looked after. My heart broke every day for my two young brothers: they were toddlers without a mother, and now without a father.

I became my brothers' caregiver. Bit by bit, I sold every piece of mother's jewellery to support my brothers and myself. They knew me as their only caregiver.

In the meantime, Father had five more children with Iran.

In World War II, Reza Shah declared neutrality for Iran and refused to allow Iranian territory to be used as a transport corridor to ship arms to Russia. Under the auspices of the Anglo-Soviet Agreement between the United Kingdom and the Soviet

Union, Iran was invaded and occupied by the British in 1941; they abdicated Reza Shah and replaced him with his son Mohammad Reza Pahlavi. We referred to him as the Shah of Iran.

All the landowners were allowed to return to their lands.

The first day after I returned to Neshta, I went for a stroll in the orange grove. Mother's presence was like the perfume in every blossom of the orange trees, sweet and everlasting.

I had been living at my Aunt Tajmah's house for a few years. Aunt Tajmah was my mother's sister. Her husband Mohammad Ali Varasteh was a cabinet minister, and, with his help, I began working at the Ministry of Revenue. Aunt Tajmah kept suggesting that we should arrange a marriage—*khastegari*—between me and my cousin Mahin, the daughter of my Aunt Aterahm. I was in my early thirties, but, even after years of being responsible for my younger brothers, I was not ready to start a family of my own.

I was enjoying the company of my friends. Farid was living in Tehran too. He could make me laugh like no one else. Once, I showed up at a dance studio to pick him up after his tango lesson. I noticed that while he was dancing with his teacher, they were both looking at me.

His teacher, a beautiful Armenian-Iranian woman, walked toward me and said, "Farid always talks about what an amazing dancer you are. May I have the honour of dancing with you?"

I told her that I was not a dancer, but she kept saying that I was simply being humble and she insisted that I dance with her. When I walked onto the dance floor, all the dance students and teachers turned their heads to watch us. I saw Farid standing in a corner and chuckling. I was so embarrassed; I kept stepping on his teacher's toes. Farid laughed alone that time.

I met my other friend, Sina, through Farid. He was a tailor. He only made clothes for women, but he loved going fabric shopping with us and picking fabric for our shirts and suits. We always wore suits and ties; even when we met in the streets of Tehran we dressed up in our trendy, elegant suits. My shoemaker was an Armenian-Iranian. He had a great touch and he used the best quality leather. It was fashionable to wear hats, so when my hair started thinning I devoted myself to finding one that suited me.

Maman and Baba, 1950s

After Mother's death, I felt lonely. I had no connection with my father, and I felt an immense responsibility for my brothers, even though my brother Jafar was only two years younger than me. Hanging out with my friends in cafés and cabarets or just strolling in the streets of Tehran lifted my soul.

Aunt Tajmah asked me again to visit Aunt Aterahm in Qazvin, and I didn't like to say no to her. Mahin, Aunt Aterahm's daughter, kept introducing me to her friends, but I was not interested in getting married. One night though, Mahin herself showed some interest in me. She was beautiful and fashionable, and she was also a smart career woman. I finally agreed to marry Mahin.

"Hedayat, I am so proud of your choice of bride. Mahin has had a difficult life, but she has earned the respect of the people of Qazvin through her dedication to helping those less fortunate." This was the first time after Mother's death that Father spoke to me lovingly. "I shall throw a seven-day wedding for you. I know that this is what your mother would have wanted."

And so we got married.

5. My Grandparents' House

AUNT MASI SPENT SO MUCH TIME at the dance clubs dancing to Elvis's music that she decided to ignore *kashtegari* tradition and married the man she was in love with, Manoocher. Uncle Manoocher looked just like one of the guys in the Elvis movies with beautiful hair, fashionable clothes, and he drove a convertible car. Aunt Masi followed her heart; she was only eighteen when she met Manoocher.

Baba liked to tease Aunt Masi. "Masi jan, are you teaching Mehrnaz dance moves again? I have no doubt when she grows up she will be just like you, a dancer and a lover. You are a bad influence!" he would say and then laugh out loud.

Baba Jafar and Maman Aterahm, my maternal grandparents, lived in a large two-storey house with a courtyard in the middle. My grandparents opened their home to people who needed their financial support. Sometimes, people just stayed for a few months until they had saved enough money to move on. Meals were prepared in a big kitchen downstairs and served there. Other people were always dropping by to help out with errands; they then stayed for meals. Sometimes there were so many people that they ate their meals upstairs as well as downstairs. My grandparents had many servants and two *naneh*, the term used for the elderly servants who had been with my grandmother since she had married.

Maman Aterahm was very spiritual. She believed in the power of prayer. Whenever I was sick, she would pray for me, holding my hand and touching me where I hurt, while her mother, Khanom jan, brewed herbs and made me drink them. At the time, there were no over-the-counter painkillers for children. Children's Aspirin didn't come to Iran until much later. I loved the little pink-flavoured tablets, but my parents would not give them to me for many years, because Khanom jan did not approve. She said that Aspirin was poison.

Instead, when I had a fever, I was given an enema. Khanom jan would write out a list of herbs that would help and then prepare them. As soon as I smelled the herbs I would start crying because I knew what the next step would be.

Maman and Baba would pull down my pajamas while I ran around and screamed, "I hate enema. I only want Maman Aterahm's prayers. I don't want an enema!"

But with the help of servants, Maman would catch me and push me onto the bed. I would fight to the last second to stop the enema from being inserted into my rectum. It would take about four adults to hold me down while Maman victoriously completed the mission. Even then, the worst was not over: they wouldn't let me go to the bathroom for what seemed like a long time. Of course, after all of this I would be so exhausted that I would fall asleep. When I awoke, my fever would have dropped, and Baba and Maman would be happy.

Naneh JiJi was the cutest *naneh* in the house with big cheeks that I loved to grab and kiss. Maman Aterahm was concerned that Naneh JiJi, who was elderly, was not allowing younger servants to assist her with washing clothes. Naneh JiJi spent all day in a room at the far side of the courtyard, washing clothes by hand for everyone in my grandparents' household. She was always happy doing this. In the evenings, she liked to give me a massage, and I loved her tender touch. How lovingly she massaged my scalp, my neck, and my shoulders. She did not like children to be around asking nosy questions when she was busy washing clothes, but she always talked to me during the massage.

"Naneh JiJi, were you ever married?"

"I was married. I had a husband and a son."

"Why are they not with you?"

"The army came and killed my husband and son, destroyed my house, and took me away."

From left to right, Aunt Masi and Maman, 1950s

This was when Russia and the United Kingdom were trying to take over some parts of Persia in the nineteenth century.

"Your great-great-grandfather Sepahsalar Khalatbari rescued me. I started living in his house. Then I was sent to your grandmother when she got married. I learned to love washing clothes, removing the stains, and staying quiet. When I am quiet I can hear my husband singing to me. Women in the village always asked him to sing. He was the most handsome man in the whole village. He was tall and his skin was pure black."

"Black? Naneh JiJi, we don't have black people here."

"My village was close to Hamadan. There were more black people there."

Arab slave traders had sold slaves to people in the southern region of Iran and the Persian Gulf in the eighteenth century.

"People kept asking me to remarry. My husband was handsome and gentle, with a beautiful voice. How could I love another man? And he gave me the most beautiful son. My son had my cheeks; otherwise he was as handsome as his father, but with lighter skin."

Naneh JiJi wiped the tears from her eyes with her white scarf. "Mehrnaz jan, I should not tell you this story. It was from a long time ago, years before you were born."

6. Vafa and My Siblings

"**N**O ONE HITS MEHRNAZ! She looks like my mother and I cannot bear to see anyone hitting her." Baba would say this with an angry tone. When he said "anyone," he meant Maman. He didn't look at her.

"She is already so spoiled," Maman would respond. "When she is a teenager then you will regret this, Hedayat."

Maman and Baba were fighting because, once again, I had made Maman angry over something and Baba did not approve of her hitting me. I loved Maman. I wanted to hug her and kiss her, but she always pushed me away.

"Mehrnaz jan, come sit on Baba's lap and kiss Baba. I would die for you, my beautiful flower. Your mother doesn't like to be hugged and kissed. If you sit on my lap, I will tell you a story."

I was the only one who loved listening to Baba's childhood stories. Sitting on Baba's lap, I would ask him to tell me about playing with Maman Aterahm in the pistachio orchard, and imagining having a velvet jacket with the same colour and texture as the pistachio peel. When Baba told stories of his childhood, his voice became soft like the velvet of the jacket he was describing.

"Baba, tell me about the time you set the cotton storage room on fire."

"Oh, that one. You remember every story that I've told you," Baba said with a big smile. And then he began.

"The Russian ambassador brought me a jacket from Russia as a present in appreciation of the official relationship between my father and Russia. It was black velvet with different-coloured gemstones on it. The fabric was so soft, and the gemstones reflected the light. I loved it very much and because I loved it so much, I only wore it on special occasions.

"One day, Mother announced that I must give that jacket to my brother Jafar, who was two years younger than me. The jacket didn't fit me anymore, but I hated seeing Jafar wear it. He always played in mud, and I couldn't bear to see my jacket get dirty. How I wished that I had worn it more often. It still looked so new. I kept my clothes very clean, but Jafar didn't care.

"One night I stole the jacket and hid it underneath the cotton balls in the special room for storing cotton. Every summer, a man would come with an instrument for refreshing the old cotton in our mattresses and comforters. He would take out the old cotton and mix it with the new cotton. Then he would put the mixture through his instrument to make the cotton fluffy before putting it back into the mattresses and comforters."

"Baba, I only want to hear about the jacket, not about the cotton."

"Okay, okay. But you can't be so selective—to hear a good story you must hear it all," Baba said before continuing.

"I lit a match and threw it in the cotton room and closed the door."

I gasped every time I heard this part of the story.

"But, Baba, even I know that you're not supposed to do that. Maman always says that, 'Girls are cotton balls and boys are fire. Do not put them in the same room.' How old were you when you did this?"

Baba was laughing so hard that he couldn't answer me.

"What's funny, Baba?"

"Oh nothing. I just can't believe your Maman is already teaching you this."

"She didn't teach me. She tells Soraya, Vafa, and Homa, and they always laugh too. But I don't find it funny. I know that I will never put cotton balls and fire together."

"I was five when I set the room on fire," Baba continued. "Everyone ran and put the fire out. To my dismay the jacket was not burnt; it only smelt smoky. Mother spanked me and then gave the jacket back to Jafar."

"Who wants to come with me tomorrow to see my shoemaker and visit Sina?" Baba asked later that night.

I was the only one who wanted to go with Baba. I couldn't fall asleep that night because I was so excited to visit the places where Baba used to hang out when he was young. In the morning, Baba brought me to the shoemakers' street. There were cobblers' stores on both sides of the street. There were even children's cobblers. I chose a pair of shiny reddish-pink leather shoes. Then we went to Baba's shoemaker, and Baba introduced me to him. I was bored in that store; there were only men's shoes.

Then we went to visit Baba's friend, Sina. He was so pleased to meet me. "Oh, little Heda! She looks just like you. She is so adorable. I will make you the prettiest dresses, even prettier than Princess Farahnaz's."

Princess Farahnaz was the Shah's daughter.

As soon as we got home, I announced to Maman, "I love Baba's friend, Sina. He is such a big and tall man, but he talks like a woman, and he is going to make me a dress like Princess Farahnaz has."

"Hedayat, did you ask how his wife was recovering from her surgery?" Maman asked.

"She's doing well. She's back at school teaching."

Maman did not respond to my excitement about Sina and the princess dress.

The next day, I got all dressed up and put on my new shoes to go and visit Great Aunt Anise. These visits were formal—government officials sometimes visited our uncles—and our parents wanted us to be properly dressed and to behave appropriately. So, while we were in the car, Maman and Baba took the opportunity to give my sister Soraya and me a lesson in good manners. They told us that girls must act like ladies, and that we should never reach across the table to get *cheerini*, Persian pastries. Instead, we should sit quietly and listen to the adults without ever interrupting.

Aunt Anise was Maman Aterahm's sister. They looked so much alike with their big green eyes, brunette hair, and petite build. Aunt Anise lived in the Shemiran region of Tehran. It was an old neighbourhood in the northern part of the city. The streets had big old trees along each side, and there was a river running through the neighbourhood. There were two houses on Aunt Anise's property: one for all the servants and another for the family, who welcomed visitors and hosted official parties. When we went to visit, we were seated in a large room with antique furniture and pieces of expensive art. I used to like to stare at the ceilings. The dome-shaped high ceiling was patterned with beautiful blue mosaics and mirrors.

We visited with Aunt Anise's husband for a long time before Aunt Anise arrived. Her bedroom was in the servants' house.

At the time, I didn't understand why Baba and Maman had given us such a lecture about manners and government officials. Nor did I understand why Aunt Anise did not live in the beautiful house with all the blue mosaics, mirrors, and chandeliers. It was like a palace. *Why did she choose not to stay and sleep there?*

I only understood later, when I was an adult. Aunt Anise was a Sufi. She believed in being one with all. The treasure was within her; the world of material belongings had no meaning for her. Poetry was the love of her life. She stayed in the servants' house and slept on the floor without a mattress so she could be reminded daily of those who suffered. She did not wish to get lost in the luxury and comfort of life.

Aunt Anise was an advocate for helping the poor. She even helped dogs, who were not cherished in Iran. In Islam, dogs are referred to as "unclean animals." If a dog touches a Muslim, then that individual has to wash her body and change her clothes. There were stray dogs in the streets of Tehran, and, at times, the city officials would poison them. They would suffer from extreme thirst before they died. This brought tears to Aunt Anise's eyes. She organized a group of people to go around the city with water so the poisoned dogs could drink before they died.

Aunt Anise's husband was Abul Hasan Amidi-Nuri. He was a legislature deputy, a prominent attorney, a deputy prime minister, and editor of the newspaper *Dada*.

Soraya listened to all of Maman and Baba's rules, but I was impatient with the adults talking while the *cheerini* were on the table staring at me. Adults were waiting for the servants to serve the pastries with tea. I did not care about the tea. I wanted the *cheerini*. I moved in slow motion toward the delicious pastries, thinking that if I were stealthy enough maybe Baba would not notice and Maman would not smack my hand. I managed to get one, and looked around furtively, but when I started eating, nothing happened. Nobody had noticed!

Later, an elderly man who was also visiting—and impatient for the servants to set down the tray—leaned forward to get a *cheerini* and broke wind.

Soraya and I tried to hold back our laughter but we did not succeed.

"Mehrnaz, go and wash your hands. Soraya, you go with her!" Maman was annoyed with our laughter.

Aunt Anise held a container of Swiss chocolates in front of Soraya and me. We knew that we must take only one, otherwise it would be rude. I took a long time to choose—the wrappings were adorned with scenes from the Swiss Alps, and I looked at each one carefully. It was hard to choose just one. I wanted more, but I glanced at Maman and she gave me a stern look.

Soraya and I got along when it was just the two of us, but when our brother Jamal was around, she followed him everywhere and did whatever he wanted. Jamal was domineering and aggressive. When I didn't follow his orders, he would get mad and hit me. I couldn't wait until Baba got home so I could tell him.

Baba Jafar and Maman Aterahm had an antique Persian wall hanging, a rug that they said would be mine when I got married. The rug depicted a scene of a princess and her friends in the forest, and Jamal loved it. He would sit underneath it on a chair in Baba Jafar and Maman Aterahm's house and create a play based on the image. Then he would determine everyone's role.

"I am the king. You are my wife, the queen. You are my daughter. You are my doormen. You are my servants. You are the queen's maid," he would dictate, pointing at each of us in turn.

Then he would kiss the queen. That always made me squirm. And it bothered me that he always made me go and collect flowers in the yard so I was hardly in the play at all. I would protest, "There is no king in this rug! There is only a princess and her friends in the forest."

But Jamal took advantage of our patriarchal society; in his

Great Aunt Anise Khalatbari, 1940s

games, girls always had subservient roles. Baba, Maman, and our society encouraged his behaviour. I would scream and cry, saying, *"There is no king in my rug."* But it was all to no avail.

I didn't get along with Jamal, so I was very fortunate when my dream brother walked into my life!

When I was six years old, a woman from Zavardasht arrived at our house with a boy. I was playing with a ball. The boy asked me if I wanted him to show me a trick. We started playing and laughing. The woman spanked him and said, "Didn't I tell you not to act like that? You are not supposed to play with little girls. They are going to send you back to the village."

He looked older and slightly taller than Jamal, but his voice was nothing like Jamal's. His voice was soft and sweet, and he was giggly. His name was Vafa.

Vafa's parents could not afford to keep him in the village because he was deemed not suited for men's work. Villagers had a very harsh life. They lived off the land, and they had to work hard in the growing season so they had enough food for winter, which always brought heavy snow to Zavardasht.

Vafa was teased by many for acting like a girl. Maman gave him chores suitable for a teenage boy, but she always found him sitting and cleaning herbs with the women, and gossiping. He knew everyone's stories. Finally, Maman gave up and assigned Vafa to kitchen chores.

Although he came to our house as a servant, Vafa became my chosen brother, a dream brother.

One day, Maman was looking for Vafa in the house. Only I knew where to find him. The government building where we lived was across the boulevard from the only chic clothing boutique in Tonekabon. Our house had a balcony overlooking the boulevard, but Maman had blocked its door with a curtain. The curtain rod stood out from the wall, leaving a deep space between the glass door and the curtain. When I got there, Vafa pulled me into his hiding place on the other side of the curtain, which he made sure was straightened behind us.

"Maman is looking for you," I whispered.

"Look," said Vafa, pointing to the good-looking son of the boutique owner. "I love the pullover he's wearing today. Isn't he handsome? He's not looking this way," Vafa continued. "Sometimes he does, and I wave at him."

I copied Vafa's style of giggling. He put his hand on his mouth and giggled. He had such white teeth, dark skin, and a big smile.

"Do you see that guy buying lottery tickets from that tiny booth? Turn your head right! Yeah, that one. He comes to my evening school."

"He's not good looking."

"Oh, right now he's wearing his work clothes. He's a mechanic. When he comes to school he puts nice clothes on. He's gorgeous."

"Vafa, Vafa!"

Maman was still looking for him. He waited until Maman's voice got farther away, then he held my hand and we ran out of the room and down the hallway, pretending that we were coming in from outside.

7. An Orange Grove and a Birthday Party

WHEN I WAS SEVEN, I asked Maman, "Why can't I have a birthday party? I go to my friends' birthday parties, and I want my friends to bring me presents too."

"Birthday parties are for spoiled children. It is not fair for the rest of the children to go to parties for rich children."

I went to public elementary schools where the majority of the students were below middle class, so only a few of us could afford to have birthday parties. But I really wanted a party, so I decided to invite my whole class of first graders—over forty children—to celebrate my birthday without telling my parents.

My birthday fell during our three-month summer holiday, so I chose a Thursday evening in May before school let out. In Iran, Friday is the only day that schools and government are closed, so naturally, Thursday evening would be the best night for a huge birthday party.

I came home from school that Thursday, and found out we were going to stay with Uncle Jafar and Aunt Banafsheh for the weekend.

"We can't go stay with Uncle Jafar and Aunt Banafsheh. My friends are coming to my birthday party," I said angrily. Maman made me go with Vafa to inform every student, at least the ones whose address I knew, that the party had been cancelled.

Uncle Jafar and Aunt Banafsheh had five children. Although I was sad about the cancelled party, I was excited about spending time with my cousins. Many of Baba's cousins lived in Tonekabon too, so there were always lots of children to play with there. They all came to my uncle's house.

When I played with my cousins at my aunt and uncle's house, I divided us into two groups: Indians and Cowboys. I loved the shows about cowboys and Indians that I watched on television. I was the leader of the band of Apaches, and I found a sharp fruit knife to carry in my hand. My cousins were the cowboys and we pretended to attack each other.

Running around with my cousins, I tripped and fell, and the sharp knife cut me above my eyes. Baba arrived on the scene, screaming with fear. He thought I had lost an eye. Dr. Toloui, who was the husband of Baba's cousin, was visiting too. He took me back to his office and gave me a few stitches. I didn't lose my eye. But when I looked in the mirror, my head was wrapped in a white bandage like a *mullah*'s turban. "I don't want to look like a *mullah*." I started crying.

The next day, my family and all our relatives were going to visit our orange grove, but they decided to leave me at home. "You lost too much blood yesterday," Maman said. "You have to stay home and rest."

"Maman, I'm not sick. I want to come to the farm and play."

Baba and most of the Massoudi family had inherited large pieces of land—orange groves and rice paddies in Neshta, in the province of Mazandaran in Northern Iran. Our orange grove was so big that I had never walked from one end to the other. But I liked walking with my cousins to the far end, where there was a big hill that we liked to roll down. On the other side, was Uncle Jafar's orange grove.

There was a farmhouse in the orange grove. There were no roads, so we had to cross a big river on horseback to get there. Baba hired a gardener who lived in the grove with his family all year round to care for the land and the horses and cows. Prior to our visit, Baba would send a message to the gardener so he could prepare some food for us. He always got us local, drained creamy yogurt, butter, feta cheese, eggs, and honey for our snacks.

There was a clay tandoor on the balcony of this farmhouse, where the gardener's wife made fresh Persian flatbread for us. I stood watching her as she put the dough into the side of the oven. Crispy warm flatbread is delicious. My favourite foods at the farm were yogurt, bread, kabobs, and tangerines.

After we built our villa by the Caspian Sea, we no longer stayed at the farmhouse. We preferred our villa with its electricity and private beachfront. The orange grove was about a twenty-minute drive from our villa, not counting the horse ride to cross the river.

Aunt Banafsheh stayed in the farmhouse once a year for a week making orange-blossom marmalade. She hired labourers to help her out. She made enough for her family and ours, and to give as presents for the relatives.

There were always visitors staying with us, both at our house and our villa. Our house felt empty and quiet when it was only my parents, my siblings, and our servants. I liked having friends and relatives staying with us, and I wished that some of our visitors would live with us forever. One of these visitors was Fereshteh, the daughter of Maman's friend Mottee. Vafa and I counted the days until her arrival. It got very hot in summer in Tehran, where Mottee and her husband lived, so the family would come to stay with us for a couple of weeks. Fereshteh was fun, charming, loud, and sophisticated. She was everything I wanted to be. She was a Tehrani girl.

The capital city of Iran, Tehran offered clubs, nightlife, fashionable boutiques full of European clothes, and dance studios for ballet and all other non-Iranian dance styles. Fereshteh was taking ballet lessons. She said that our dance moves were *dahati*, small townish, so she taught Vafa and me new ones. She was even allowed to date boys.

Vafa and I loved hearing her stories about her dates. Fereshteh was four years older than Jamal, so whenever we went to the beach, Maman left Fereshteh in charge. Jamal hated it when someone else was in charge, especially a girl, so they would often fight. But Fereshteh was not afraid of getting into physical fights with Jamal.

One night we learned that something exciting would be happening. "The Shah and his family will be cruising the main street tomorrow evening, and spectators are being invited. I'll be standing at the front greeting them. If you all behave well, you can stand beside me so you can have a good view," Baba told us. The Shah's villa was in Nowshahr; it was a beautiful house on the shoreline of the Caspian Sea.

Fereshteh

"Oh my God. I hope the Shah's brother will be there too." Fereshteh was so excited at the idea of seeing the Shah's youngest brother, the dream of every young woman. Fereshteh and Vafa started jumping up and down.

Fereshteh had a bob cut, but her hair was curly like mine, and it got even curlier in Nowshahr because of the humidity. She spent a whole day straightening it and rolling it. She wore a thick white hairband and put on makeup. She looked so beautiful with her tanned skin in a sleeveless, low-cut, summer dress. She dressed me nicely too.

The Shah's brother did not come, but I was happy because I got to see the prince, who was a few months younger than me. He was driving a big white car that was the size of an actual truck. We loved the royal family, and we were all happy to see them close up that evening.

Vafa's parents came once a year from Zavardasht to visit him. My parents gave them money annually, because Vafa was not getting paid. His parents were so kind. They brought us *naan sarsheer*, the dehydrated creamy flatbread. Maman always told us that it had been her favourite when she was a child, spending summers in Zavardasht. At night, Vafa's mother rubbed my back and told me stories.

"Vafa, take your parents shopping today. Buy souvenirs for your siblings," Baba said one day.

"I'm busy in the kitchen today," Vafa answered sharply.

"Vafa, I don't want to hear another word. We don't need you in the kitchen," Maman said sternly.

Vafa did not want to be seen with his parents in Nowshahr. Vafa avoided acting or looking like a *dahati* like the plague.

I never gave up on my dream of having a birthday party.

"Baba Jafar, Maman won't let me have a birthday party. I go to them all the time for my friends, and I bring them presents. But I never get birthday presents," I told my grandfather.

Baba Jafar had come to stay with us for a couple of weeks in winter. When he was around, I was the most spoiled creature on earth because Maman was not allowed to spank me.

"Mahin, why hasn't this child had a birthday party yet? Throw her a big one while I'm here."

"You spoiled girl. You will get a spanking after Baba Jafar leaves," Maman threatened. I didn't care. I stayed close to Baba Jafar; while he was there, I was untouchable. And Maman finally, grudgingly, agreed.

Iran is a densely populated country. Our classroom sizes were anything from forty to seventy students, and once again I invited the entire class.

In Iran, throwing a party means providing a meal. All day, everyone was busy cooking dinner in the kitchen while Baba

Jafar and I organized the party room. I told him I wanted our big coffee table in the corner of the room. I wanted my chair to be by the coffee table and all the presents to be put on the table. Children started arriving, and each one of them brought me a present.

"Why did you bring presents? We just wanted you to celebrate with us," Maman kept saying to each one of them.

I kept thinking that this wasn't true. I wanted their presents. I sat by the coffee table and didn't socialize with anyone.

Maman was so irritated. "Go and dance with your friends."

I kept staring at the presents. I was too tired to play or to dance. I wanted everyone to go home so I could open the presents. I wasn't allowed to do so in front of the guests—this was an Iranian tradition. The only present I can still remember today was a small blue teddy bear statue covered with sprinkles.

The first and only birthday party of my childhood took place on that winter day, even though my actual birthday was later in the summer.

8. Tehran and Pomegranates

OUR ANNUAL FAMILY TRIP to the pomegranate orchards near the City of Saveh, southwest of Tehran, was one of my favourite outings. Every autumn, we travelled with Baba Jafar and Maman Aterahm, Aunt Masi and Uncle Manoocher and their three daughters, a couple of *naneh*, and four or five of our servants. Meals were prepared early in the morning, and the warm pots of Persian mixed rice and patties were wrapped in cloth tea towels. Enough Persian tea was made for everyone and poured into thermoses. There were snacks of roasted and salted seeds, pistachios, and nuts. All the people and the food were packed into two cars; children sat on adults' laps.

Whenever I walked in the pomegranate orchards, I thought of the Islamic stories of heaven and hell, and I knew that this is what heaven would look and taste like: a deep blue sky dotted with hundreds of blood-red pomegranates, the creek running through the orchard and babbling in my ears.

I grabbed the biggest and reddest pomegranate I could find. The red skin was so thin and shiny, and the seeds popped in my mouth. Heavenly juice ran down my chin onto my red dress.

By this time, we had moved to an upper middle-class neighbourhood in the northern part of Tehran, in the foothills of the Alborz Mountains. Maman had become tired of following Baba's job, which required us to move every two or three years. There were no universities in Northern Iran, and most of the schools for higher learning were located in Tehran itself. In the Middle East, Tehran was like Paris and New York combined: it offered art, culture, fashion, and nightlife. People dressed up in the latest European fashions and went for strolls along the main streets.

Maman's rheumatoid arthritis had become chronic and she was in a lot of pain. Maman and Baba consulted with Aunt Anise's son, Dr. Hushang Amidi Nuri, a physician in London. He recommended that both Maman and I come to England for further treatment.

I had had a skin graft and plastic surgery in Tehran right after I had been burned, but the surgery was unsuccessful. My legs had not been burned in the fire, but now I had deep scarring on the insides of both my thighs from the knees up from the failed skin grafts. I had learned to hide those scars too. I could never wear shorts or the mini-skirts that were popular then without also wearing thick pantyhose. There were such deep scars under my right arm that, as a result, I couldn't raise it above my head. Baba and Maman were very disappointed with the Iranian surgeon who had operated on me, but Doctor Hushang gave my parents hope that plastic surgery could help me with my arm movement.

Maman and I stayed with her cousin Rana in London, England. On the first day, while she was showing us around London, Rana instructed us to say "sorry" if we accidentally bumped into someone. Tehran was so crowded that we constantly bumped into people in the streets, buses, or lineups, but we didn't always say sorry—it happened so often that we would have quickly sounded like a broken record. In London, "sorry" became my first English word. If Rana wasn't watching me, I would purposefully bump into someone just so I could say it.

Maman and I started seeing doctors. My surgery was scheduled for a few weeks after we arrived. Rana took us shopping and sightseeing early on because Maman thought that after my surgery I might not be up to it. A few of Baba's cousins were living and studying in England too, and all of them were happy to take us on tours of London.

One day I found my dream: the biggest box of individually wrapped Swiss chocolates I had ever seen, each with the Swiss Alps wrapping that I liked so much. They were just like the ones Aunt Anise had offered us, but there were even more of them

Mehrnaz, 1960s

because the box was enormous. It was also very expensive. I convinced Maman to buy one for me and one for Baba Jafar. I knew how much he loved Swiss chocolates.

I ate a few each day, but I kept the wrappings and put them back in the box. How delicious and how pretty!

I kept both boxes under my bed. The flat where we were staying was very small, and there was nowhere else to put my suitcase and souvenirs. One day I reached to get a chocolate from my box and was disappointed to find that I'd finished them all; only the empty wrappers were left.

Maman bought me other kinds of chocolates when we were out, but the Swiss Alps chocolates were expensive and she wouldn't buy me another box. I wouldn't eat Baba Jafar's because I wanted him to have them all. Every night, I kept thinking of the chocolates under my bed and I couldn't sleep.

Then one night, I decided that I would have only one and that Baba Jafar could have the rest when we got back to Iran. But a couple of weeks later, I had to face the truth.

"Mehrnaz, why are you crying?" Maman had said when she found me sobbing in my bed.

"There's no chocolate left for Baba Jafar. I bought that box for him and then I ate them all."

When I was in hospital, Maman told me that she had bought another box of chocolates for Baba Jafar, but that this time she would find another place to keep it. I smiled, imagining looking at the chocolates with Baba Jafar and telling him which ones were more delicious.

Baba phoned once a week, and every time I talked to him I started crying. I missed him. We ended up staying in London for three months. The first time Baba called, I couldn't wait to tell him about the English cucumbers. "Baba, they have these long cucumbers but there is no flavour in them. They just *look* like cucumbers." I was shocked the first time I ate an English cucumber. In Iran, we ate cucumbers as if it were a fruit; they are small, but flavourful. I was also shocked to see boys and girls kiss in public. I liked looking at them, but I was embarrassed if Maman or Rana caught me looking. They were touching, kissing, and doing almost everything in public. I could see their tongues going into each other's mouths. I was a young girl so I thought that was gross. But I really liked seeing boys and girls holding hands. The fashion in the streets of London was similar to Tehran, except Tehrani women wore mini skirts and dresses more often than jeans, and they wore more makeup.

After my surgery, I had to wear a cast in the shape of a short-sleeved t-shirt for one month. The recovery was painful and itchy. Maman would use a long knitting needle to reach in and relieve the relentless irritation on my back while I cried. "Maman, it's not fair that my siblings and cousins are at the villa going swimming and having fun, while I'm in the hospital with this cast around my body."

"God loves those who suffer," Maman would say.

"I don't want God's love," I would cry.

The surgeon in England said that there was nothing more he could do at that time, and that I would have to return for further surgery when I was eighteen. I had to practise raising my right arm above my head on a daily basis; it was really painful. But the doctor said that it would stop hurting when the new scars from the surgery healed.

9. The Shah of Iran

OUR ROSY NEIGHBOURHOOD IN TEHRAN only had one thorn. While there were no beggars like there were in the rest of the city, there was an empty lot across the street from us that was occupied by eighteen families. The police couldn't get them out.

These families were living in poverty. They had built one room per family with mud and clay, and they had two holes for toilets. Maman discouraged me from going inside the complex. "Some of them are drug dealers," she said. "You must be very cautious—do not go there. Bring your friends from the complex to our house."

I made friends with two sisters from the complex, and they spent a lot of time in my house. I was closest to the younger of the two, Azam, who was about my age. They sometimes slept on a futon on the floor of my bedroom. To them, this was a luxury.

"Maman, are Azam and Ashraf's mom and stepfather drug dealers?" I asked "They only sell gum and cigarettes from their push cart. They're so nice; they can't be drug dealers."

"Don't be a *foozul*!" Maman frowned at me and then turned to Baba as they both tried to hide their smiles. *Foozul* means "busybody."

I hardly ever went inside the complex. It always smelled like excrement, and besides Maman had told me not to go there. I thought maybe that was why. Instead, I would stand at the entrance and send the little kids to get Azam and Ashraf so that we could play outside together.

But, as I got to know the family, I eventually did go inside. I was surprised to see that their home consisted of only one room where they all ate and slept. It was made of clay and it was very clean. Their bedding was wrapped in colourful handmade fabrics, then rolled up and placed against the wall. They wrapped the bedding so skilfully that they looked like big cushions. Azam's mother made me tea and asked me to sit. I sat on the floor and leaned against one of their cushions. She made sure that I had the nicest cushion behind me.

"Sit here," she said. "The bedding inside that wrapping behind you is for our guests. It is all washed and clean."

I leaned against it and felt very comfortable. When she said "clean," it made me think of the smell of excrement again. I wondered how they could eat their meals with this smell all around their house.

Azam's mother served me *cheerini* and tea when I came to visit. She had many stories from their village, and she always laughed loudly when she told them. When it was time for me to go home, I was surprised to realize that while I was listening to her stories, I couldn't smell the excrement at all.

Azam's mother seemed so happy. She laughed more than my maman. She was missing her lower front teeth, and she dyed her hair with henna. Maman allowed me to dye my hair with henna too. Azam's mother created a mixture of henna, yogurt, and chamomile, and put it on my hair and toes. When I was younger, my *naneh* used to put henna on my nails and toes, even though henna-dyed nails was usually only for old people. Now I preferred nail polish, which Aunt Masi was always happy to buy me.

There was no electricity or water in the complex. Most of the adults did not have jobs. Maman found jobs for one or two of the men at the city hall. They became janitors, sweeping the sidewalks and removing garbage from homes. They emptied all the garbage into a big bin and pushed it to the dump. Every time they saw Maman, they thanked her for her kindness. I never understood why they were thankful for that job. The bin they pushed was so heavy and smelly. I always covered my nose when I walked by them. What were they thankful for?

In our living room, we had a large and splendid chandelier facing this complex, and, for a while, there were no curtains in the window. Many of the children and some of the adults from across the street would stand outside admiring our chandelier.

I was living a charmed life, but I didn't know it until Maman drove me to see her cousin. He was a physician practising in a public hospital in the southern part of Tehran. I had never been to that part of the city before, and I had never been in a public hospital.

I saw shacks made of tin with thick fabric over their doorways. Children scurried about like colonies of ants. This area shocked me. It was called Halaby Abad, the town of tin shacks. The compound in front of our house where the poor people lived looked luxurious compared to homes in this area.

The media was heavily censored during the Shah's regime. There was no coverage on the news about this tin town without doors, water, or electricity, where poor people dug deep wells to drink and wash. Families in Halaby Abad had many children. They could not afford birth control. Some of the children fell into the wells and died.

In October 1971, over the course of four days, the Shah celebrated the 2,500-year anniversary of the Persian Empire with elaborate festivities. In the palace, six hundred guests, including many world leaders, dined for over five and a half hours—it was the longest and most lavish official banquet in modern history. Iranian television had live coverage of the event. As a family, we sat in front of the television and admired every minute of this elaborate celebration. We particularly admired the ornate dresses of the queen and the guests.

Baba and Maman liked the Shah and the royal family, but they were disappointed about the White Revolution's negative effect on the lives of farmers.

The Shah introduced the White Revolution in 1963. The primary intention of this action was to strip power and influence from the landed elites of Iran. The law forced the long-established landlords to sell their lands at bargain prices to the government. Then the government offered the peasants inflated loans to buy the land. The majority of the peasants were unable to make their land profitable or to pay back their loans. They were ultimately forced to leave the land and move to cities to look for jobs, leaving the government to take back the land.

The people who lived in the compound across the street were just one example of the exodus of farmers leaving their homes and coming to Tehran to find employment. But there were no jobs. Many of these families became involved with the underground drug trade, mainly in opium. The Shah had legalized medical opium, and it was readily accessible in Iran. Smoking opium was common among olde and wealthier people. It was considered a social activity.

My parents were passionate about helping people in trouble, and our family home became an unofficial, part-time social service office. They did not approve of many of the Shah's policies, but they never discussed the country's unfair social gap. In those days, no one spoke out against the regime of the Shah. There were small, underground movements of opposition parties, but when they were discovered their members were tortured, imprisoned, or killed by the Shah's guards or his dreaded spy agency known as SAVAK (Sazeman-e Ettela'at va Amniyat-e Keshvar). We were taught to never say anything to our friends against the Shah's regime.

"You just don't know who is a SAVAKi," Baba whispered.

Universities were private in Iran, so low-income families could not even dream of sending their children to school. There was no healthcare for people with low incomes. There were public hospitals, but they were poorly funded. People around the world saw the extravagant lifestyle of Iran's royal family, but they didn't see the overwhelming poverty of the rest of the country.

Shortly after the anniversary festivities, my whole family sat in front of the television yet again to watch the trial of Khosrow Golsorkhi, an Iranian journalist, poet, and communist activist, and Keramat Daneshian, a film director. They had been accused of anti-government activities by SAVAK. But it was merely a show trial, in which Golsorkhi and Daneshian were expected to renounce their affiliation with the left wing. Instead, both spoke strongly against the Shah's regime, delineating the harm that programs such as the White Revolution had inflicted on Iran and the Iranian people. Since the two men were disobeying orders to support the government, their trial was cut short, and they were executed.

We did not dare to share our opinions about their execution, but young Iranians began to describe Golsorkhi as an Iranian Che Guevara.

10. Mecca and High School

"I DON'T BELIEVE IN GOING TO MECCA. Mecca must reside in our hearts. Why would I spend so much money going to Mecca when there are so many hungry people in Tehran? My duty to my religion is here, helping people; it is not in Mecca."

I always felt fearful when I heard Maman arguing against going to Mecca. Mecca is the birthplace of the Prophet Mohammad and the site of Mohammad's first revelation of the Quran. Making a pilgrimage to Mecca, in Saudi Arabia, is an obligation for every Muslim, at least once in one's lifetime. A Muslim is only exempt if she is physically and financially unable to make such a pilgrimage.

I was confused by Maman's protest against going to Mecca. She was very religious. She did not wear a *chador*—the long scarf that Muslim women wear to cover their hair and body—but she prayed daily and practised many other Islamic rituals.

Just a couple of years earlier, we had made a family trip to the Imam Reza shrine in Mashhad. He was the eighth imam of the Twelve Shiite Imams who succeeded Mohammad's leadership spiritually and politically. Imam Reza's shrine is one of the largest mosques in the world. Baba had rented a minibus with a driver, and we filled it with Uncle Jafar's family, our family, servants, and *naneh*, and headed toward Mashhad, a nine-hour drive east of Tehran.

Hundreds of people thronged around the mausoleum. We stayed for a week, making daily visits to the shrine and the Bazaar of Mashhad, a mall inside an ancient building intricately constructed with high-ceilinged domes. Each store was just as wonderful as the last. The bazaar was packed with people buying jewellery, fabric, and holy souvenirs like prayer beads and rugs.

There were many stories about spontaneous healings taking place at Imam Reza. One night, Maman and Aunt Banafsheh planned to stay overnight to burn candles and to pray. The older children were allowed to stay, but I was too young. I cried and I begged to stay too, and Maman caved in.

There were many rooms around the mausoleum where we could sit, but no one was allowed to sleep. The rooms were packed with people, so Aunt Banafsheh and Maman took turns doing the walking-praying around the mausoleum in order to save our seats.

Some men walked around carrying big tanks of rose water on their backs. Their job was to make sure that no one slept even while we sat. We could close our eyes to pray, but if they saw we were falling asleep, they sprayed our faces with rose water to wake us up.

All night, we lit candles and prayed, pacing around the mausoleum or sitting facing the mausoleum. I was sleepy, so I kept asking Maman's permission to walk around the mausoleum to keep myself awake. After a while, Maman and Aunt Banafsheh got tired of walking, so Maman allowed me to go with Soraya and Aunt Banafsheh's daughters, Ghazal and Katayun.

There were still hundreds of people walking around, and we could only go in one direction. It felt like a big wave of people was pushing us forward. Everyone was praying, crying, and chanting. Suddenly, I felt a big push, and I lost Soraya's and Ghazal's hands. I looked around, and there was no sign of Soraya, Ghazal, and Katayun. I screamed and called their names, but no one could hear me. The masses of people kept pushing around the mausoleum, but no one could see or hear me. Everything was so loud. The group around me began to move toward one of the exits. I was pushed with them toward the exit too. Outside, I stopped crying and wiped my tears. I didn't want people to know that I was lost. I was afraid that someone would steal me.

Finally, I spotted one of the men with the rose water. I told him that I was lost. It was dark outside and I was scared. He told me he would bring me to the office. Everything was dark except the blue mosaic pond and the shiny golden dome above the Imam Reza shrine. I was shaking with fear. Suddenly, I remembered to pray for my safety. I was praying while we were walking to the office.

The men in the office noticed that I was praying.

"Who taught you that prayer?"

"No one taught it to me. I hear my Maman Aterahm reciting it when she's worried about something."

They prayed with me and talked to me for a long time, until I spotted Baba running outside. I could see the reflection of sunrise on the pond. Baba was so surprised that I was not scared or crying. The men told Baba that we had been praying together. When Maman saw me, she was not even mad at me. Later on, Soraya and my cousins told me that Maman had been crying all night.

"Mahin, the men loved Mehrnaz. They said that she entertained them all by reciting different prayers and telling them stories. They were men of faith. They did not hurt her," Baba shared this with Maman.

"Do not say that in front of the girls! Girls must not trust men just because they are 'the men of faith' or *mullahs!*"

"Why was Maman mad at Baba and not at me?" I thought to myself.

On the way back to our hotel, I asked for ice cream.

"But you haven't had breakfast yet."

I just wanted the *akbar mashti* style ice cream. My stomach had been feeling funny since I had gotten lost the night before. Maman noticed I wasn't feeling well and asked nervously, "Why are you holding your stomach? Where does it hurt? We must bring you to the doctor."

I didn't understand why Maman was acting so strangely. She checked my underwear. I didn't know why.

Baba said, "We'll go back to our hotel and get everyone. Then we'll all go for *akbar mashti* ice cream."

We got all the *naneh,* servants, and younger kids, and got a big table at the ice cream shop. When I had the first bite of the ice cream, I stopped making eye contact with Maman. I leaned against Baba and ate my ice cream slowly. The taste and smell of rose water and saffron in my mouth made my stomach feel better. I didn't want to swallow each bite of the frozen cream. I wanted it to melt slowly in my mouth.

"Mehrnaz, do you see the white hair on my head? It's all because of you," Baba said with a smile on his face. Everyone laughed.

Finally Maman was smiling too. She said, "Hedayat, not only has she given you white hair, but she will make you go completely bald. It's your fault. You spoil her. If only she had not come to stay overnight at the shrine like the other younger kids, or if she had sat like Soraya, Ghazal, and Katayun…"

Baba pulled a thread from the corner of his handkerchief and lit it on fire. He shook it to put the fire out and then circled the smoke of the thread around my head, praying. Baba believed in smudging for keeping the evil eye away. At home, he would smudge with *esphand*, wild rue seeds, but when we were out he used a thread from his clothing or a handkerchief.

After our trip to Imam Reza, all Baba could talk about was going to Mecca. If a person is sick but financially can afford to go, then she is obliged to send someone else on her behalf. People are given a title after their pilgrimage to Mecca: *haji* for men and *hajieh* for women. So, if Maman bought hers, she would get the title of *hajieh*.

After Baba's pilgrimage, people called him *haji* Massoudi, and some just called him *haji*.

"Mahin, this is our obligation. Allow me to buy your pilgrimage."

"No!"

This was not the only thing Maman and Baba did not agree on. They fought a lot. When Baba was home, they slept in separate bedrooms. I did not like sleeping alone in my bedroom, so some nights I slept in Baba's bedroom and sometimes in Maman's bedroom. Baba would massage my head and sing me Persian folk songs before falling asleep and snoring loudly. My favourite song was *"Be darya bengarom."*

Be darya bengarom darya tou binom
Be sahra bengarom sahra tou binom

Be harja bengarom koho daro dasht
Neshan az yare zibaye tou binom
Delom ey delbarom debar kojaii?

When I look at the sea, I see you.
When I look at the meadow, I see you.
Wherever I look, mountains, meadows,
I see your beautiful face.
My love, my beloved, where are you?

As I got older, sleeping in Maman's bedroom was more fun. She didn't sleep well at night because she was in so much pain. She had a radio beside her bed. It would air a storytelling program starting on Saturday night, the first night of the week. I didn't want to miss the exciting parts of the stories, so I would fight sleep every night so I could hear the end. The final night of the week, when the story ended, was always the most exciting. The stories were mystery dramas. In the mornings, I always checked with Maman to make sure that I had not missed the ending.

When I started grade eight, Maman decided I would go to a reputable private high school called Kharazami. It had a high success rate for university admissions. There were over three thousand students in Kharazami, with nine classes of grade eight alone. Students were put in classes based on their academic average. I was put in grade eight-one. All the students in this class had an average of over ninety-five percent. This was the first time in my life that I had been placed in a segregated classroom.

Maman and Baba were extremely proud of me, but I was not happy in this class. At recess, none of my classmates played. They studied or read scientific magazines. I was lonely.

"Maman, please change my classroom. I want to go to grade eight-three," I begged. A relative of ours was in that class. I had started playing with her and her friends, and they were fun.

"Everyone dreams about being in grade eight-one. It's good for your future. Those students will be the next generation's doctors, lawyers, and engineers. You will be one of them," said Maman.

Not long after that, there came a middle-of-the-night phone

call bearing the terrible news that Baba Jafar had died from a massive heart attack. We were shocked because he was in his early sixties and had been in good health.

After spending a week in Qazvin with Maman Aterahm, we came back to Tehran. The thought of sitting in that lonely, boring classroom on top of the heartache I was going through was unbearable. I cried all through class thinking of my Baba Jafar. I had always loved being at school, but now I was so unhappy.

The next day, right in the middle of a class, I packed my red leather briefcase and walked out. I did not turn my head around to answer the teacher. I headed straight to the principal's office.

The principal was so busy that it was impossible to see her. There were also nine vice principals, two of whom were Maman's friends, but I didn't want to go to either of them.

I strutted into the huge administrative office and up to the big desk with the tiny woman sitting behind it, but when I opened my mouth to speak all I could do was cry. The tiny principal came out from behind her desk and kindly invited me to sit down. I told her about losing my Baba Jafar. I was so heartbroken. I told her about the classroom and how eight-one was so quiet and boring.

"No one laughs there. It makes me think of Baba Jafar, and I cry during class," I told her.

"Is there a class you want to go to?" she asked.

"Yes, eight-three," I told her. "Students are fun in that class."

My girlfriends, Sholeh, Roshi, and Sima remember the day I walked into their classroom with my red eyes and my red briefcase. There was only one seat available in that class of sixty-two students. In just a couple of months, my academic average dropped from ninety-eight to low nineties or high eighties, but my social life was on the rise.

I joined the cool group of students and began smoking cigarettes in the smelly, dirty bathrooms and on the school's fire escape. The beautiful leather briefcase that I had carried so proudly before no longer fit this Mehrnaz, and I gave it away. I pestered Maman to give me money for lunch. I wanted to buy a hot dog, potato chips, and pop like the children from the more westernized families. They were the cool families.

"Maman, why don't we eat hot dogs and hamburgers at home? Many of my friends do. I'm so tired of eating Persian food every single day."

Persian lunch boxes consist of three stainless steel dishes buckled together. Salad goes in the top container, and the other two are filled with rice and stew. I kept the salad container with me in my desk and dropped the two other containers on the heated shelves in the warming room. Our containers were nice and warm when we picked them up, but, like my red briefcase, I no longer wanted these home-cooked meals, so I learned to exchange my lunch with some of the students who had hot dogs.

The schools in Iran were segregated by gender. We weren't allowed to wear any makeup at school. When we arrived in the morning, the principal and the vice principals stood at the entrance door and screened us for makeup and the length of our uniform skirts. When the school day was over, the boys ran out of their classes and lined up outside the girls' schools, waiting for the girls to come out. During the day, we would have collected the shavings from our red pencils, mixed it with Vaseline, and smeared this red potion on our lips and cheeks just before leaving the school.

It was a rule that when a teacher entered the room, we had to rise and say, "Hello, Mr. or Mrs. _____." Most of us were bored during the religious study class. One day, we made a plan to cover our hair with scarves and wear stilettos to class. Many of our mothers had a pair or two of these old-fashioned shoes from the fifties. When the religious study teacher walked in, all sixty-three of us clicked our heels on the tile floor and began complaining about the scarves not covering our hair.

"Oh my God, my hair is showing!" we cried out.

We did not have to wear the *hijab* at that time—we were just trying to be funny. The teacher stormed angrily out of the room to ask for help from the principal. Of course, by the time the principal walked in, we had removed our scarves and shoes and were sitting quietly, as though nothing had happened.

"Mehrnaz, I want you to smoke a cigarette with me. If you want to smoke, I would prefer that you have your first cigarette with me." Maman had no idea that I had been smoking since grade five; she didn't know about the butts stolen from the fancy ashtrays filled by our houseguests, smoked in secret with my cousins. So Maman and I smoked.

"Mehrnaz, you are smart. Go to medical school, not for money but to help out the villagers. I'll come with you when you go to the villages. They need people like you. I am so proud of Dariush. He is in medical school, and his only purpose is to help the underprivileged people. You and your uncle Dariush could become a team. There are no medical services in the villages. And believe me, men want only one thing from women. You could get hurt because of your body. But when you're a doctor, they cannot hurt you. You do not need a man when you have your degree. Frame your degree and put it on the wall. Marry your degree."

I told Uncle Dariush that Maman wanted me to become a medical doctor.

"Mehrnaz jan, your mother has dreams for you, but your life must be made of *your* dreams. Going to medical school and helping the destitute people of our country was a dream of mine from the time I was a young boy. What is your dream?"

I was shy to tell him that my dream was for my scars to disappear and then to marry a man I loved.

Uncle Dariush was Maman's half-brother on her father's side. I met him for the first time when he came to visit me at the hospital when I was four. He came with his father, who was my biological grandfather, and his sister. They were all so kind and nice. I couldn't understand why I had not met them before. At that time, I didn't know that Maman had been separated from her father when she was a child.

Uncle Dariush sat beside me and read me books. He was only a couple of years older than Jamal, but they were so different. Uncle Dariush was quiet and kind, and acted so much older than Jamal.

56

11. Aunt Banafsheh's Food

I HAD NEVER SPENT TIME in the rice paddies. We had always driven by them and watched the women working. One day, I asked Baba to take me to Uncle Jafar's rice farm in Neshta, which was near our orange grove. We ate lunch with all the workers at my uncle's farmhouse. The shiny green colour of the vegetation and the smell of the rice paddies were comforting and relaxing. I was fascinated by the female workers, who showed up early in the morning with their babies wrapped around their backs to work in the rice paddies. They were bent over all day long in water up to their knees. They worked in rows and sang songs together as they harvested the rice. The view was spectacular, and the sound of their singing was magnificent. I wanted to join them and experience what it was like to work all day in those lush green paddies.

I had a brand-new camera, and I began taking photos of the rice paddies and the workers. The scene was beautiful: women in colourful clothes, working in rows, moving in unison among slender, deep green stalks waving in the flooded field.

First, I had lunch with the workers on the floor of the farmhouse balcony. Then, I followed the women into the water, and they assigned me a row. I bent down and began harvesting the rice side by side with the other workers. I suddenly realized, to my horror, that I was surrounded by snakes. I let out a blood-chilling scream and leapt onto the back of one of the workers. I could not get down; I would not get down, and I could not stop screaming.

Baba had to run to rescue the poor worker and peel me off her back. He carried me piggyback all the way out of the rice paddy. Everyone was laughing except me.

"They're water snakes," Baba explained. "They're harmless." He couldn't stop laughing.

To my surprise, I realized that I was a true city girl, even though I spent so much time in our orange grove and in our villa by the Caspian Sea. Although the villa was remote—twenty minutes from the next town—it was nothing like country life. Servants and gardeners did all the work while I simply read books and magazines about the lives of celebrities in Iran, Europe, and America.

During those days, the favourite television show of many Iranian families, including my own, was *Days of Our Lives,* an American soap opera. It was broadcast once a week for an hour on Wednesday evenings. It was all Homa talked about all week. By this time, Vafa was the cook and Homa did the errands, including serving tea, an all day and evening job. But there was a rule: when *Days of Our Lives* was on, Homa was off the hook from getting anyone tea. She sat the closest to the television set, and she would make us all be quiet, even when the commercials came on. Maman and Baba sat with us too and didn't let us distract Homa. She paid special attention to the Oil of Olay commercials because she was obsessed with her complexion, and she bought every product she saw.

"I told you that you are not allowed to waste your money on skin products. You have to save your money for when you get married and leave our house. This money will buy your independence in your marriage," Maman always insisted.

When friends and relatives stayed with us, they gave Homa and Vafa huge tips. Maman wanted them to save their tips. But Homa did not listen to Maman, unlike Vafa, who loved and adored Maman and always tried to please her.

Vafa didn't want me in the kitchen; he didn't like me distracting him. But if he was cooking just for us and not for a big dinner party, he liked it when I sat in the kitchen and read him romantic stories from women's magazines while he was cooking. Vafa became famous for his cooking among our relatives and friends. At first, he was asked to go to their homes when they hosted large dinner parties to assist the chef, but soon Vafa became the chef himself.

His specialties were Tehrani dishes cooked with spices like saffron, turmeric, cinnamon, and cumin. They were flavourful without being too spicy. Vafa's *tahchin* was the best: he marinated boneless chicken pieces overnight in yogurt, saffron, onion, and salt. Rice was boiled in plenty of water and then drained. Yogurt flavoured with beaten egg yolks, saffron, butter, salt, and pepper was placed at the bottom of a pot while the cooked marinated chicken and drained rice were layered on top. This creamy, buttery, and saffron-flavoured rice was a crispy yellow-orange on the bottom.

Vafa remained Aunt Banafsheh's student when it came to Northern Iran's dishes, which were mainly vegetarian and seafood, flavoured with garlic and green herbs. They were different from Tehrani dishes. We did not use garlic or eat the northern dishes in Tehran because our dry climate was not forgiving of the smell of garlic on the breath. But we could not wait to go to Aunt Banafsheh's house in Tonekabon—the whole place exuded garlic. She had a touch for making the best garlic pickles, and she had big jars of them in her attic. I loved watching Aunt Banafsheh grind herbs with a stone in her round clay dish. Her hands moved so quickly, mincing garlic or herbs. She even made her own rice flour by hand in that clay mortar. Years later, when food processors came to the market, she refused to use them. "They take the flavour away," she claimed.

Uncle Jafar and Aunt Banafsheh's oldest daughter, Ghazal, was getting engaged. This was the first engagement party among my Massoudi cousins. When the groom came with his family for the *khastegari*, Maman and Baba were invited to attend as well.

Typically parents negotiate the *mehrieh* and the location for the wedding reception. The *mehrieh* is a sum of money that the families of the bride and the groom agree upon; this is the amount that the husband would be obligated to pay if he were to divorce his wife.

Traditionally, the groom's family pays for the reception hall, so they frequently offer to host it in a less expensive place. The bride's family, on the other hand, often have a better place in mind.

For Ghazal's wedding, the adults made all the final decisions, including planning a huge engagement party for over one hundred people. We decided to host it in our villa.

Our home was perfectly set up for such an event. When Maman and Baba were going over the plans for building our villa, Maman had wanted a liquor and tea bar off the kitchen big enough to host wedding parties. The architect had designed a window from the kitchen to open up to the bar area of the living room. There was a large half-circle bar for serving drinks, and the meals were handed through a window to the people standing behind the bar. Maman didn't want heavy traffic going through the kitchen. Only the cooks were allowed in the kitchen, and they handed the dishes out through the window.

It took Aunt Banafsheh, Vafa, and Maman days and days to plan the menu for the engagement party. They were trying to balance the meal so it would appeal to both Tehrani guests, who didn't like garlic, and Tonekaboni guests, who loved it. In the end, garlic won! Vafa was in charge of Tehrani dishes, and a chef was hired for Northern Iran dishes. But Aunt Banafsheh still prepared her specialties in advance, and Maman could not keep her away from the kitchen during the engagement party.

"Mahin jan, I just have to do one more thing, then I'll leave the kitchen."

Aunt Banafsheh could not bear the idea that the meals might not be made to her standards of perfection. The only one she trusted was Vafa. He made the Tehrani dishes better than even Aunt Banafsheh could.

The future groom's younger cousins were very handsome. All of us girls did our best dance moves to see whose attention we could get. I was obsessed with boys. I had one crush after another, but the boys didn't even know that I liked them. We didn't call what we felt a *crush*; we called it *love*.

We weren't allowed to have boyfriends. Girls *had* to remain virgins until they got married. I had a poster of a Charlie Chaplin quote on my wall: "Your naked body should only belong to those who fall in love with your naked soul." Baba and Maman did not understand what this poster meant to me. I wondered if they ever even read it.

There was even a custom-made fabric that was used on the wedding night to collect the blood from the virgin bride, proof of the bride's chastity. Once in a while, there was no blood on the fabric, and the family began to gossip. Then the bride would have to be checked by a doctor to find out if she had indeed been a virgin on her wedding night or not.

"You know what some brides do, when they are not virgins? They bring a small bottle of blood that they collected from cutting their fingers, and pour it on that fancy fabric. They pretend they were virgins." I heard this at school.

"Those men deserve to be cheated like that. If they don't remain virgins themselves, why do they expect women to stay virgins?" The girls and young women in my generation started having these kinds of conversations, but as a teenager, I didn't really think that I had the courage to break this tradition.

I was in love with a young man, Navid, who lived on the same street as my grandparents. He had long curly black hair, deep black eyes, and a hairy chest. He used to wear a black shirt with the top buttons open and a big skull necklace.

"Mehrnaz jan, what do you find attractive in this guy? The jewellery he wears is so weird. This guy is a bum."

"Baba, you are so old fashioned. Skull necklaces are in style!"

12. Maman and Vafaii

A COUPLE OF YEARS LATER, we had our own family wedding to plan. My brother Jamal was engaged to marry Gita, a daughter of one of the most prominent lawyers in Tehran. She and Jamal had been together for years, and Maman and Baba had always wanted her to become their daughter-in-law. I had never seen Maman so happy.

"But it's too expensive to have Vafaii perform at the wedding," Baba said, hoping to change Maman's mind.

Vafaii was among the top ten pop singers in Iran. He was around Maman's age, early forties. Maman loved a song of his, "Nayer." He had straight, layered thick hair down to his shoulders, and when he sang "Nayer" he shook his head, making his hair fall over his face. It melted Maman's heart when Vafaii did this.

Maman and Baba finally agreed on one thing: they were going to have a big wedding for Jamal. Five hundred people were invited. The reception was held at an exquisite hall. They hired one live band and two of the top ten pop singers: Shamaii Zadeh and Vafaii. A traditional folk band was also hired to play when the bride and groom entered the room.

Soraya and I were excited about our dresses for the reception, which were being sent from London. My mother's cousin, Rana, who had been our host when we visited, chose beautiful dresses for us and mailed them to Iran. I was fifteen, and as always, extremely conscious of my scars. My cousin knew me well, so she made sure my dress covered my scars, but Soraya's dress was low cut and sexy.

Baba and Maman stood with the bride's parents at the door and greeted the guests. Vafaii started singing, and the dance floor was soon packed with young and old. There was no room to move. After a couple of songs, the band started playing "Nayer." All of a sudden, a huge throng of people began to move, making room on the dance floor. When I turned around, I saw Maman in her beautiful blue, low-cut, long dress, dancing and walking toward the floor. She flowed from the entrance door, where she had been greeting the guests. Everyone backed off to watch Maman. I had never seen Maman move and dance so freely without limping.

"Look at the beautiful mother of the groom," guests were saying as they cleared a space for her. Vafaii jumped down from the stage and met Maman on the dance floor. The crowd—especially her old friends from Qazvin—cheered loudly.

I had only ever seen Maman in pain and limping. I had heard from so many of her friends, especially Mottee, that Maman had been a great dancer before she got sick, but I never believed them. Soon, only Maman and Vafaii were on the dance floor. When he shook his hair, Maman also shook her beautiful long hair. I didn't want the song to stop.

A week after Jamal's wedding, we were invited to our tenant's son's wedding. They lived on the second floor of our building. Before the wedding, I had gone to a hairdresser to straighten my curly hair, and I was very proud of how I looked that night, with my hair straight and shiny. The family's youngest son Kyan asked me to dance. I had never noticed him before. We danced together all night.

Kyan was in the army. I assumed he was nineteen or twenty, because if boys didn't go to university after grade twelve they were required to serve in Iran's army for two years. It became my mission, and that of our servants, to figure out which weekend Kyan would come home. As soon as his car pulled up in front of our house, the servants would notify me. Then I would show up in the hallway, all dressed up, pretending that I was going somewhere, and then just say hello. I couldn't understand why he didn't ask me out on a date. It didn't occur to me that he was actually much older than I thought.

Second only to my crush on Kyan was my obsession with fashion. Most of our clothes were custom-made by my favourite tailor, Baba's friend, the flamboyant Sina. His shop in Tehran was about an hour away from our house. Sina's large waiting room was always packed with men sitting around knitting, sewing, crocheting, and chatting while music played in the background. The room smelt of saffron, cinnamon, turmeric, and sautéed onions. Sina's friends always had a pot of stew and Persian saffron rice on the stove. Most of these men were middle-aged. But there was one young man with a very athletic body who brought tea for us. Sina was very friendly with him.

Framed photos of Sina's wife and children hung from the walls, gazing down on the flamboyant Sina and his friends.

Sina made my dresses for everyday use, but he also made my dresses for big Persian weddings, which we were invited to often. Sina loved making dresses for weddings. For these special gowns, I had to go for two fittings. On the second fitting, Sina would ask me to try on my dress and show it to his friends in the waiting room. As I twirled around them, Sina's friends always described every detail of my dress articulately and passionately, and I loved their admiration. They made me feel so good, like a supermodel, while Sina put his exquisite, final feminine touches to my clothes.

I was hoping my beautiful dresses would catch Kyan's attention. I could not understand why he never showed any interest in me after dancing all night with me at his brother's wedding several months before. In Iran, we did not have sex before we were married, but Persian dancing was the next best thing. Men and women would gaze into each other's eyes and move their bodies in sensual and flirtatious ways that would be considered inappropriate at any other time. Dancing was like foreplay, but it ended as soon as the music stopped.

After Kyan's brother's wedding, I tried for months to get his attention hoping he would ask me out. I asked my girlfriends to call him and pretend that they were interested in him while I was sitting next to them. I wanted them to find out if he had a girlfriend. Of course, I always returned the favour when they asked me to do this for me as well. But we never let the boys know who we were. The day finally arrived when Kyan asked me out. I had not been on a date before; this was my first. After consulting for days about what clothes to wear, what colour eye shadow and lipstick to put on, and of course, spending hours straightening my hair, I was ready to go on our first date.

"Where would you like to go?" he asked.

"I'm fine with just driving around," I answered. I did not wish to go to any cafés or restaurants. I was terrified that I might be seen by relatives or friends on my secret date. I had not told my parents I was going out on a date. This would not have been allowed.

"I would prefer to go to a café or a restaurant so I can see your face when we talk," he said.

I proposed that we drive to the Shemiran area. The alleys in Shemiran were considered very romantic. I had read many love stories and passionate Persian poems, and I thought it would be romantic to sit in the car underneath a lamppost in an alley with big old trees. And we wouldn't be seen by anyone!

"I want you to give me both your hands and close your eyes," Kyan whispered. He held my hands and it took my breath away. I had dreamed about this from the night we had danced together. Then I felt his face brush against mine as he tried to kiss me.

"*Yah Ghamar Bani Hashem,*" I cried out startled, and jumped back.

This was the prayer that I said when I was really afraid of something, but saying this prayer out loud while on a date was embarrassing. I had thought he was going to tell me that he loved me. Instead, Kyan turned the interior car light on.

"Are you okay? I am so sorry for scaring you. I had no intention of kissing you on our first date—that is why I wanted to go to a café or a restaurant—but you brought me to a dark alley with no one around, so I thought you wanted to make out."

"I have never kissed a man. This is my first date."

"But I always see you all dressed up with lots of makeup looking like you are going on a date."

"Oh, that's just how I dress when I go out with my friends."

"How old are you, Mehrnaz?" he asked, looking puzzled.

"Fifteen."

"Oh!"

He started the car and drove me back home.

I didn't tell him that most of the time I dressed up and put on makeup just to say hello to him in the hallway. Kyan never asked me out on a second date.

Baba was living and working in Lahijan in the north. This region was famous for growing tea, the main beverage in Iran. Since his job in the ministry required him to move so often, the government provided him with a car, a driver, and a house in the middle of the tea hills.

Brewing Persian tea is an art. We are very particular about the taste and the colour of the tea and how it is served. When brewed too long, it becomes bitter and cloudy. Any time of the day, when visitors drop by, they are offered tea, served strong, in small clear glasses with small irregular cubes of sugar.

Vafa spread a large tablecloth on the floor of the kitchen and broke a one-foot-tall sugar cone into small chunks, skilfully tapping at the edges with a brass sugar hammer. It took many hours to prepare enough to supply our household for a few months. The cubes were dense and dissolved very slowly. They added just a hint of sweetness to the flavour of the strong tea. We did not have dessert after meals, only tea with cubes of sugar. For children, the tea was poured into the saucer with one small sugar cube stirred in to cool and sweeten it.

Sometimes Dr. Farhangi, Kyan's father, came downstairs to our apartment for teatime with Maman. Maman was an intellectual woman, and she enjoyed her highbrow conversations with Dr. Farhangi. "Dr. Farhangi is a professor at the University of Tehran. He speaks seven languages," Maman said.

I sometimes wondered if Maman would have been happier with a man like Dr. Farhangi rather than with Baba.

"I want to share my life with a man who I can have intellectual conversations with. I just don't understand why we still allow the custom of *khastegari*. There are so many unhappy couples who do not share common interests. It's not acceptable that my parents are allowing *khastegars* to come and evaluate Soraya." Roshi and I were at Sholeh for tea.

"There is so much pressure on us to marry a suitable man.

66

Every time I go to a wedding, people turn to my mother and say that they wish the next wedding would be for Sholeh jan. It makes me so upset that they think we are just objects waiting to be selected by a suitor. What about love and common interests? *Khastegari* is an undignified tradition for women."

Roshi said, "Oh, how about this expression: 'You go to your husband's house in a white dress, and you leave your husband's house in a white dress?'"

The dead body of a Muslim is wrapped in white fabric, and then the wrapped body is buried in the ground.

It was time for Soraya's *khastegari*, and the family of one of her suitors was coming over. He was a doctor. She put on a fancy dress, but she still wasn't allowed to wear makeup. It was traditional for the girl to bring tea for the family of the *khastegar*, and for them to judge whether she had brewed a good tea and presented it well. Maman did not believe in this tradition, however, so Homa brought the tea. Soraya could only enter the room a few minutes after everyone was seated, and she had to stay seated while the *khastegar*'s family was there. I was dressed up too, but I was allowed to go in and out of the room as I pleased.

"Oh my God, the doctor is old and ugly," I announced to Soraya before she'd had a chance to see him.

"Shut up! You are so *foozul*." Soraya pushed me out of her room, but then Vafa ran to her room and put his hands on his cheeks and said the same thing.

The sisters of the doctor had seen Soraya in the waiting room of our neighbourhood public bath and thought that she would make a good bride for their brother.

Once a week, we went to the public bath for a thorough cleaning. We showered at home, but we loved the ritual of going to the public bath. We only used the private rooms, but there was another part that had a pool in the middle of a room and shower stalls. People sat by the pool to exfoliate their bodies and wash their hair before rinsing in the shower. Maman never let us use the public room; she thought it was dirty. Instead, she always phoned in advance to book a private room for us, and she gave a generous tip to the manager for making sure it was extra clean. But she still brought a portion of powdered potassium permanganate, which she dissolved in hot water and poured over the whole surface area of the room. The room had a sitting area that held six or seven people, and one big shower head hanging from the ceiling, which ran all the time. The walls and the sitting area were covered with white tiles. There were staff in the public bath who would come to exfoliate our bodies and wash our hair for an extra charge. Maman's favourite worker was Nargess, and Maman booked her at the same time that she booked the room.

"Nargess is great at exfoliation. When we get someone else I can see dead skin afterwards, but not with Nargess." Maman recommended Nargess to our neighbours. This was a neighbourhood public bath. Maman always bought the best *kisseh,* not too soft but not too hard that it would hurt our skin. *Kisseh* was a mitten for exfoliation. When we were waiting for our turn to be exfoliated by Nargess, we asked the manager to bring us drinks and snacks. I asked for chips or cheese puffs and pop. The room would get hot and steamy, and Nargess would wait for a while because she wanted us to sweat before she exfoliated us.

The sister of Soraya's suitor had called our home several times hoping to learn whether her brother was accepted for marriage. Maman put Homa in charge of communicating with the family while Maman did her research about them.

Homa, Soraya, and I were in the public bath with Nargess when there was a knock on the door. The sisters of the doctor knew Nargess well, and they asked her if they could share our room. Later on, Maman found out that when the manager had booked Nargess for us, Nargess had told the sisters. She wanted this marriage to happen because she knew the doctor's family, and she kept trying to convince Maman that they were very reputable and respectable. Nargess was acting as a matchmaker because she would get a huge tip from the groom's family if the marriage was a success. The sisters, who were closer to Maman's age, took off their clothes and joined us in the shower room. Nargess carried on a conversation with them. Homa, Soraya, and I were awkwardly quiet. We knew they were there to inspect Soraya's body.

In very devoted Muslim families, the tradition of *khastegari* dictates that the female family members of the *khastegar* have to check the naked body of the woman to make sure that it is perfect.

The sisters of the doctor wore *chador*. This was their way to sneak into the bath to check Soraya's body. Poor Soraya—even with her flawless body, she felt so shy under their staring eyes. I asked Nargess to wash me first so I could leave the room. I didn't care about hiding my deformed body from them. They were not there to judge my body, but I was appalled by their intentions.

Soraya also emerged from the bath quickly. We sat in the main lobby, waiting for Homa, drinking pop and eating chips, and laughing about how disgusting it was that the sisters had invited themselves in, and had stared at Soraya, and asked stupid questions like, "Do you say your daily prayers?"

Soraya lied and had said yes, but she didn't look at me because she knew we would burst into laughter. Soraya was lucky that they didn't ask her to recite the daily prayers. I was the one who prayed on and off, so I knew the prayers off by heart, but she did not. The sisters waited a while for Baba and Maman to make their decision. The doctor was in his late thirties. Baba and Maman liked that he was a doctor, but they didn't feel that the family was a good match for us. Although they did not mention anything about Soraya wearing a *chador*, Maman and Baba felt that after the marriage they might pressure Soraya to do so. Finally, Homa phoned the sister and politely rejected them.

13. Soraya Gets Married

TWO CARS PULLED INTO THE DRIVEWAY of our villa. A suitor was coming to ask for Soraya's hand. "Oh look! I like his car," I said to Vafa. The suitor was driving a beautiful BMW.

"But he's not good looking at all!" I exclaimed.

"I agree," Vafa nodded solemnly.

"You two be quiet now. No one is asking for your opinions," Maman said. She was always so nervous when the suitors came. Everything had to be orchestrated—when the tea would come, who would bring the tea, when Soraya would enter the room, and so on.

"Homa, you had better bring the tea. I only bring tea when the suitor is good-looking," instructed Vafa, raising his hands to emphasize that he would not be serving this time.

"Don't you remember that I am not supposed to bring tea anymore," Homa snapped, "after that freak suitor who thought I was Soraya? Every time I entered the room to bring tea and serve sweets and fruits, he got up and wouldn't sit down while I was serving. He was checking me out from head to toe." Homa made a face to show how dismaying it had been.

"Poor man," she continued. "Perhaps his Maman had taken him to see a girl every day and he couldn't remember the name of the girl he was going to see. Soraya was introduced when she entered the room, and my name is not even close to Soraya's."

"Homa, you made him fall in love with your green eyes. He wanted to kiss you," I teased.

"Stop it, you're making me nauseous." She scowled.

The father of the suitor was a colleague of Baba's. Baba and

Maman approved of his family. The suitor, Iraj, had a degree in Russian and English languages and worked as a translator for a large company. He was ten years older than Soraya.

A few days after the *khastegari*, Iraj dropped by with Farang, a close family friend of ours.

"It looks like Iraj's BMW just pulled in," Vafa said.

"Iraj would like to have a chance to talk to Soraya in private, so I brought him over. I hope you don't mind?" asked Farang.

Soraya and Iraj walked toward the beach. Vafa and I trailed them to the edge of the villa, and then we hid and watched from behind a tree.

Maman frowned at me. "Mehrnaz, come inside. Vafa, you go follow them, but give them some space."

"I really like him," Soraya said afterwards. "He seems very kind. We decided to get engaged so we can spend more time with each other." Soraya sounded so different. She had been easily persuaded by Iraj, I thought.

"Soraya, just take your time. Iraj's family are pressuring us because they all love you, but you don't have to give them an answer right away," advised Maman.

A few months later, a big engagement party was held in our house. The families had agreed that Iraj and Soraya would be engaged for one year. After the engagement party, Iraj, who lived in the city of Rasht in Northern Iran, was allowed to come and stay in our house on the weekends, as long as he and Soraya slept in different rooms. When he visited, they included me in most of their outings to movies and restaurants, visits with friends, and strolling in parks. And I began to like Iraj.

"So I heard that when I came for *khastegari*, someone said that I was ugly," Iraj said to me teasingly.

"Soraya, how dare you?" I was so embarrassed.

Maman and Baba were busy preparing for *jahazieh*—furnishing a home for the newlyweds with custom-made furniture for the bedroom, living, and dining rooms, and new appliances for the kitchen—and shopping for Persian rugs, Baba's favourite task, for most of the rooms in the house.

Sina was disappointed that he was not chosen to make the wedding dress for Soraya. He was a great tailor, but not of the

Uncle Dariush Rashvand Sardari

calibre that we would have chosen to make a wedding gown. Nevertheless, he was delighted to make my dress.

"I want a dress just like Miss Iran's—the one that she wore the night she was crowned," I instructed.

"Let me find the magazine," Sina replied. He was proud of his collection of women's magazines.

"I want it just like hers: white gauze for the chest and shoulder area, white fabric for the dress, and a pink belt with a pink orchid." He did not disappoint me.

Soraya looked stunning in her sleeveless, low-cut and body-hugging, white silk wedding dress. The ceremony was held at our house and the reception at a hotel. I was happy for my sister, but mostly I was excited because I knew Kyan would be attending the reception.

"Oh my, who is that gorgeous man?" Roshi said, fanning her face with her hand and directing me with her eyes.

"Oh my God, stay away from him. He is my Uncle Dariush. He is Maman's youngest brother."

At the reception, Roshi, a few of my cousins who were around my age, Kyan's sister Sara, and Kyan and I danced in a circle for the whole night. I still had a crush on him, although he hadn't asked me out again since our last disastrous date when he had tried to kiss me.

Uncle Dariush was not dancing, so Roshi made sure we could see him from the dance floor. Even after the wedding, Roshi couldn't stop talking about him. Our friends couldn't believe that I had never told them I had such a handsome uncle.

"Look, he is really serious," I said. "He always talks about books with me. I think you guys would feel like a little girl with him. He is so mature for his age."

"Excuse me. Not 'you guys!' They weren't at the wedding. I discovered him. He's mine," Roshi declared. "When Dariush entered the hall in that navy blue suit at Soraya's wedding, I gasped. He had such a presence, with his beautiful mystic eyes and his genuine smile."

Roshi still talks about him to this day.

Unlike most Persian girls, Roshi has sandy blonde hair, olive skin, and big hazel eyes. So many men in my family admired Roshi's beauty, even men in their forties. Roshi finally asked me for Uncle Dariush's phone number. She couldn't get him out of her heart. I gave her his number and made her promise not to tell him that she was my friend. She started phoning Uncle Dariush and with every conversation she fell more in love with him. Then she couldn't resist any longer and she told him who she was.

"Roshi, you are too young. You are just like Mehrnaz to me," he told her.

Roshi was not heartbroken that he had rejected her. On the contrary, it made her love him more. Whenever we met men, they always gravitated toward Roshi first; I was the second choice. Men of all ages wanted Roshi, and now Uncle Dariush treated her with the respect and integrity that every young girl wishes for deep down.

"Everyone treats me like a beautiful object," Roshi exclaimed. "They see my hair, my body, my eyes, but what I want them to see is my soul. Dariush was that man I was searching for. A man who does not objectify a woman!"

We both sighed.

14. Reza and Ashura

"A NEW FAMILY MOVED IN next door to my uncle's house. Mehrnaz, I know you would love their son, Reza. He looks just like your favourite water polo player." Roshi gave me Reza's phone number. Reza was at university studying architecture and was often there late into the evening. The only time he and I could talk on the phone was late at night, after he got home.

"Mehrnaz, are you on the phone? Are you sleeping?"

Maman slowly opened my bedroom door. Reza knew not to say anything when the phone went dead. We had been talking so quietly. Baba's bedroom was next to mine, and I could hear him snoring. Maman's bedroom was next to Baba's, but she could still hear someone talking on the phone. Reza and I would usually talk till two or three in the morning. Getting up for school the next day was always difficult.

When Maman walked into the room, I would hide the phone under my comforter and start snoring. Maman was always worried about my congested sinuses and allergies.

"I heard someone talking last night," she said. "I came to your room and you were snoring. You sounded congested. You don't listen to me—you must wear a hat and cover your nose with a scarf in winter. I'll make an appointment with your ear, nose, and throat specialist. He needs to look at your sinuses."

"I cannot come to Qazvin for Ashura. I have to study," I fibbed and looked at my parents with what I hoped was my most studious face.

The Day of Ashura marks the Remembrance of Muharram.

Muharram is the first month of the Islamic lunar calendar, when Shia Muslims begin mourning for the grandson of the Prophet Mohammad, Imam Hussein, who was martyred at the Battle of Karbala. The mourning starts from the first day of Muharram and continues for ten nights. The tenth day of Muharram is Ashura. That is the day that Imam Hussein, his wife, and his children were all murdered.

Iran is predominantly Shia. Since the Prophet Mohammad didn't have a son, Shia Muslims believe that his successor is his son-in-law, Hazrate Ali. Sunni Muslims believe the successor is Caliph Abu Bakr. Both Hazrate Ali and Caliph Abu Bakr were very close to Mohammad. Shia have twelve leaders who are called Imam, and the first four leaders in Sunni are called the Caliphs. Sadly, there have been many wars between Sunni and Shia Muslims. The Battle of Karbala was between a small group of supporters and relatives of Imam Hussein, the son of Hazrate Ali, and a much larger military detachment of the forces of Yazid I, the Caliph of Sunni.

I was in grade twelve, and every time I didn't want to do something, I said that I needed to study. My parents knew that I had to study hard if I wanted to get into a good university, and so they always believed me.

Maman looked at Vafa.

"I won't be missing Ashura's ceremony in Qazvin," Vafa said sharply.

"Maman, I talked to Ashraf, and her mother agreed for her to stay with me. Her mother said she would check on us." I was still friendly with Ashraf, from the compound across the street.

My parents agreed to travel to Qazvin on their own and leave me behind. As soon as it was settled, I called Reza and asked him if he would like to come over for dinner with my friends.

I had attended the Day of Ashura ceremonies in Qazvin the previous year. It was our tradition to wear black for the ten days of Muharram. On the evening of Ashura, men met at the mosque and marched through the streets. They all wore black and, while they marched, they chanted and flogged themselves on the chest; some of them used small whips with chains to hit themselves on their backs and shoulders. The men in front led the chanting and the rhythm of the flagellation. The chains were held together with a handgrip that made a musical sound as the men lifted their whips and slapped their backs.

I loved watching their holy march. The rhythmic sound and movement were mesmerizing and spiritual.

The shoulders of these men were bruised for days afterwards; sometimes they bled. In some rare cases, men cut themselves on the forehead with machetes. They believed that by hurting themselves physically, they would remember and sympathize with the murder of Imam Hussein.

Two or three men carried an *alam*, a heavy, metal installation that was filled with intricate figurines and engravings and that could weigh up to three hundred kilograms. Candles were lit throughout the *alam*.

"Mottee, it's Mahin," Maman had knocked at the door of the *takieh*, the building used to perform the Ashura rituals.

Mottee's family owned a heritage building in Qazvin. It was like an old arena. There was a spacious courtyard with a stage in the middle that was open to the public. The building around the courtyard was two storeys high, and contained several small rooms. It was this building in Qazin that was used as the *takieh*. Mottee's brother hosted ceremonies during the ten days of Muharram, but Ashura was the climax of the celebration; more than a thousand people attended the ceremony.

Theatrical performances and re-enactments of the events of Ashura would take place on the stage, and Mottee reserved a big room on the second floor that had a good view. Actors portrayed Imam Hussein and his family. Then a *mullah* would give a speech and sing prayers. Men and women would weep throughout the entire ceremony.

"Marjan, how is my skirt?" I had asked my cousin who lived in Qazvin. We were fussing with our clothing and our hair as we got ready for the day's ritual ceremonies.

Marjan and I were so excited about going to the *takieh*. I also loved hanging out with Fereshteh, Mottee's daughter. Mottee had the best room in the *takieh*, facing her brother's room. Baba and many of our relatives and friends were invited into her brother's room. But the women were only allowed in Mottee's room. I could see the boys on the first floor, but they couldn't see us very well.

All women had to wear *chadors* in the *takieh*. Formal *chadors* were transparent with patterns in cut velvet, and women wore them over their black dresses at funerals. But we couldn't wear transparent *chadors* to the *takieh* or to the mosque. Maman Aterahm had many different *chadors*, so we chose the ones we liked to go to the *tekieh*.

Marjan and I were wearing mini skirts with black pantyhose hidden under our *chadors*.

"Excuse me, excuse me," I said, as Marjan and I passed through a crowd of Mottee's friends on the way to the bathroom. We had to walk down the stairs and wind our way through hundreds of women wearing black and sitting in the courtyard, just so we could go to the bathroom. Our sole purpose, however, was to pass the room where the boys we knew were standing. Marjan and I were excellent at walking with the *chador*. We held the *chador* under our chins with one hand and let the rest of the material fly back, showing our mini skirts and stockinged legs to the boys.

"Talaan wants you to go downstairs to bless the entry of a group who have just arrived from mosque." Ashraf was looking at me as she answered the door. Talaan and his wife and children lived in the compound across the street from us. I had forgotten that this year, he had asked my parents' permission to host the ten-day commemoration for Muharram in our basement. We had a big finished basement with a bathroom and kitchen, and my parents had said yes.

"Oh God, I'm covered with makeup and I have nail polish on. I can't go. It would be disrespectful."

Ashraf grabbed *chadors* for herself and for me. "Cover everything and only leave your eyes open."

"But what about my hands? They would see my nail polish."

"Give them a hand gesture of blessing with your hands under the *chador*."

I did not expect such a big group at the front door to our

basement. The men who were carrying the *alam* bowed holding it in front of me. I gestured, inviting them in. Talaan put his hand on his heart and bowed to me.

"I felt so guilty standing there with all that makeup on and those men bowing to me," I told my friends later. "We shouldn't have put on makeup during Ashura." They agreed. We also scolded each other for not having worn black and mourned as was the tradition. Then we were all remorseful.

"Oh God, oh God, Reza is here. Do I look good?" I was nervous about meeting Reza in person for the first time. I had told him that my family had gone to Qazvin for Ashura and he had agreed to join me and my friends for dinner.

I had only spoken to him on the phone and I was shocked when I saw Reza. He did not look like my favourite Iranian water polo player. Why had Roshi said that to me? He was cute, but I was expecting him to look like the tall, wide-shouldered, handsome water polo player. Instead, he was of average height, and he had a petite build. But the moment he started talking to me, I stopped thinking about his looks and found myself charmed by the familiar voice from our nightly talks.

"Oh, I thought you said only Roshi would be here," Reza said quietly. He knew Roshi, but he didn't know Ashraf or our five high school friends.

My friends and I always talked *about* boys, and we talked on the *phone* with boys, but we did not go out on *dates* with boys, at least not officially. We put on makeup and went out to movies and cafés and restaurants, but if one of us did have a date in a café, the rest of us would sit at the next table, without the guy knowing that we were friends of his date. This way we felt safe, and we could check the guy out. Our families did not approve of us dating. All of us were raised in moderately religious families. Islam was our religion and our deeply rooted culture.

Reza ate dinner with seven girls that evening, and then he asked if he could go to my room. My friends and I laughed at how embarrassed Reza was; we didn't think it would be so awkward. Reza and I had tea in my room. We sat next to each other on the Persian rug cushion, our legs outstretched and touching.

"This is such a good feeling, but it is a sin, especially at Ashura."

I was feeling two emotions at the same time: guilt and desire.

Reza left shortly afterwards, and I told my friends about how good it felt sitting right next to him. I continued my phone relationship with Reza until Kyan finally asked me out again in the spring of grade twelve.

Afterwards, when my parents returned from Qazvin, my Baba was very pleased with me. "Talaan was so touched by your showing up at the door with *chador*. He congratulated me for raising a daughter like you," he said.

Talaan had also told Baba, "These days, young people have no respect for Ashura. Haji, you raised such a good daughter."

15. In America with Baba

GRADE TWELVE WAS A NIGHTMARE for many students. Our grade twelve average and the outcome of our university entrance exams determined which university and subjects we could apply for. I studied very hard and maintained a high average until spring arrived, but it got more challenging to stay focused. I woke up early in the morning to study, but the fragrance of honeysuckle and wisteria from our neighbours' yard made me close my science textbooks and write poetry.

Poetry was my companion when I was sad and when I was in love—the words just poured onto the paper. Iran is the land of Rumi, Hafiz, Khayyam, and many other great, lasting romantic poets, all of whom inspired me.

My hard work and dedication to romancing Kyan had finally paid off, and we began dating regularly. We adhered to tradition and did not have sex. We liked to walk along the ponds in Tehran's parks, sit in the rose gardens, and inhale the intoxicating perfume.

Sometimes, I brought with me a book of poetry by the young female Persian poet named Forugh Farrokhzad. I would ask Kyan to read some poems aloud while I closed my eyes and let his voice fill my heart. Once when Maman and Baba were not home, Kyan came to my room and read my favourite poem from that book, "Another Birth," into a tape recorder.

> *Perhaps life is that second when my gaze*
> *Loses itself in the depth of your eyes*
> *And it is in that sensation*

That I become one with the moon
And the darkness of the night.
I know a sad little fairy
Who resides in the ocean
And she plays the song of her heart,
So ever gently
On her Ney.
A sad little fairy
Who dies at night with one kiss
And at dawn, she rises with one kiss.

I brought this poetry book and tape recording to soothe me while I was away from Kyan, travelling again, this time to America for my third plastic surgery.

Kyan had not been accepted to university in Iran, and he was leaving to go to university in England where his brother was. I was sad to be separating from him, but I was also planning to study in America while fulfilling my life-long dream of getting plastic surgery at the age of eighteen. The hope that my scars would soon go away with surgery had made my teenage years bearable. I dreamed about having a party after I returned to Iran and showing off my body with no scars to all my friends. I dreamed almost every night of the story that my aunt Masi used to tell me of the girl with the porcelain skin.

Roshi gave me a beautiful tank top as a going-away gift. She also believed that after this surgery my scars would go away and I would be able to wear tank tops like all my friends did.

My trip to America started with a family trip to London. Baba, Maman, and Maman Aterahm flew over with Aunt Masi, Uncle Manoocher, and their three daughters. Aunt Masi and Uncle Manoocher had purchased a town house in Basildon, a town outside London, from a cousin of ours who was in real estate in England. They had only seen photos of this house before purchasing it. The temperature in Tehran was over forty degrees Celsius when we left, but when we arrived in Basildon we had to wear cardigans and turn the gas fireplace on; we all loved it. At night when everyone was in bed, I was so inspired by the coolness of the night and the flames of the fireplace that I stayed up and wrote poetry until the early hours of the morning.

Baba and I only stayed one week; then we left for America to join Jamal and his wife, and Soraya and her husband. Maman stayed in Basildon for a month before going back to Iran to take care of the house and all the servants. Vafa had been left in charge of everything.

Jamal and I consulted with many plastic surgeons in different states in America. I did not like any of them; when we were in their offices, they faced Jamal and talked to him. There was more conversation about the cost of the surgery than its outcome. I had loved Dr. Thompson, my plastic surgeon in London; at the age of twelve, I hardly understood any English, but he had always faced me and spoken with such a gentle manner. Dr. Hushang had translated it for me.

Jamal and Soraya lived in Washington, DC. We all found the summer in Washington hot and humid, but Jamal and Soraya told us that the winters were very cold. We decided to move to Scranton, Pennsylvania. We were so relieved to find pleasant summer weather in Scranton. Although Tehran was hot, it was always a dry heat, and some relief could be found in the shade or after sunset. At our villa, the weather was hot and humid, but nothing like what we experienced in Washington.

I applied for pre-dentistry; to my surprise I was accepted at Marywood University in Scranton after only one interview. My grade twelve average was very low for an Iranian university, but I was accepted in a pre-dentistry program in America.

I was taking science courses. My English was not very strong, but grade twelve in Iran covered chemistry, calculus, physics, and biology at the same level as they were offered at the college. So I knew the subjects; I just had to learn new vocabulary. The tests were also mostly multiple choice, which made things easier.

Baba was buying souvenirs and getting ready to go back to England to stay with Aunt Masi and her family before returning to Iran. I was supposed to stay in Scranton to study and then have the surgery when the semester was over.

I lived with Jamal and Gita. Every day he drove me to the college and picked me up in the afternoon. He was also busy studying to complete his MBA. I was not motivated to study. I was homesick and bored, and Jamal was controlling. I told Baba that I would rather live with Soraya and Iraj, who were much more easy-going and fun.

"Oh, daughter, you must stay with your brother," Baba said. "It's not respectful to him if you go and live with your sister and her husband. He is your older brother. I am paying for this nice two-bedroom apartment so you can have your own bedroom and bathroom."

I was sad at the thought of Baba leaving, and I really missed the fun I'd had in Iran with my friends. I hung out a few times with my classmates from Marywood University. We went to the McDonalds drive-through, but my stomach could not digest the food. In Iran we ate lamb, not beef, though we did not eat that much meat; at home, I mainly ate whole foods. My classmates also asked me to go to bars, but I didn't drink alcohol. I missed the crowd in Pahlavi Street, the main street running from the north to the south of the city in Tehran.

In Iran, my girlfriends and I strolled along the streets of Tehran nearly every night. Ancient Cypress trees filled with songbirds lined both sides of Pahlavi Street, adding to the clamour of busy stores and food vendors. Our favourite hang-outs were American or European-style high-end cafés and restaurants, the Chattanooga and the Sorrento on Pahlavi Street. But Western-style food was expensive and not tasty. When we wanted delicious cuisine, we ate at traditional Persian restaurants. But we were not on Pahlavi Street for the food; we were there to feast with our eyes: to watch the boys, critique fashions, and, most importantly, to look alluring sipping on our elegant non-alcoholic cocktails.

There were many eventful evenings on Pahlavi Street, like the night Maman's friend Mottee came for a visit. Mottee was a stylish woman who usually wore very elegant clothing, but sometimes when she did not feel like dressing up and styling her hair, she wore a *chador*. I was bored, and I pestered Maman for us to take a walk, but Mottee was reluctant because she didn't want to go to the high-end part of Pahlavi Street in a *chador*. Finally, I convinced them to come for a short walk with me and Vafa. Then I insisted on going to the Chattanooga. The server at the entrance quietly informed us that women wearing *chadors* were not allowed to come in. So I pulled poor Mottee's *chador* down and we all walked in. We were laughing so hard at embarrassed Mottee in her house clothes with her messy hair.

Now I was stuck in Scranton where it was dead quiet after five o'clock.

"Baba, I've decided that I'm coming with you to London. I want Dr. Thompson to be my surgeon. I have such fond memories of him when he operated on me when I was twelve."

"Mehrnaz jan, I am so happy that you made this decision. The thought of separating from you was breaking my heart."

"Baba, I don't think I want to be a doctor or a dentist. I've decided to become a fashion designer. I am thinking of turning the big room in the basement of our apartment building in Tehran into my fashion design studio."

"We could remove the wall between the kitchen and the bathroom and create a spacious fitting room and a small bathroom." Baba sounded so excited.

"Mehrnaz, when you talked to Sina about design, I could see your excitement. You will be so good at it."

I was so happy to be back at Basildon with Aunt Masi, Uncle Manoocher, Maman Aterahm, and my cousins. Dr. Hushang was pleased to see me again too. My surgery was booked with Dr. Thompson, who was as kind and gentle as I remembered him. He suggested that for the next five to six years, he would schedule a new surgery for me every six months. In the meantime, I could enrol in a degree program.

Baba and I went to the Paris Academy in London and I enrolled in the fashion design program. I window-shopped in the streets of London with Baba and dreamed about my career.

Every morning, Baba and I took the train from Basildon to London. Baba dropped me at the academy and explored London until lunchtime, and then we went for lunch together. At the end of the day, we took the train back to Basildon and arrived home to the smell of Persian dinner being cooked.

Being with Baba out on the streets of London was sometimes embarrassing. "Baba, don't always start a conversation in the streets or on the train with Iranians; it's so embarrassing. We don't have to talk to them just because they're Iranian." I would have to say this to him almost every day.

And, everytime, Baba would respond solemenly, "Mehrnaz, don't ever forget your roots," and then shake his head solemnly.

So when we went shopping one day, I had to warn my cousin. "Pari, go ask Baba to come to the fitting area but tell him not to speak Farsi because there are two Iranian women here. I don't want Baba starting a conversation with them."

Pari was Aunt Masi's oldest daughter. She was thirteen years old and she loved to come shopping with us.

"Mehrnaz *vaat* me." Baba kept repeating this as he waited for me outside the fitting room. He wanted to say *what*, but it sounded like *vaat*. He was translating from Farsi to English a phrase that meant "What would you like from me?"

Pari and I were so embarrassed. We were certain everyone was looking at him.

"Pari, please take Baba out of the store. I beg you. Oh my God, I'm so embarrassed." I left the store without buying anything.

Baba was mad at Pari and me for being embarrassed by him talking to fellow Iranians. But it took less than five minutes before Baba had started talking to two Iranian men in the street. "Mehrnaz, could you tell these gentlemen which school you attend?"

Baba used to meet his friends and go for a walk every late afternoon and evening in Iran. He was used to chatting with friends while walking. He found it strange that people walked in such a rush on the streets of London.

"Look, no one makes eye contact here." Baba also couldn't believe no one talked on the train from Basildon to London, even though they were sitting next to us or in front of us.

"Baba, don't look at them," I would plead. "It's rude. They want to read their books and newspapers."

"They should read their books and newspapers when they're alone. The train is a place to meet, chat, and hear each other's stories." Baba was used to reading the Iranian newspapers daily, but only at home.

"Now you're telling the British what to do. Iran is being controlled by the British and the Americans. They do not waste a minute of the day. They are productive and successful nations." I tried to persuade him that he had to change his way of thinking.

Baba was nothing if not consistent. "Daughter, success does not translate into happiness. When I walk on the streets of Basildon, I can see people through the windows of their homes sitting on their couches and watching television. I do not see people talking together or visitors dropping by. They are not connected; this makes people unhappy."

I started getting bored of the conversation, though, so I changed topic.

"Baba, look! Women here wear nylons without shaving their legs. That's really disgusting," I said. In Iran, all the women shaved their legs before putting on nylon stockings.

I did not look at the faces of people in the train, but I did look at their legs and feet. I noticed that the men's shoes were so highly polished. I thought they must polish their shoes every single night.

I only lasted three weeks in the fashion design program. "Baba, the class is too slow. The teacher gives us a number that we have to add, subtract, or divide to make our own patterns, but then it takes so long for most of the students to calculate and draw the lines. I wish he would just let us work on our own pace. I am so bored in this class. I don't want to be a fashion designer anymore."

"I paid a big fee for you to enrol in this program. It's a very reputable academy. How about staying a few more weeks? There is no other program you can join now before your surgery date."

"No, Baba, I can't stand to be there one more day." And, as usual, he indulged me.

I started to do the touristy things with Baba. We explored London, but mostly we ended up at Harrods, our favourite department store.

Baba, Baba's cousin, and I checked in at the same hospital, London Clinic, where I had had my other surgery at the age of twelve. We were told that it would be a long surgery. Baba looked pale and nervous.

The procedure was long and extremely painful. I stayed in the hospital for over a month. There was no cast this time. My chest was open and exposed. Dr. Thompson came every day, taking stitches out of my chest and from under my arm. I was in extreme pain. Baba stayed with me in the hospital every day. He arrived every morning to wake me up for breakfast, and left late in the evening, catching the last train to Basildon.

Kyan was living just a few hours away from London. I sent him a card while I was in the hospital, and he called me. I loved hearing his sweet voice; it was salve for my suffering. I was hoping that we could see each other once I was released from the hospital. I didn't want him to see me in the hospital. But he never contacted me again while I was in England, and I was heartbroken that he did not make an effort to see me. I missed him so much.

Baba and Maman were happy with the arrangement that we had discussed with Dr. Thompson. They wanted me to stay in London, go to school, and continue with my surgeries, but I decided to go back to Iran. I announced to them that I would not continue with any further plastic surgery on my burn scars. My body looked worse after this third surgery than before, because of the new skin graft on the outside of my thigh and the redness from the stitches on my chest. There were about two hundred stitches from the surgery on my chest and under my arm. I had had enough.

"My body is good for me. I cannot imagine spending another day in the hospital. I also cannot justify the amount of money you are spending on me. If a man wants to marry me, he will have to love all of me."

Many of our relatives who lived in London advised me not to go back to Iran. They were concerned about the unstable political conditions there. The Shah's regime was getting weaker, and the opposition parties were growing in popularity, even though they were still operating underground. Many demonstrations against the Shah's regime were being organized outside Iran by Iranian students who were studying abroad.

I was stubborn, however, so in January 1977, I returned to my beloved home in Tehran. I never did have that party to show off my body to my friends, and I never wore the tank top that Roshi gave me.

I started living life without the hope that the scars would ever go away. I hated my scarred chest. I felt like I was living two lives. Clothed, I felt beautiful, but naked, I felt ugly.

Every night, I cried for my shattered dreams, for the torture I had endured for nothing, for the endless stream of surgeries, the disappointments, and now for the long healing process and the knowledge that this was it.

I replayed Aunt Masi's story in my head one more time.

"*When she was a child, her whole body was covered with burn scars. Then when she turned eighteen, she went to England for plastic surgery. We didn't see her for a whole year. When she came back, she had a big party. She was wearing a beautiful sleeveless dress. After the party ended, a few of us stayed for a sleepover. We asked to see her body. The room was lit by moonlight. She took off her dress. She was beautiful—her long black hair hung down on her porcelain body. She had beautiful breasts with no scars. Her body was flawless except for one strand of hair on the side. When I went to remove the hair, I discovered it wasn't a hair at all: it was the only scar from the plastic surgery. Her other scars were all gone.*"

It was only then that I understood that Aunt Masi's story was fictional. It was based on her hopes and dreams for me.

16. A Motorcycle Ride

"I CRIED EVERY DAY while you were away. I didn't want you to go for another surgery. I remember how your body looked after you came back from London when you were twelve—there were so many new red marks from stitches and your leg where the skin graft was taken was so red and sensitive. The only person you allowed to put ointment on your thigh was me, but you still cried because it was so painful. I rubbed the ointment as gently as I could, but your skin was so raw. I didn't want you to go through all of that again."

Vafa was still crying.

The first week I was back in Iran, I was invited to a party on the first floor of our apartment building. Maman had rented the first floor to a couple while I was away. At the party, Aly introduced himself to me as the brother of our new tenant, and he asked me to dance. The next day, he phoned me and said he was in love with me.

"How is that possible? You just met me last night," I said.

"When you were away, Vafa came to visit my sister regularly. He always talked about you. He shared so many stories about you. He cried when you were having surgery—he didn't want you to have any more. He believes you are the most beautiful girl in the whole world, and he carried your framed photo with him. I fell in love with you before I even met you. Vafa told me that you were going to stay for a few years until all the plastic surgeries were done, and I was sad that I wouldn't get the chance to meet you. I think Vafa knew that I was falling in love with you, because when he found out you were coming back home, I was the first person he shared the news with."

Aly was ten years older than me. He was so mature and serious that he seemed even older. The age difference was acceptable in Iran. Parents approved of men with higher education, usually engineers, physicians, and lawyers. If a man was older, it meant that he was settled down and financially independent; it was very common for men over thirty to marry young women of seventeen or eighteen.

We went on a few dates and we talked on the phone. After a couple of months, we unofficially got engaged at Aly's insistence. He saw no reason for us to date in secret. "I love you and I want the whole world to see us together," he said. Engagement was the key for Iranian young people to date openly.

I didn't want to have an official *khastegari* and engagement party. My parents liked Aly. He knew every detail about my body, thanks to Vafa; it was very tempting to marry a man who loved me in spite of the scars on my body. The only thing that was missing was that I did not love him.

Most girls married this way, including my friends, cousins, and my sister. They did not fall in love with their suitors; when they chose a husband, they used logic rather than their hearts.

And then it hit me. I thought, "Oh my, what have I done? My heart is filled with love for Kyan. I will be unhappy for the rest of my life if I marry Aly."

I sent a letter to Kyan. Even though he had not contacted me or visited me after his phone call to the hospital, I still believed that he loved me.

"A man proposed to me," I wrote, "and my parents have approved. I will wait for you to come back, if you want me to. I love you."

Kyan wrote back and asked me not to wait for him. Heartbroken once again, I burned all our photos.

Once we were engaged, Aly was so happy that he was able to officially pick me up from my house. We went to cafés and walked in parks, but I had no feelings for him. Everyone was excited at home, but I told them that I didn't want to talk about wedding plans.

"It stresses me out," I said, dodging the issue.

Vafa was the only one who could not control his excitement. He talked constantly about Aly and the wedding, repeating to himself, "The first time I met Aly, I fell in love with his genuine smile. I wanted him to become the groom, the husband of Mehrnaz."

I was taking classes for the university entrance exam. I studied very hard and managed not to be distracted by Aly. My main focus was to get into university. Uncle Dariush was thrilled to see my enthusiasm about continuing my education. "Mehrnaz jan," he asked, "what subject interests you?"

"My grade twelve average is not high enough for me to go into medicine and fulfill Maman's dream. I'll just have to see what my mark will be on the entrance exam, and then I can decide which subjects I will be qualified to apply for."

"But you must follow your own passion. Entering university in Iran is extremely difficult and subjective. It's only based on marks. Not every student with an A plus average will make a good doctor! Why don't you find out what your passion is? Don't worry about your mother's dream or society's expectations. If you can't follow your passion in Iran, then go back to America to study."

I envied Uncle Dariush when he talked about passion and purpose in life. Uncle Dariush had one passion: providing poor people with adequate healthcare. Maman referred a few relatives to Uncle Dariush, but he refused to take them because he told Maman that his time was devoted only to people who could not afford to get medical help.

I wished I could be as passionate as Uncle Dariush. I wished I knew what I wanted to do with my life.

"So Mehrnaz jan, what is this news about your unofficial engagement?" Uncle Dariush teased.

"Oh, Aly is a nice man and he loves me." I didn't look him in the eye. I knew that he would be disappointed with my decision. He believed in me—he thought that I would do more in my life than follow the tradition of our society—but he was a man, and he had no idea how difficult it was for me as a woman to not follow tradition.

"You are too young for marriage. Our society puts so much

pressure on women to get married at a young age. Follow your dream—be courageous, be different, and be independent."

Uncle Dariush saw me as a beautiful young woman with unlimited potential, but he didn't understand what I was facing in our misogynistic society. Kyan, I thought, did not love me back because of my body, but Aly loved me in spite of it. Uncle Dariush had the power to choose whom he was going to marry—he was handsome, wealthy, and a physician. I didn't have the same opportunity to choose—a man had to accept my body. So, I changed the subject.

"Did Maman tell you about my motorcycle accident?"

"Yes!" He smiled. "I had no idea that you loved riding motorcycles. I asked your Maman why she doesn't buy one for you. She didn't think your Baba would go for it."

We went to our villa for Nowruz, the celebration of the Persian New Year that begins on the first day of spring and continues for two weeks. Prior to Nowruz, Iranians spring-clean their homes, inside and out. Nowruz is not a Muslim celebration; it's a cultural celebration of rejuvenation. It is a custom to wear new clothes on the New Year, so Baba and I walked along the busy street of Pahlavi, buying new clothes for everyone in our house. Baba was at his happiest: he was shopping.

On the first day of Nowruz, we visited with our elders. On the second day, we stayed in our villa and the relatives came to visit us. Because Baba was the oldest among his siblings and many of his cousins, we had visitors all day long. Many stayed for lunch and dinner. Children received money instead of presents, so Baba got a stack of new paper money from the bank and handed it to the children as they left the house. Adults didn't get money or presents. My grandparents gave us gold coins.

During these two weeks, we played cards with our cousins and hung out in Motel Ghoo. Our villa was located between two of the most popular resort cities on the Caspian Sea; it was twenty minutes to Motel Ghoo and thirty minutes in the opposite direction to Ramesar.

Motel Ghoo was like any other resort town in the world. Men and women walked around the city in their bathing suits. The religious storeowners had a notice at their doors: "Please do not enter the store in bikinis." Alcohol was served in all the restaurants and cafés.

The thirteenth day of Nowruz was a national picnic day, and thirty or forty of us were picnicking outside the city. A relative of ours, Abdul, had arrived with his brand new motorcycle and joined us. I was passionate about riding, but there was no chance that my parents would buy me a motorcycle, so when the opportunity arose I always asked to ride other people's bikes.

Abdul's motorcycle was a new model. I had never ridden such a powerful bike. He gave me a ride on a freshly paved stretch of highway that had not yet been opened. It was heavenly riding on a fast motorcycle on the smooth pavement with no cars. When we were away from my parents' eyes, Abdul let me ride by myself. I was impressed with my speed. When we got back to the picnic area, I asked Abdul if I could ride some more. My cousin Taraneh, Aunt Banafsheh's daughter, ran to me and asked for a ride to Motel Ghoo, where her boyfriend was spending the afternoon. She climbed on behind me and then her younger brother started crying that he wanted to ride with us too. When I turned around to tell him that the next turn would be his, I hit the curb and the motorcycle took off into the air, spilling my cousin onto the highway.

"I am going to die," I thought to myself as the motorcycle flew into a concrete canal by the side of the road. I landed a few metres from the bike in the canal that had not yet been filled with water.

I got up and started waving my arms to the forty-plus people who were running toward me with Baba in the lead screaming, "God help me, my daughter is dead!"

The canal was deep and they couldn't see me, but the moment I came into view Baba yelled, "DAUGHTER, YOU ARE GOING TO KILL ME!"

He was shaking with fear. It was typical for Baba to overreact when I was hurt.

So there I was, standing by myself, getting dirty looks from aunts and uncles for being such a rebel while Baba was getting all of the attention. Abdul's new bike was damaged. Baba offered to pay for the repair, but Abdul would not accept any money. He was a lovely and kind young man. I felt badly for damaging his bike, but he was more concerned about me not being hurt.

We left the picnic right away. Baba was shaken and went to his best friend's villa to recover.

Farid's villa was close to Motel Ghoo. Farid spoke with a gentle voice and moved with graceful gestures. He was a small man with light brown hair and green eyes. Baba and Farid had many memories together. They were childhood friends. Whenever our families gathered, I asked Baba if he could tell us stories about his adventures with Farid. I especially loved the story about Farid embarrassing Baba in front of his tango teacher.

"Baba and dear Farid, could you tell your funny stories?" I would ask each time we gathered around. I could hear them again and again.

"Oh, Heda, stop telling those stories," Farid would say with a chuckle. Only Baba's closest friends and a couple of his aunts called him Heda.

The sleeve on my new shirt was ripped from my fall. I was wearing a pair of jeans, so my legs were not scratched, and luckily I had no broken bones. Maman was shaken too, but she said nothing. Farid's wife made a special syrup for Baba's racing heart, and he slowly stopped shaking. Then Farid gave me a lecture about being so hard on Baba.

"Your Baba's heart is very fragile. You must be considerate of your Baba's sensitive nature."

17. The University of Damavand

I WAS ACCEPTED INTO THE English Literature program at the University of Damavand in Tehran. I had achieved my goal to get my education in Iran. Many young people who didn't make it in Iran were sent to Europe or America for their education, but I didn't want to leave my country again. Tehran was a vibrant city, alive with music and food vendors, a dream city for young people. Life did not wait for weekends; I was out with my friends every evening.

One afternoon while riding in a taxi on my way to meet some friends for lunch, I noticed a white Mercedes Benz inching along through the congested traffic. The driver was handsome beyond description. He stopped and parked the car to let out an old man; then he got out.

I asked the taxi to stop, jumped out, and followed him to a juice vendor. He did not notice me as he walked back to the car. Mesmerized by his looks, I knocked on his window; I had no idea what I was doing. I asked him if we had met on the ski hill last week. He said that he had been on the hill, but he didn't remember meeting me. He gave me his card. His name was Ashkan. I wasn't a skier, but it was cool to hang out at the Dizin ski resort in the Alborz mountain range, which was less than a two-hour drive from Tehran. It was a high-altitude resort—over three thousand metres above sea level. And it was a great place to people-watch; I had made a lucky guess.

However, I couldn't believe that I was using a pick-up line that I had heard a hundred times from men in Iran. I felt like I was in a dream where the roles of men and women were reversed. I had never chosen a man. Kyan had chosen me first and asked me to dance with him. I hadn't noticed him beforehand. Aly too was the one who had approached me. Women did not pick up men, but I had just done it!

I needed to end things with Aly, so I waited painfully for two weeks before I called him.

Then Ashkan and I started dating. He would pick me up two blocks from our house. My parents knew about him, but he was not allowed to pick me up. I would never say that I was "going out with Ashkan" or I would have to endure Maman's favourite line: "What would the neighbours say?" She was especially worried about this now that everyone had seen me with Aly over the last few months.

Ashkan took me to very elite and ritzy restaurants and cafés for our dates. He knew all the managers and servers, and he tipped them well. We got special treatment and never had to wait to be seated. Walking beside Ashkan made me feel attractive and glamorous; men and women turned around to look at us.

I continued to date Ashkan. We did not have sex. We did not kiss. We kept going on dates at posh cafés and restaurants. After six months, he finally came to ask my parents for my hand.

There were three major bus companies in Iran, and Ashkan's father owned one of them. Ashkan was managing the company with his father. He was twenty-five years old. Baba did not like the fact that Ashkan's family was *nouveau riche*, and he wasn't very friendly to Ashkan when he came to ask for my hand. Baba told Ashkan that he needed some time to think about it.

Baba was obviously against our marriage, and he said he had to investigate Ashkan's history. Baba asked a couple of his friends who were very connected in the business community to find out whatever he could about Ashkan. When the investigation report came back, Baba announced that Ashkan was a heroin addict. I was hysterical.

One day, Roshi and I were driving in Tehran when I saw Ashkan's white Mercedes Benz parked in front of a hospital. The next day, I drove around the front of the hospital again and his car was still there. I called the hospital and talked to him. Ashkan was trying to quit his heroin addiction. I went to see him. My prince looked so handsome, even in his blue hospital gown. That was the last time I saw him. He asked me to give him space while he tried to quit his addiction and I never heard from him again.

The University of Damavand was an all-female university that had a mix of wealthy and working-class students. Recently the Shah had introduced a policy: if students signed an agreement to work for the government after graduation, their university fee would be covered by the government. This law finally made secondary education possible for all young people in Iran.

The university was located in the foothills of the Damavand Mountains, north of Tehran. It was a quiet place with no traffic, surrounded by cherry trees. Most of our professors were British or American, and they loved the lifestyle in Iran. Many of them lived in small villages nearby and rode their bicycles to the university.

Oil made Iran a rich country, and foreigners could make a high income compared to what they might earn in their homelands. Life was good in cosmopolitan Tehran with its pleasant four-season climate and short winters.

In the meantime, the Shah's regime was getting weaker, and there were many anti-government demonstrations. The Shah's army announced that peaceful demonstrations would be allowed. He understood that his dictatorship was backfiring.

I didn't believe in the dictatorship, and I participated in many demonstrations. As a young university student, I loved the freedom of attending political demonstrations, but I knew it was dangerous. The army would often start firing into an unarmed crowd, killing or injuring hundreds of people. Groups of us would go up to the rooftops to chant anti-Shah slogans.

My family was pro-Shah, and they didn't like me to attend any demonstrations against the regime. They were afraid for my safety, even for my life. I started reading books about revolutions and different ideologies. These books were only available underground. I believed that every voice should be heard. The poor citizens of Iran needed education, healthcare, housing, food, and jobs, not a royal family who lived in golden castles. There were many arguments in our house. Even though Baba had been involved in politics when he was young, he still tried to keep me away from the demonstrations.

Baba had a particular understanding of the influence of foreign policies—specifically those of Great Britain, the Soviet Union, and the United States—on the Iranian political sphere and oil industry. "This movement is not real," he would say. "The youth are being manipulated. The Shah wants a new agreement to be signed about the profit that foreign countries are making from our oil industry, a modern agreement for 1979. The last agreement was signed after Mohammad Mosaddegh, Prime Minister of Iran in the early fifties, was overthrown in 1954. America is not supporting the Shah anymore because he is trying to lessen American control over our oil industry.

"I became involved in politics when Mosaddegh tried to nationalize the Iranian oil industry. The British were taking most of the profit from our oil. We are a rich country because of oil, but we are also cursed because of our oil. Countries like the United States, the Soviet Union, and the United Kingdom control politics in Iran, because they want the ruling party on their side. We are like a puppet in their hands."

Vafa brought tea for Baba but not me. "What about me?"

"I only serve tea to Shah's supporters," Vafa said and frowned at me.

Baba laughed and he continued, "I was in the streets with thousands of people when we elected Mohammad Mosaddegh as Prime Minister of Iran in 1951. He was the voice of the people. He was against the British having control over our oil industry. He even took some power away from the Shah. But during this time, because of the British boycott, Iranians were becoming poorer and unhappier.

"Mosaddegh graduated from law school in France. He was an advocate of democracy and resisted foreign domination. On August 19, 1953, Mosaddegh's government was terminated in a coup d'état orchestrated by the Americans and the British. That was a sad day in Iranian history. That was the day I knew that our country was being controlled by foreign policies, and that only those politicians who had ties with one of the powerful countries would stay in power. Mosaddegh was imprisoned for three years, and then he was put under house arrest until his death; he was buried in his own home in order to prevent a political uproar. Many of Mosaddegh's supporters were imprisoned, tortured, and killed."

Baba's tone of voice changed, "I admit that the Shah needed to reform his government. When Ayatollah Khomeini opposed the Shah's White Revolution in 1963, the Shah sent Khomeini into exile because of the uproar that he caused. The Shah's army killed thousands of demonstrators. My Uncle Mohammad Ali Varasteh was the Finance Minister and later the Deputy Leader of the Senate during the Shah's regime. He didn't vote for the exile of Khomeini; he believed that sending Khomeini into exile would make him a hero. The Shah didn't like my uncle voting against Khomeini's exile; he didn't value my uncle's loyalty, integrity, and his intellectual decision, and he expelled him from his government. It is disappointing that the Shah surrounded himself mainly with disloyal members of government. But we do not need a revolution. What we need is a government whose priority is loyalty to the royal family and people of Iran."

At university, classes let out early so we could be home before four in the afternoon. The Shah's army had recently announced a curfew. I was excited by the energy of the movement and the promise of democracy, and I was in favour of getting rid of the royals and bringing in a new government. The opposition parties encouraged us to gather in the streets after the curfew. I was not afraid, and I even began organizing many of the young people in my neighbourhood myself. I started a demonstration on the corner of our main street. Fereshteh, Mottee's daughter, came to stay with us that night and joined me in the demonstration. Old rubber tires were dropped off in the streets to be lit on fire and rolled toward army tanks. The smiles on people's faces were contagious. It was remarkable to witness rich and poor young people, all standing together against oppression. It was the people's movement.

I was pushing one of the tires down the street when I turned around and saw a familiar face—familiar but changed. I barely recognized Kyan. He had long hair and a beard. I didn't know that he had returned from England. His family didn't live in our building anymore.

In the next second, the army began attacking us and we turned and ran toward my house. Maman and Baba were standing anxiously on the balcony. As soon as they saw me running toward the house, they opened the door. The hallways from the first to the fifth floors were filled with demonstrators. We ran to the rooftop. A soldier banged at the door with his gun, but we were on the roof chanting the political slogan, "Brother soldiers, why are you killing your brothers?" When everyone was quiet, Fereshteh yelled, "Brother soldier, you are so gorgeous!"

The soldier stopped banging at the door and looked up to see if he could see this woman who had yelled. We could see him because of the light above the door, but he couldn't see us.

"I really didn't mean to say that," Fereshteh said later. "I was so scared, but I looked down and he was standing under the light and he was so handsome and it just came out of my mouth." We were sitting around in our house, laughing about how Fereshteh's flirtation with the soldier had saved our lives. The truth was that many army soldiers who were supporting the revolution did not want to lose their jobs. He was doing his job, but he didn't intend to kill us; he just wanted to frighten us.

The Shah left Iran in exile on January 16, 1979.

Ayatollah Khomeini returned to Iran after living in exile for fifteen years. I watched the arrival of Khomeini at the Tehran airport live on television until the screen went black unexpectedly. After the television stopped broadcasting the event, millions of people showed up at the University of Tehran and on the streets in front of the university where Ayatollah Khomeini was giving a speech. I left the house to join the crowd. Although Baba was not in support of this movement, he came along because he was afraid for my life. There were still random attacks on anti-Shah groups. Millions of people cheered the arrival of Khomeini in the streets of Tehran. There was happiness in the air.

Soon after, Iran held an election. Each party, including the Islamic Republic of Iran, had its candidates. People were still afraid of the Shah army's coup d'état. We were told to vote for the Islamic Republic led by Khomeini; it was safer to be united and stay strong against the Shah. I voted for the Islamic Republic.

We were practising freedom of speech; people were free belonging to different parties and to declare their views openly. At universities, students promoted their political beliefs; communist parties and Islamic parties were side by side. The sense of freedom was priceless.

"Mehrnaz, when I saw you in the street during the protest, I had no doubt that by this time you would be married. But then I looked at your hand and saw no wedding ring, and I looked into your eyes and saw what I have always seen: love."

Kyan and I started dating again. It felt like we had never been apart. My parents were happy that he was back in my life.

18. Kyan and Sia

FOR A FEW MONTHS, Kyan and I did what we used to do—walk in parks hand in hand, go to cafés, and read poetry. Then Kyan proposed to me, and my dream finally came true. I talked for hours with Vafa about my future with Kyan. Maman and Baba discussed moving to our villa and giving the second floor of our apartment building to Kyan and me.

"Vafa, I want you to move in with Kyan and me. He really likes you, and I want you to love him."

"Do you remember when you came back from England after your surgery? Kyan broke your heart. He didn't visit you in the hospital, and then he never contacted you when you were in England! I will never forgive him for that."

"But Vafa, I didn't want him to see me while I was at the hospital. Kyan loves me; please forgive him. I have forgiven him."

"Kyan should have come to see you in the hospital every day. This is what a man does when he knows he is lucky to have a precious princess like you in his life."

The day finally came that I decided to have a conversation about my body with Kyan. He knew about my burn and plastic surgeries.

"Are you concerned about my body?"

Kyan said that he had talked to his mother about it. She told him, "As long as Mehrnaz's womb is not damaged and she can have children, then it will be fine."

As he spoke, my heart began to break into pieces.

He continued, "My mother was sad when my brother's wife could not have children. She feels happier now that my brother and his ex-wife are divorced and he and his new wife are expecting." Then he held my hand and added, "Marriage is a risk, and marrying you will be one more risk that I will take."

"Kyan, I think I am coming down with the flu. I need to go home. I feel nauseous."

I went home, closed the door, and cried.

I was busy writing my final exams, and I didn't share what Kyan said with my family, Roshi, or Vafa. I had declined what I considered to be the humiliating tradition of an arranged marriage to an acceptable suitor and had chosen to marry for love. And yet Kyan, the man who had held my heart since I was a young girl of fifteen, had discussed my body with his mother. I had passed her test because my womb was not defective.

I didn't tell him that he had broken my heart. I told him that I needed space to think about things.

Part of me still didn't believe that I had the right to express my disappointment and sorrow to him—the part of me that judged myself and saw myself as ugly and as a beast.

After my last exam, I organized a trip for Baba, Roshi, Vafa, and me to go to our villa. I needed to be by the Caspian Sea, away from Kyan. I wanted the sea breeze to heal my heart. Roshi and Vafa knew that I was breaking up with Kyan, but my pride would not allow me to share his words with them.

"Finally, you're breaking up with Kyan. He has never loved you the way you loved him. Aly still loves you."

"Oh Vafa, stop it. While I was engaged to Aly, I picked up Ashkan in the street. I don't want any other man in my life right now!"

In the daytime, we swam and suntanned. In the evenings, we went to Motel Ghoo, where I could forget myself on the crowded streets and on the beach, among the happy tourists in the cafés and bars.

One night in Motel Ghoo we ran into my cousin Mahyar, Aunt Banafsheh's son. Mahyar introduced me to his friend Sia. Sia's father was a friend of Baba; he was the ear, nose, and throat specialist who had diagnosed me with allergies. Sia was my age and a third-year university student at medical school. He asked me for my phone number.

When we went back to Tehran, I was still hoping to hear from Kyan. I wanted him to say that I was the love of his life, but that call never came. Instead, Sia phoned me and asked me out. He said that for him it was "love at first sight." He was romantic, funny, and thoughtful. He praised my beauty. He loved my eyes and wrote short stories and poems for me.

But my love for Kyan was still rooted deeply in my heart. I wrote this poem when I finally knew in my heart that Kyan did not love me the way I had loved him.

"You had no love for me"

I put my heart in a suitcase and went on a journey.
Love made me believe that our dance was eternal.
Your smile is engraved
on the peak of the mountain of my heart.
Yet you had no love for me!

I met a man who ever so gently opened my suitcase.
I held him and his smell was of love.
Our naked bodies intertwined
like the long green grasses in the summer breeze.

With him next to me I fell asleep,
and I dreamed of you.
Dreamed of that hot summer day in Tehran,
under the willow tree,
holding hands,
sitting beside the blue pond.
You read love poems and whispered love in my ear.

Where are you now?
I left the table of love hungry.
You had no love for me!

19. Vafa Gets Married

OUR HOUSE BECAME QUIETER after Jamal, Soraya, and Homa got married. And, after everyone left, Vafa and I became even closer.

Then the day arrived when Baba and Maman had a special conversation with Vafa.

"Vafa, we are very proud of you. You are respected at your work. You have saved money. It's time for you to get serious and settle down," they advised. While he was still living with us, Vafa had been working now for a few years at a company where he earned a decent income.

It was time and he knew it, so he returned to Zavardasht, the village where he was from, and his family found him a young bride. He came home and told me all about Shamsi. "She is young and beautiful, and I am going to marry her."

"But...!"

Vafa interrupted me and said, "No but, missy!" When he used this tone, I knew better than to say any more.

We had two wedding celebrations for Vafa and his bride, one at Maman Aterahm's house in Qazvin, which was closer to Zavardasht and easier for Vafa's family to attend, and one at our home in Tehran.

"I'm getting so stressed about my suit. The tailor made the waistline of my jacket too straight. It does not give me a curve. And I keep asking him to make the pants tighter and he keeps saying, 'Sir, you chose chiffon velvet. Women use chiffon velvet for dresses; it's not a good fabric for pants, so it is best not to have it too tight.' I should have chosen a younger tailor."

"What about Shamsi's dress? Where is she getting her dress made?" I asked.

"Oh yeah, I forgot to tell you. Shamsi is really easygoing about these things. She told me to choose her a wedding dress. I told her all about the white dress that you wore at Soraya's wedding and how much I loved it, so she decided to wear it."

"Then I need to send it to her so she can get it fitted."

"She's your size. It's going to fit her."

Vafa was enjoying all the attention and the excitement of the wedding preparations. I was in charge of the music and styling Vafa's hair. I blew it dry and locked it in with lots of hairspray. My beautiful Vafa, with his fitted shiny black velvet suit, thick wavy black hair, and glowing smile stole the show from the bride.

"Vafa, go and welcome your friends," Maman urged, trying to get him off the dance floor. Shamsi was very shy and didn't dance. Most of the guests were Vafa's friends and family. Only a few of Shamsi's relatives were able to attend the wedding in Qazvin.

After the wedding, the bride and groom drove from Qazvin to Tehran, with many cars following behind them. One of the guests was Shahram, the owner of the company where Vafa worked. Shahram and I chased the bride and groom down the highway, Shahram in his green BMW, and I in my cheap Citroen that Maman had given me when I was accepted at university. The car was packed to the gills with people, including Maman, and blasted dance music from the windows.

Baba complained later on, "You were giving me a heart attack. A Citroen is a cheap, unstable car. You don't race a Citroen against a BMW. That was so dangerous!"

A week later, we had a big celebration in Tehran. We invited many Tehrani friends and relatives. Fereshteh, Roshi, Vafa, and I did not leave the dance floor.

Uncle Dariush was not planning to come to the wedding because he was on call—Roshi was very disappointed because she had never stopped loving him—but then he showed up late, coming directly from work. Many men at Vafa's wedding were flirting with Roshi, but they didn't mean anything to her. Uncle Dariush came over and chatted with us, but it was awkward. This was first time that Uncle Dariush had talked to us since

Vafa and Mehrnaz, 1979

Roshi's persistent phone calls three or four years earlier. We were now in our early twenties and we thought of ourselves as very sophisticated and intelligent. Uncle Dariush was as collected and genuine as always, and Roshi gathered all she had to carry on a small conversation with him, hoping that might finally garner his admiration.

"Mehrnaz, my heart was beating so fast that I could hardly breathe," she said afterwards.

"Roshi, I have never ever seen you like this with any other man. You're always so smooth and flirtatious, but with Uncle Dariush..."

Roshi interrupted me. "Mehrnaz, if this is how love is then may I never stop loving him."

Vafa didn't move far from home. He and Shamsi moved in next door, into the basement of Aunt Roohi's house.

One afternoon, Vafa came to my room and closed the door behind him. I knew he was up to something. "My boss Shahram is in love with you," he announced. "He wants his parents to come visit your family, and he wants me to organize it. I'm not letting you go back to Kyan."

"No, Vafa. You know there's no way I would agree to that. No *khastegar*!"

"I always talk to him about you, and I'm so happy that he fell in love with you at my wedding. He is sweet, handsome, and wealthy. I told him that you want to complete your education, and he said that he supports that."

Vafa would not stop talking about Shahram to me. He talked to Baba and Maman as well. Even though Shahram was Iranian-Jewish, Baba and Maman were pleased with his marriage proposal, so Vafa went ahead and organized a day for us to visit Shahram's parents at their home.

Of course, this was all arranged without my consent. When the afternoon arrived for our meeting, I didn't plan to go. Baba, Maman, and Vafa were all dressed up and waiting. Baba and Maman begged me to go, and Vafa started crying and telling Maman and Baba how disrespectful my behaviour was. He wouldn't stop crying and making a scene.

"I have done everything for you. I always spoil you. Now I am asking one favour from you. I would be so embarrassed if you don't come."

I agreed to go, but I did not agree to dress up. I wore a casual top with jeans and sandals.

We arrived at Shahram's parents' home. Shahram was wearing a suit and tie. Their house was luxurious. I was the only one who did not fit in.

Vafa was heartbroken that I would not agree to marry the wealthy and handsome Shahram. Vafa, who knew all about the scars all over my body, never saw me as anything but beautiful. When he met a nice, handsome man he simply wanted to make a match for me. His dreams for me were always big. I was such a fortunate girl to be loved unconditionally by two men. When I looked at myself, I saw a body ravaged with scars, but Baba and Vafa only ever saw me as perfect.

20. Uncle Dariush

THE FREEDOM I HAD BEEN FIGHTING FOR soon became a nightmare. After the Islamic Republic of Iran took power, the opposition parties were forced into operating underground; their members' lives were now in danger.

The government was soon enmeshed in a civil war with Iranian Kurds who were asking for autonomy for Kurdistan, a province of Iran. Kurdistan is the mountainous area where the borders of Iraq and Iran meet, south of Syria, Turkey, Armenia, and Azerbaijan. Much of the land is difficult to reach because of the high altitude.

The Kurds had supported the revolution. They had fought for their autonomy in the Shah's time, and now they were being attacked by the Islamic government for the same plea. In trying to force the Kurds into submission, the government destroyed countless villages and towns.

My Aunt Munir was Kurdish. Maman Aterahm had brought her to live with her family in Qazvin when she was a teenager. She stayed with Maman Aterahm until she became a teacher; then she moved back to Sanandaj in Kurdistan to teach. Every summer, Aunt Munir came and stayed with us at our villa.

"Our language is Kurdish. We have our own dance," she liked to say. I loved listening to Aunt Munir talking about Kurdistan.

"Kurdistan was only independent for three years, from 1920 to 1923. Since then it has been divided between Iran, Iraq, Syria, and Turkey. The Kurds want their autonomy, but the governments of these countries have been fighting against it."

"Why are you not fighting to free Kurdistan?" I asked.

"It is too dangerous to fight. But I fight my way—without guns. That is the reason that I became an educator."

When I was still very young, we took a family trip to visit Sanandaj and stayed at a friend of Aunt Munir's.

When we got to Sanandaj, Baba mentioned our desire for dance costumes to Aunt Munir.

"We must take the children to see the fabric shop at night,"she said. "It is glorious to see the light shining on the colourful patterned fabrics, some with golden threads. I would love for Soraya and Mehrnaz to have Kurdish outfits."

Aunt Munir was so proud that we were visiting her beloved city and province, and delighted that we were interested in Kurdish folk traditions. I didn't want to leave the fabric shop. I had asked Baba if he would buy me a Kurdish costume. The dresses were long and made of beautiful bright-coloured fabric with gold threads woven throughout.

"If we get one for you, then we have to get one for Soraya too. The car is full; we don't have the room for two sets of Kurdish costumes." I was disappointed that we left the shop without a Kurdish costume for me.

Aunt Munir was our passionate unofficial tour guide. "Now let's go and see the most majestic view ever, one that you'll remember for the rest of your life."

"Oh wow!" I had never seen a city like Sanandaj before. There were tiny two-storey buildings with flat rooftops terraced into the slope of the mountain, each roof providing a yard for the house above. Small lights flickering from each house created a fascinating design against the black sky—big stars and rows and rows of lights all along the slope of the mountain.

I had such beautiful memories of that family trip to Sanandaj. Knowing that the government of the Islamic Republic was officially in civil war with Kurdistan, and the people of Kurdistan were being killed, was heart wrenching.

Every year, Maman, Baba, and I visited the mountainous village of Kelardasht, in Northern Iran for a couple of weeks to escape the heat of summer of Tehran. Maman always insisted on renting a place close to the river, which ran through the city. It was peaceful to fall asleep in the cool night air, under the beautiful night sky with big stars, listening to the sound of the river.

"Hedayat, one of the names of these nine Kurds in the newspaper is like Dariush's name," Maman said with worry.

Baba walked to the village daily to get the newspaper. The newspaper showed a photo of nine Kurdish men who had been killed by the order of Ayatollah Khalkhali. He had been chosen by Ayatollah Khomeini to be the head of the newly established Revolutionary Courts of the Islamic Republic.

Baba looked and noticed the name was in fact very similar to my Uncle Dariush's—only one letter was different.

"It's reported that they were Kurdish. Mahin stop being worried. Dariush is not Kurdish. And he's a doctor. If it were him, they would have included his title with his name."

"As soon as I heard on the radio that the government was asking for doctors to volunteer in Kurdistan, I started getting worried," said Maman. "I know Dariush. I know he would volunteer his time to help others, but I was hoping he wouldn't go. It is too dangerous."

There was no phone service in Kelardasht, so Maman stayed close to the radio, hoping to hear the full details of this event. She couldn't stop worrying about Uncle Dariush.

"Hedayat, I did not sleep all night. Let's go back to the villa. I need to phone Dariush, to hear his voice. I prayed all night for the families of the nine Kurds who were killed by Khalkhali. He's a criminal."

Maman's fears for her brother were justified. In late August 1979, while Uncle Dariush was operating on an injured Kurd, he was ordered to leave his patient in the middle of the operation and attend to another wounded person who was a member of the Islamic Revolutionary Guard. As a doctor, he would not leave the patient he was operating on, and he requested that they wait until he was finished. He was told that he must save the life of the Islamic guard first.

We were told that this is how he responded: "As a doctor, I have sworn to treat every patient equally."

Within hours, my Uncle Dariush, Dr. Abolghasem Rashvand Sardari, an orthopaedic surgeon, at the age of twenty-seven, was prosecuted with no trial, and executed by orders of Ayatollah Khalkhali.

His body was not delivered to his family. We could not go to that region. He was buried in Paveh in the province of Kurdistan because Paveh and all those regions were under the control of the Revolutionary Guards of the Islamic Republic. The government forbade his family any official funeral, but friends and family still gathered at my aunt's house. They wrote letters to Amnesty International to record his murder.

Friends of Uncle Dariush, mainly doctors and medical students, organized a peaceful demonstration in a boulevard in Tehran; they did not notify the Revolutionary Guards of this gathering since it would not have been approved. By then, newspapers were controlled by the regime. The press printed several pages about all the illegal acts that Dariush and the others had been accused of. The Ayatollah Khalkhali portrayed my uncle as a lunatic criminal.

Friends of Uncle Dariush organized activities to raise awareness about his murder. Maman, Baba, and my siblings stayed away from these activities, but I attended the meetings. My grieving parents tried to discourage me from risking my life.

"We don't want to lose another loved one to this regime," they pleaded.

Roshi was grieving in seclusion. "Mehrnaz, I have stayed in my room for the last three days and cried. Dariush's caring voice is replaying over and over in my head. How I loved his beautiful, genuine smile and the sound of his laughter. My love for him was pure. I can't imagine what Vida is going through."

At the time, Uncle Dariush was engaged to a colleague, Vida.

I wanted the news of my uncle's murder to reach every newspaper in the world. I didn't fear for my life; I feared living a life of fear.

I gave copies of Tehran's phone book to friends, and told them to call as many numbers as they could to spread the news. I also asked them to join us in a peaceful demonstration, and I pasted flyers for it on street posts around the city.

Afternoons during naptime, I assembled groups of young people, including our servants, and we all went separately to post the announcements. I told each one of them that if they were arrested by the Revolutionary Guards, they were to tell the guards, "I was paid by Mehrnaz Massoudi to post these announcements."

I had read books and reports about how prisoners were treated in the Islamic Republic jails. I was aware of the risk I was taking. Women were raped and tortured in damp, cold prison cells. I prepared a bag with woollen socks and sweaters in case I was arrested.

It wasn't long before the Revolutionary Guards were at our door. Hamid, one of our servants, was arrested while he was putting up announcements. Uncle Hushang, who was a chief of police during the Shah's regime but had been fired by the Islamic Republic, was visiting us. He didn't know what was going on, but he knew that I had over a hundred books that were banned by this government. While Baba was talking to the guards at the door, Uncle Hushang wrapped the books in linen sheets and took them to the vacant lot behind our house with the help of the servants. He also put someone in charge of emptying all the alcohol down the toilet.

I was sitting in my room unable to comprehend that the moment had finally arrived. I had believed that I had no fear of being arrested, but now that it was about to happen, the thought of being raped and tortured was making me sick to my stomach.

I prayed to my uncle. *"Uncle Dariush, may your soul be with me. I am scared. May I have courage."*

Maman opened the door to my room. "Mehrnaz, your guardian angels kept you safe! The guards arrested your Baba and Hamid."

Despite Maman's pleas, the guards took Baba and Hamid away without telling us where they were going. They were gone for twenty-four hours. We could not locate them. Everyone was angry with me, but, at the same time, they were relieved that *I* had not been taken. The Revolutionary Guards were looking for educated young people who were against the Islamic Republic. They were not interested in a religious Haji and a young boy from the village, so Baba and Hamid were released the next day.

Hamid had come to work at our house when he was only eight

or nine years old. I knew that he must have said something to the guards that day. "Hamid, why did you give Baba's name to the guards?" I asked.

"I know what they do to female university students in jail—I didn't want them to rape you and kill you. Your Baba is old and he is a Haji, so I knew they wouldn't do anything to him." Hamid had saved my life.

"Mehrnaz, these men were brutal, scary; their eyes were filled with hatred," Baba told me with tears in his eyes. "I can't sleep because of the thought of what they might have done to you if they had arrested you. Mehrnaz, please have mercy on me and stop your protests."

For the first time since the murder of Uncle Dariush, I started sobbing. This government had murdered my uncle, and the only thing we could do was to stay silent. I promised myself that one day I would let the world know that this government had murdered my uncle in the name of Islam!

21. My Friend, Fereshteh

"I HAD SUCH A SAD DREAM LAST NIGHT," Sia began. "I dreamed that you and your daughter, a little girl whose eyes looked just like yours, came to my office. She was sick. I examined her. Then I took off the pendant that you gave me for my birthday and put it around her neck. But she was not my daughter. We weren't together."

For his birthday, I had given Sia a white-and-yellow gold chain with a pendant shaped like his zodiac sign, Pisces. Once I put it around his neck, he never took it off. Sia completed me with his poetry, passion, and love of music.

We were both going to university in Tehran, and we saw each other every day. When I went to Tonekabon with my family, he went to visit his parents too so we could see each other there as well. We met every day, kissing, hugging, and melting into each other's bodies.

After months of seeing each other daily, I felt like I was ready to share my secret. One winter's day, we were driving along the shore of the Caspian Sea.

"Sia, can you see the burn scars under my chin? They cover my chest as well. My breasts are covered with scars. I have no nipples."

Sia kissed me and held me. "I've had sex with many girls, and I've touched beautiful breasts; they are just flesh. I am becoming a doctor, and I am passionate about the body's healing powers. Your scars are a masterpiece of healing. I will worship you and your body. It is my dream for my children to have your eyes."

I shared every word of what Sia had said with Aunt Masi and

Maman, and they fell in love with him instantly. On a spring day, I made love with the man of my dreams, with my shirt on. I kept the buttons of my shirt closed, but opened the door of my heart to Sia.

Sia was a Baha'i. He followed the monotheistic religion founded by Bahaullah in the mid-nineteenth century in Persia. In Iran, marriage between a Muslim and a Baha'i was not common.

It was around the same time that I overheard a conversation between Baba and one of his brothers. "I won't agree to Mana marrying this Englishman. Not unless he becomes Muslim," my uncle insisted. "He has to get circumcised."

My cousin Mana had been living in London for a couple of years and had recently announced that she was engaged to be married to an Englishman. When I heard the word "circumcised," I burst out laughing. What was my uncle thinking asking an Englishman to agree to circumscision? She had sent my uncle beautiful, professionally taken, black-and-white photos of herself and her fiancé. He was a handsome man, and Mana was gorgeous and stylish. Then, just as surprisingly, Mana and her Englishman broke up, but not because of the requested looming circumcision. Mana had returned to Iran with a new skill: channelling the spirit world with a Ouija board.

Mana had loved trying new things. For example, at thirteen, she had been the first person in our family to take karate lessons. I had no idea what karate was, so when she asked me if she could demonstrate, I said yes. Then I had to beg her to stop hurting me! I was only seven at the time.

Baba had organized a day with his brothers to gather around the table for "channelling" at Aunt Roohi's house next door. Mana was all set for the big event. I was not allowed to attend.

I was exasperated. I knew that channelling was not a supernatural skill that Mana had somehow acquired; it was just a fad that had caught her interest. Nevertheless, I was curious. "Mana, tell me all about it." It was such a big event. My uncles were all so serious, whispering to each other.

"No. I'm not going to share this with you. It's private. But I will tell you this one thing: your Baba asked our grandfather if you will be marrying Sia."

"And?" I said laughingly.

"Our grandfather said yes."

Baba seemed upset for the next few days. He was concerned about me marrying a Baha'i. But at least I didn't have to ask Sia to be circumcised! Baha'is practise circumcision, just like Muslims.

One afternoon, Fereshteh teased me. "I want to meet this handsome prince who stole my little sister's heart."

After graduating from university, Fereshteh had married her handsome boyfriend Armin. They were an attractive and stylish couple. Shortly after, they went to America to continue their education. When Fereshteh returned from America without Armin—they were getting a divorce—she and I started spending more time together. When I was a child, I had always looked up to chic and cool Fereshteh as a role model, but now we hung out as friends.

"We're going to our villa next week and Sia is coming too. He'll be staying at his parents' place, but we're planning to see each other every day," I told Fereshteh. "Please come. I want you to meet him."

"I need time off from work, and I need to get a tan so I can wear my bikini," she replied.

"It's not really safe to wear a bikini on the beach anymore."

"I'm not scared of them. They can't tell me what to wear and what not to wear!" Fereshteh was defiant.

The following week, when we got to the villa, Sia and I made plans to meet. Our plan was for Sia to park his car at a nearby public beach and then walk up the coast toward the villa. Fereshteh and I would then walk along the beach until we ran into him.

Just as we were leaving, Baba stopped us. "Fereshteh, your dress is very revealing—put a shirt on over it. I have heard that the Revolutionary Guards drive by in their boats to check out the beach. They arrest women wearing bathing suits or revealing too much skin," he said.

Baba didn't know that underneath Fereshteh was wearing a bikini under her dress. Women had worn bikinis for years in Iran, but this was the first summer that the rumour was going around that the guards were harassing women on beaches.

Fereshteh ignored him, determined to do what she wanted.

Our plan worked beautifully. I introduced Fereshteh to Sia, and after they had exchanged pleasantries, she moved a bit away from us to a spot where she could suntan, leaving Sia and me alone. We found a spot in the shade of some trees, close enough that we could see Fereshteh and that we could spot Baba if he came by. We loved sitting beside each other, holding hands, kissing, and talking.

Not long afterward we heard Fereshteh call out to us. "Mehrnaz, I'm frying out here; it's time to go back inside."

Sia and I had no idea that two hours had passed. We were not ready to part.

"Mehrnaz, it's time to go in. My skin is getting red," she urged me again.

I wanted to go back, but I didn't want to leave Sia. Then I saw Fereshteh jumping up and down waving her arms and yelling, "Oh, look who's here!"

I ran into the water and started swimming, and pretended I hadn't heard her. When I lifted my head from the water, Baba was standing on the shore.

"Mehrnaz, I told you never to swim by yourself."

"Baba, I was just swimming in the shallow water." I stammered. I had a summer dress over my bathing suit, that I pulled down over my legs as I waded out.

"Fereshteh, I can't believe you're in a bikini. It's so dangerous," said Baba, turning his attention to her.

Fereshteh was sunburned all over. Her skin was an olive tone like mine but if we stayed under the sun from noon to three in the afternoon, we could get sunburned. Growing up, we never used suntan lotion, but usually we were not allowed to be in the sun in the early afternoon; our parents made sure to keep us at home for a nap during those three hours.

"I'm so red; it's not sexy. I wanted to have a sexy tan."

When we got back to villa, I rubbed olive oil on Fereshteh's sunburned skin. We thought it would help.

"I was going to put that special dress on to go out to see my friends tonight, but it's too tight—it will hurt my skin," she moaned. Then, under her breath, she whispered, "By the way, Sia is handsome and charming. I approve of him."

That evening, Fereshteh and I went out. She took me to a very luxurious villa. "This is Laleh's parents' place," she told me.

"Laleh is fooling around with someone, right? What did you say his name was again?" I asked.

"His name is Sepehr. You'll recognize him because he'll be the most handsome guy there."

Tall, slim Laleh, with straight, long blonde hair, tanned skin, big eyes, and a beautiful smile ran toward us, and the two friends gave each other a big hug.

"This is Mehrnaz," Fereshteh introduced me. "I've told her all about Sepehr." Laleh greeted me with a shy smile. "Fereshteh, you're so bad," she said.

Of course, I could pick out Sepehr in the crowd. He was a stunningly handsome man wearing a white linen shirt and tan beach pants. There were three couples there with their children, plus Sepehr. The women were all Fereshteh's friends from high school, now in their thirties. The husbands were older, but Sepehr looked as though he was in his early thirties as well.

"Laleh married in her early twenties," Fereshteh filled me in. "Mohsen was one of many of Laleh's suitors. Her parents liked Mohsen because his father is a multimillionaire and Mohsen works for him, so Laleh decided to marry him, but she never loved him. Then they had two daughters."

"How did she meet Sepehr?"

"He's a member of our tennis club."

"Since when do you play tennis?" I said laughing.

"I've been taking tennis lessons at the club. I go with my friends to watch the handsome, athletic men. You must come with me if only to see those men. We sit there for hours having drinks and watching them play."

"I feel bad for Mohsen," I said.

"Oh Mehrnaz! Not poor Mohsen; poor Laleh. Mohsen was in his mid-thirties when he came for Laleh's *khastegari*. He had had so many girlfriends before then, but he wanted to marry a beautiful young virgin from a rich family."

"Why doesn't Laleh leave him?"

"Mohsen told her that she could leave, but after ten years of marriage she will not get her *mehrieh* and he would get custody of their daughters.

"Another friend of ours left her husband and took him to court so she could have her children, but the court voted in favour of her husband. She's heartbroken. So poor Laleh, she can't leave Mohsen! She doesn't want to leave her children."

22. Closed Universities

IN 1980, THE GOVERNMENT ANNOUNCED that all universities in Iran would be closed after the spring semester. Despite the horrors of arrests, jailing, and executions, university students and opposition parties were still organizing many anti-government activities. The government also declared that when they decided to reopen the universities, students would be interviewed and only the ones who supported the Islamic Republic would be allowed to return. Students from opposition parties encouraged us to show up at the university to participate in what was to be a peaceful and silent demonstration against this decision.

Baba insisted on driving me to the demonstration. The front gate was locked; there were no walls around the building, just a big elaborate iron gate at the entrance. I joined the rest of the students while Baba waited in the car.

Suddenly, the Revolutionary Guards and a mob of people from the nearby village came running toward us, yelling, "Kill these communists; they have burned the Quran! Death to America."

The people from the village had been brainwashed by the Revolutionary Guards into thinking that we were communists. At the same time, we were also accused of supporting America because there were American faculties in our university.

This was my university. This was where we discussed *Jane Eyre* by Charlotte Brontë, where we shared our enthusiasm for democracy and revolution. This was where I entered the garden of love, and read the poems of Hafiz, the great Persian Sufi poet from the fourteenth century. All we were asking for was to keep the doors to our university open, and we were being attacked and killed for it. Guards swung chains at us, targeting our faces. I was terrified. I wasn't brave enough to be in the front row. Blood ran down students' faces.

A guard came from behind me and picked me up by the neck. I was screaming. He opened the door to Baba's car and threw me inside. Baba sped away. I was hysterical. I didn't want to leave the group, but Baba wouldn't stop the car.

After I had calmed down, Baba told me that he had climbed up the pillar beside the front gate, where many people had gathered to watch the attack. Baba started screaming, "*Allah O Akbar*, God is Great, I am a Haji! My daughter is among them. These girls did not burn the Quran." He had pointed at me over and over again.

The guards yelled at Baba to come down, but he would not budge. Finally they told him that if he got down and into the car, they would pull me out of the crowd.

I was not a member of any opposition party, but I was publicly opposed to the Islamic Republic of Iran. Many followers of the regime, fellow students, and friends knew my beliefs. I never stopped sharing openly the murder of my uncle Dariush by Khalkhali and the Revolutionary Guards, and I was known to the Islamic group at my university as the niece of Dr. Abolghasem Rashvand Sardari. I spent hours at the table of Kurdish student activists; some whom I knew personally were later arrested. The future of my education had become uncertain and the lives of my friends and fellow students were threatened.

As for Sia, students of the Baha'i faith were not allowed to return to university. Our school curriculum did not discuss Baha'i as a world religion, even during the Shah's regime, so I didn't know much about it.

Later, it was explained to me like this: In the middle of the nineteenth century, a young Iranian merchant announced that he was the bearer of a message that would change the world. He took the name Bab, meaning "the gate" in Arabic. He claimed that he was the gate to spiritual reform. Iranian Shia Muslim leaders saw Bab as a threat to Islam. Bab's mission was to prepare the way for the coming of Bahaullah, the prophet of the Baha'i.

"Mehrnaz, wake up! Sia is on the phone."

Sia was sobbing, "Hamid and Majid have been killed. Someone threw a bomb into their boutique."

Hamid was Majid's older brother and Sia's friend. Hamid and Majid owned the boutique together; they were in their twenties. They were Muslims, but Hamid's wife Roxana was a Baha'i. They had a baby boy. I had met Hamid and Roxana only a few months before.

"Hamid and Roxana would love to meet you," Sia had said. "They want to show off their baby boy. They're having a small party at their home and they asked me to bring my big speakers for the dancing. I believe Hamid's brother Majid is proposing to Roxana's niece."

Hamid had green eyes and light brown hair, and Roxana had black hair and dark skin. Their baby had such a beautiful complexion, a combination of his parents' light and dark. Majid did not look like his brother. He was tall with dark skin and dark hair—so handsome—and he knew all the modern dance moves to top Persian, European, and American pop songs.

"I had to go and identify their bodies. Their parents and Roxana were in no condition to do that," Sia was shocked and stricken with grief.

"But why would anyone throw a bomb into their boutique?"

"The neighbouring store owners think it was because Hamid is married to a Baha'i. It was an act of the Revolutionary Guards. I can't get the picture of their burned bodies out of my head. The entrance door with the metal rolling shutter came down after the bomb was thrown at the store, so Hamid and Majid couldn't get out. Mehrnaz, what if they do this to you when we get married?"

I decided to leave Iran with Sia. Our aim was to go to America and continue our education. It was difficult for us to arrange, because there was no American Embassy in Iran at that time as a result of the Iran Hostage Crisis. From November 1979 to January 1981, fifty-two American diplomats and citizens had been held hostage after a group of Iranian students belonging to the Muslim Student Followers of the Imam's Line took over the American Embassy in Tehran. Sia and I had decided to go to Germany to apply for our visas to the United States.

Sia left before me, and we planned for me to join him in one month. My girlfriend Sholeh and I decided to go to Paris to visit our friend Sima, and then I planned to go to Frankfurt to be with Sia. I didn't tell Baba and Maman that I was going on to Germany. They thought I would be staying in Paris.

Roshi was envious of Sholeh, Sima, and me getting together in Paris. Roshi had just gotten married and couldn't join us in Paris.

A year ago, Roshi's father had dropped by at our house unannounced. "I am here to ask you for help. You're the only one Roshi will listen to."

Roshi's father had pleaded with me to persuade Roshi not to marry Mehdi, her boyfriend. "I have asked Mrs. Massoudi's permission for Roshi to stay with you at your villa. Please take her away from Mehdi. He is not suitable for Roshi. There's another man, Majid, who is asking for Roshi's hand. He is from a good family, and he's a respected dentist. He is the man I want Roshi to marry."

Roshi's father was a principal of a well-known boys' high school in Tehran. He always sounded determined and powerful, but that day he sounded weak. He was asking me for help, and I did not hesitate to give it. Roshi had lost her mother when she was seven years old. She was the only daughter. After Uncle Dariush had rejected her, she hadn't dated anyone for a while until she met Mehdi.

"I am also hoping that you and Roshi can come to a wedding of our relatives in Shahi, which is only few hours away from your villa. Majid will be there, and I want Roshi to meet him," Roshi's father said. I did as he asked and soon Roshi was engaged to Majid. They had gotten married this past summer.

Sholeh and I met in front of the French Embassy in Tehran at eight at night. We knew that in order to get into any European embassy, we must show up the night before and line up. We brought tea, fruits, watermelon seeds, pistachios, bread, and feta cheese. We were excited to spend the night in the line-up. We'd heard many sad and funny stories of Iranians trying to leave the country.

"My friends and I drank a bottle of vodka, and then showed up drunk, singing and dancing in front of Komiteh, the building of the Revolutionary Guards, in our neighbourhood. We were all arrested and got lashes. Here, these are the marks on my back." A young man was sharing his story. We laughed with him while he told his story, until we saw the marks on his back.

I never stopped thinking about Kyan. He had not phoned in the months after I told him that I needed to go away to our villa to have a break from everything. But when he finally called, I was happy to tell him that I was dating Sia. He was hurt. He wanted to see me, and I wanted to see him too, but I didn't want to tell Sia about it. He would get upset if he found out I was seeing my ex-boyfriend. But now that Sia was in Germany, I arranged to meet Kyan the day before I left for Paris. I intentionally did not meet him earlier because I was afraid that I would go back to Kyan again. But seeing him a day before leaving Iran I thought was safe.

We met in a romantic restaurant. A violinist was playing passionate music. Kyan's eyes were filled with admiration and sorrow at the same time.

"My angel is growing into a dazzlingly beautiful woman," he said, taking my hand.

My ticket to Paris had been purchased and I was leaving the next day, but his hand holding mine felt like an anchor that I didn't want to let go of.

There were so many questions I wanted to ask him: "Why didn't you call me? Why did you betray me by talking to your mother about my body? Was I wrong all these years assuming that you loved me?"

But I didn't. He had broken my heart many times. Did I still hope he loved me? I wasn't sure.

My parents held a farewell party for me the night before I left for Paris. Many friends and relatives came, and to my surprise Kyan walked in. I wondered if Baba had invited him. Music was playing loudly and people were dancing. I joined Baba and Kyan, who were standing in a corner of the room. Baba had told Kyan that, "If Mehrnaz comes back in two weeks, I will buy her an Austin Mini."

I had been wanting this car for so long, but Baba would not buy it for me. Now he was bribing me with it, but it was too late, even though the thought of my own Austin Mini was tempting.

Fereshteh joined us. "Kyan, have you met Fereshteh?" Baba asked.

"Oh yes, how could I forget Fereshteh? I remember the night she saved our lives."

Fereshteh started laughing. "Kyan, you have such a good memory."

"What trouble was Fereshteh up to that time?" Baba asked smiling.

"The night during the revolution when we all ran inside your building, and the soldier was banging at the door to get in, we were on the roof chanting the political slogan, 'Brother soldiers, why are you killing your brothers?' But when everyone was quiet, Fereshteh yelled, 'Brother soldier, you are so gorgeous!' The soldier was so surprised, he stopped banging at the door."

I was laughing so hard, remembering the shock of the people around us after Fereshteh had yelled at the officer.

"I thought it was me pleading that made him go away," Baba said, laughing.

"Oh, Fereshteh, this is your music. Please do your solo dance."

I loved to watch Fereshteh dance; she blended classical ballet and sensuous Persian dance moves.

"Only if you join me halfway," she said and smiled.

"I promise," I told her. "Kyan, you haven't danced tonight. Why don't you join us?"

"I don't feel like dancing tonight. I will dance with you when you come back to me," he said, smiling.

23. The Iran-Iraq War

WHAT DELICIOUS FREEDOM! We could walk along the Champs-Élysées, speaking openly about the Islamic Republic's oppression, without fear of being arrested by the Revolutionary Guards. We were all hoping the Islamic Republic of Iran would soon collapse. The walls along the streets in our beloved Tehran might have been covered with the slogan "Death to America," but all of us young people in Paris had one goal: to get visas for the United States.

I was nervous about how to break the news to Baba and Maman that I was leaving Paris to go to Frankfurt to join Sia, but soon fate provided a delay. One morning, the phone rang, and Sima, Sholeh, and I learned the shocking news that Iran had officially declared war on Iraq. Then Iraq invaded Iran. Iran had been bombed, and all telephone connections had gone dead. I did not have to share the news of my leaving Paris to go to Frankfurt. I couldn't call home at all.

Hundreds of concerned Iranians gathered by the office of Iran Air, desperate to get news from home. All flights were cancelled. In the romantic city of Paris, we were filled with heartache and fear over our loved ones in Iran. We got the news that people in Tehran were safe. Bombs were targeting an area close to the border of Iran and Iraq. Iran and Iraq had a long history of border disputes, but, once we heard that the U.S. was supporting Iraq in this war, we became very concerned. The U.S. was not concerned about the border disputes; the U.S. was interested in invading Iran with the help of Iraq for the purpose of removing the Islamic Republic of Iran. We hoped for the removal of the regime of the

Islamic Republic, but not if the cost was the destruction of Iran and the loss of civilians' lives.

After a couple of weeks in Paris, I flew to Frankfort. Sia found me a cozy one-bedroom apartment in a heritage building in the beautiful town of Bad Homburg, close to Frankfurt. We began living together there without our parents knowing.

"Sia, where's the shower?" I asked when I moved in.

"That's one thing this place doesn't have. The owner said it is only one bus ride to a sports club. There are clean showers there."

The bus didn't come very often, so I only went to shower at the club once. I found a public bath in the town centre, but it was only open on Saturdays and Sundays. I disliked taking sponge baths, but it was my only option. I loved living with Sia. He also kept an apartment for himself so his parents wouldn't find out that we were living together. In Iran, we had never spent a night together, and it was lovely waking up in the morning in each other's arms.

We took German language courses, while still hoping to find a way to get to America. But soon our hopes faded. The American Embassy had stopped accepting Iranian applications for student visas, so it was very difficult to get them. News of the Iranian hostage crisis—still ongoing in 1980—was all over the German press, and we began to feel the fear and anger pointing at us.

When I had been in America and England prior to the revolution, we were recognized as rich oil people, respected, even admired. The staff in the shops paid extra attention to us, knowing we were there to spend money, and they enjoyed talking to us about the Shah's affluent lifestyle. But now, with the hostage crisis, a radical religious regime in power, and the economic sanctions that were being levied by the United Nations, the Iranian currency had lost its value and so had we, its people.

Younger Germans were the exception. They accepted us, while their elders began to regard us as terrorists. The owner of my apartment was complaining about Sia staying overnight. We went away for the weekend and when we came back we found an eviction notice on our door. Sia and I had not understood the lease agreement, and it turned out that my lease was only for three months. My apartment was shown to others without my permission and rented out to another tenant. Sia and I started looking for another place to live.

We had been asked several times if we were Spanish, so we decided to tell people we were from Spain, even though neither of us spoke a word of Spanish. We were having such a hard time finding housing. Sia's bachelor apartment was in the basement and it was in bad condition—dirty and damp. The unit next door was used as a chicken coop. Sia had an Iranian roommate, so I couldn't live with him there. I was so homesick for Iran.

We kept hearing horrible news about the war in Iran. Beautiful Tehran—a city of life and light, the Paris of the Middle East—was shrouded in complete darkness. Every window was covered with thick paper or curtains. For light, people were only allowed to have candles. Driving at night was forbidden for fear of Iraq dropping more bombs.

I wanted desperately to go where my heart was: with my family in Iran. Sia and I were in love with our country. We wanted to grow old in Iran with our people. We missed our lives with our families so much that we didn't care about the terror of the regime. Sia's father didn't encourage his son's return. The government was targeting the Baha'i, and Sia's father had been fired from his job at the hospital. He was seeing patients and operating at his own private clinic, but there were many threats against him.

"Mehrnaz, stay. Don't come back there is nothing here for you. All universities are still closed. It is not safe here, stay." Maman wanted me to stay as long as it was necessary. But I only lasted six months. I left Germany and returned to Iran and the welcoming arms of my family and friends at the airport. I felt completely surrounded by my loved ones, knowing that Sia would be following shortly.

Baba and Maman held a big lunch party at our house. The day I arrived was the anniversary of the Iranian Revolution, and the government had announced that the blackout was over. Tehran did not have to exist in the dark any longer.

It was a beautiful, sunny winter's day. I took a moment to take a walk along my street with Roshi and Sholeh, where I had lived since childhood, where I was not seen as a foreigner, and where I was not considered a terrorist. I let the sun caress my skin and my hair, and I promised myself that I would never ever leave the land of Persia again. My brother Jamal and my sister Soraya, and Aunt Masi and her family, were all back in Iran. This was the centre of my universe: Homa and her husband Mansour and their two daughters lived on the fourth floor; after returning from the U.S., my brother Jamal and his wife Gita lived on the third floor; my parents and I lived on the second floor; and my sister Soraya and her husband Iraj lived in the basement. My siblings had stayed in the U.S. for only three years—long enough for Jamal and Iraj to graduate with their MBAs. Our first floor was still rented to Aly's sister's family; Aunt Roohi, her husband, and their children lived next door; and Vafa and Shamsi lived in the basement of Aunt Roohi's house.

This was the ground that had centred and nourished me; I was surrounded by love. I would not let the government keep me away from my land, my family, and my friends.

24. Dark Days

AYATOLLAH KHOMEINI'S DECREE IN 1980 made the *hijab* for women mandatory in Iran. In order to disrupt any uprising against his government, Khomeini placed an absolute ban on all forms of dissent. Ayatollah Khomeini also called for the foundation of a youth militia—Basij. Now Basij was called out onto the streets at times of crisis to dispel dissent.

Basij became the police of their neighbours' morals: their main focus was placed on locating and persecuting bad *hijab* practise. Women were not allowed to show their hair and skin in public. We had a choice of wearing a scarf, loose and non-fitting coats, and long pants. Only the faces and hands of women were allowed to be seen in public. It was not mandatory to wear a *chador*—the one piece of fabric that covers a woman from head to toe.

It was a sad day for me when the law first came into effect: I still walked the streets of Tehran under the beautiful sun, but I had to cover my hair with a scarf. There were many demonstrations against the mandatory *hijab*. Women who refused to wear the *hijab* were arrested and sentenced to lashes. There were even some incidents where random people in the street attacked women, throwing acid into their faces or slicing them with knives.

Baba told me the story of Reza Shah who had banned the *hijab* in 1935.

"In those days, Mother and my aunt tried to wear dresses and coats with elegant hats to stroll in the streets of Tehran. They felt awkward leaving the house without their *hijab*s; they only walked a few steps before running back inside. They felt naked without their *hijab*s, and they laughed at their failed attempts. I witnessed my mother being forced out of wearing her *hijab*, and now my daughters are being forced into wearing them. Mother had a great selection of chadors. I remember a black one that was made of a tightly woven mesh-like fabric displaying patterns of leaves in silk velvet. My favourite one was black with a turquoise lining. When she walked, the turquoise showed. She had a beautiful wardrobe of elegant clothes, chador, and jewellery."

I think he hoped to make me feel better about being forced to wear a *hijab*.

He continued: "Reza Shah was passionate about modernizing our country, including involving women in education. For the first time in the history of Iran, women were being accepted into universities. Your Great Aunt Nayer Samii was a member of parliament. I fear that the Islamic Republic is going backwards by denying women their freedom."

Baba had a friend who had passed away when he was young. Whenever we ran into his widow in Tonekabon, Baba stopped to pay his respects. She was beautiful and serene.

"I remember the day my friend married the most beautiful young woman in Tonekabon," Baba would say. He liked telling me about her and describing her beauty. She did not remarry after her husband died, and she raised her two sons on her own. Baba was devastated when he found out that the Revolutionary Guards had accused her of adultery and put her in jail. She was not a prostitute, and she had never been seen with another man. There was no case against her. She was in her forties. People gathered around and listened to her begging for her life while the Revolutionary Guards and the bystanders stoned her to death. This happened in the city of Tonekabon.

Baba said that she begged the guards not to kill her. "Let me live and I promise that I will serve the community for the rest of my life. I will clean mosques. I will pray every day."

Is this the law of my Islam? I could not understand these actions.

Despite his father's warning, Sia flew back. It was dangerous for me to walk in the streets of Tehran with him. If young men and women were seen together in public, they could get arrested and interrogated, and if they were found to be dating, then they

Mehrnaz's passport photo, under the regime of the Islamic Republic of Iran, 1983.

were jailed or whipped. That didn't stop Sia and me from seeing each other every day. We were young and fearless and in love.

In Tehran, we became immune to the sound of anti-missiles; there were many false alarms. Still, every time the sound filled the air we froze until we were sure it was an anti-missile and not a bomb. Certain foods, which had been imported prior to the war, were rationed. In the mornings, long lines of people formed, waited to get food with their government-issued coupons. My family managed to buy everything on the black market. Gasoline was rationed as well, and there was always a discussion in my house about where to buy black market coupons for gasoline.

Baba spent a lot of time in his room trying to connect to BBC Radio in London. Media in Iran was censored, so we only heard what the Islamic Republic wanted us to hear.

Since Baba had retired from his job, he had taken up collecting antiques. Our formal guest-receiving room was decorated with antique wall hangings, lamps, plates, and many other treasures. Baba's new passion was finding rare pieces of *termeh*, a sumptuous and ornate Iranian cloth handwoven by experts. In the evenings, he sat on the Persian rug cushion in his navy velvet housecoat, hand stitching fabric to the back of *termeh*, to keep the hems from unraveling. Baba and his friend, Farid, were passionate about *termeh*, and they often shopped for golden ribbons to sew along the edges of their latest acquisitions. When we visited Farid's family, he was proud to show us his *termeh* collection.

Baba started losing weight and complaining of feeling tired. After a couple of months, he went to see his doctor only to find out that he had leukemia. Baba and Jamal travelled to Europe for medical advice.

Baba was only in his late fifties, but he was told that he had only a few years to live. I couldn't imagine Baba leaving my life so early. For me, he was bigger than life itself. How could I define my life without him?

Meanwhile, Sia and I were shocked when the government announced another new law: it was illegal for Muslims to marry Baha'is. Sia also found out that medical universities had banned Baha'is from going back to their universities. He had already completed three years of medical school and now all of his efforts meant nothing in Iran. Sia's greatest dream was to become a doctor. We began making plans to leave Iran yet again, only to find that the government was no longer issuing passports for Baha'is. Sia could not leave the country.

Life became one horror story after another.

One quiet afternoon, I heard a gunshot and ran out into the street. Two young men were lying bleeding in the road. One was my neighbour's son, Mohammad, who belonged to a pro-Islamic group. He was alive, but his friend wasn't moving. I held Mohammad and screamed for help. Neighbours arrived, including his mother. When I went home, Maman was angry with me for running to the scene. "Don't you know they come back to finish them off? You could have been killed!"

They had been attacked by anti-Islamic activists. It had happened directly in front of a corner store, but at first no one had shown up to hold Mohammad's bleeding body except me. Afterwards, others had arrived slowly. No doubt they had the same concerns as Maman. Mohammad survived the shooting, but his friend did not.

When my brother-in-law Iraj opened a private school in our building to teach English, he asked me to teach the beginners. Although we didn't need a permit to open the school, we still aroused suspicion. One afternoon while we were walking in our street, the Revolutionary Guards stopped Iraj and interrogated him about all the young people going in and out of our house. With that, my short teaching career was over. The Revolutionary Guards had our house under surveillance.

One day, our tenant's son ran to get me. "My mother is bleeding. She has to go to the hospital." His mother, Aly's sister, had cut her finger while she was opening a tin can; she was bleeding heavily. I quickly put on my coat and scarf, and drove her to the nearest hospital, about five minutes away from our house. I stayed with her until her husband arrived.

As I was driving home, I noticed a car filled with young men chasing me. This happened a lot in Iran. I loved driving, and I especially loved it when guys chased me. They assumed they were better drivers than women, but I was proud to say that I always managed to surprise them with my fast and fierce driving skills. This was my neighbourhood. I knew every turn and every little street. They were trying to pass me, but I wouldn't let them, and kept cutting them off. I was having a blast at first, but then I realized that this chase was different: they weren't playing music or laughing, and, a few times at the intersections, they almost crashed into cars driving in the opposite direction.

When I slowed down to park in front of our building, the car cut me off, blocking me from parking. Then five armed men surrounded my car and wouldn't let me out. One of them held the door. I screamed, "MAMAN!" Maman heard me and ran to the balcony, but she was hardly walking those days, so instead of running over to me, she started screaming for help. The armed men were taking me away. Now the neighbours all poured into the street.

"Someone go get Mohammad!" Maman kept screaming. "Mohammaaaad!" He was the neighbour's son who had been shot and a pro-Islamic activist.

Mohammad arrived and began speaking with one of the armed men. Fortunately, he knew them. They were undercover Revolutionary Guards. They were always watching for suspicious activity around the hospital, and they told Mohammad that they thought I had taken an injured anti-government activist in for treatment. Aly's sister was not an activist!

I didn't leave the house again for many days. I didn't even go to see Sia. Finally, the fear of this regime had rooted itself in my very being.

25. Pregnancy and Abortion

BABA RETURNED AFTER HAVING SPENT a month in Europe visiting specialists. His diagnosis was confirmed—leukemia— and the doctors whom he consulted in Europe recommended the same treatment as his doctor in Tehran.

Baba had missed our trip to Tonekabon, so, soon after his arrival we left Tehran to go and stay with Aunt Masi and her family for a few days. We drove on Chalus Road, one of the most spectacular roads in Iran, which connected Tehran to the City of Chalus in Northern Iran. It was a four- to five-hour drive beginning with windy roads in the rocky mountains of Alborz. As we got farther away from Tehran, the mountains became less rocky and more covered with trees. Then we dropped to sea level, where the air was humid and the landscape green. The smell of the Caspian Sea was the smell of home. It made me so sad to drive past our own beautiful villa and not stay there; its remote location was not safe anymore. People were disappearing without a trace.

"I've been feeling nauseous for the past couple of weeks," I told Sia a little while after we returned. "It's been going on ever since my trip to Tonekabon. I was carsick going through the switchbacks on Chalus Road."

We went for a blood test.

"Mehrnaz, I got the blood test results. You're pregnant," Sia said.

Shocked, I touched my belly. How did I not notice the change in my body? I wondered. My period had always been irregular. When I went to England and America I did not menstruate for six months. In the beginning, Sia and I were careful; there were accidents, but I never got pregnant. I couldn't imagine asking a doctor for birth control pills as an unmarried woman.

"I called my father," Sia told me, "and he'll arrange for an abortion with one of his colleagues."

"No! I'm not aborting my baby."

"Mehrnaz, my dream is to be a doctor. There is no way that I can stay in Iran; I have to live where I can go to university. We can't have a baby. If we do, I'll have to stay here and give up on my dream."

"Sia, I feel like I don't even know you. This is our baby. All you're talking about is your career."

I cried for many days. We fought and fought, but finally I agreed to have an abortion.

The Islamic Republic had made abortion illegal. Sia's father was a physician, and his colleague agreed to perform the abortion in the hospital and to document it as a different procedure. Sia's father paid a huge fee. Every staff member in the operating room was paid a large sum for keeping our secret, thereby risking their lives.

A woman could not have an operation without her parents' or her husband's signature, so Sia and I decided to get married rather than ask my parents. Sia's father called to arrange for a formal visit. Maman organized a time.

"Mahin, why did you agree for them to come to ask for Mehrnaz's hand? Her life will be in danger. The government could kill her. Marriage between Baha'is and Muslims is against the law now." Baba was angry, but we needed his signature for the marriage to be legal, so we did our best to convince him.

"If you don't agree, then I will go and live with Sia," I threatened. Of course, that would be an embarrassment to my family and to any family in Iran.

Later, Sia phoned me, his voice shaking, and said, "Your Baba, Jamal, and Iraj showed up at my apartment. Your Baba said if I love you then I must not put your life in danger by marrying you. He was crying."

When Baba came home, I had packed my bag and was ready to go and live with Sia. Baba sat down, his head in his hands.

"This regime murdered my uncle in the name of Islam, and you kept asking me to be silent in the face of tyranny for my own safety," I told him. "Now this regime is prohibiting a Muslim from marrying a Baha'i. Is it a sin to marry a Baha'i? You're asking once again for me to obey the law of this regime and not marry a man whom I love. Am I committing a sin marrying my beloved Sia? The hands of this regime are stained with the blood of innocent people. Marrying a Baha'i is not a sin."

I was so angry that for the first time I wanted to talk about all the secrets in our home. The secrets, the unspoken words and lies, which had broken so many hearts.

"Arranged marriage should be a SIN!" I shouted. "It should be a sin to allow young women to be judged by their bodies, and men by their education and wealth. Marriage of a gay man to a woman should also be a sin."

Vafa ran from the other side of the room. He tried to grab me and bring me to my room. "Missy, you're going too far. Don't say any more!"

I pushed his hand away and continued. "What do you think happens to all the homosexuals in this country? Do the prayers of their parents get answered and they finally become straight? Do they end up happily ever after when they marry the opposite sex?"

Vafa was trying to carry me to my room, but I wouldn't let him. "Allowing men to marry four wives is a sin. They beat their wives to get their agreement so they can marry another woman. Marrying a Baha'i IS NOT A SIN."

Vafa was still dragging me behind him and trying to close my bedroom door.

"Vafa, stop it. I am not you. You obeyed Maman and Baba. It was not your decision to get married. You chose silence, but I can't."

Vafa managed to put me on my bed and closed the door. He started crying, "Haji and Mahin jan love me. Whatever they did was for my best." He sounded so defeated.

He cleared his throat and continued. "You know that I love Haji and Mahin jan. But I love you more than anyone else, and this time I am on their side. You are risking your life by marrying Sia, and I will not support that."

He walked to the drawer where I kept my cigarettes. My bedroom, with its light blue walls, dark blue carpet, and white curtains, was my oasis. When I needed to calm down and feel balanced, I would stay in my room and play classical music, drink tea, and smoke cigarettes.

"Oh, the pack is empty," he said. "Don't you have another one?"

"I forgot to get more."

I only smoked when I felt sad or angry, so Vafa knew that I always kept a pack on hand.

I wanted to hug him and tell him that I was pregnant, but I couldn't do it. It would break his heart. And I knew that Vafa couldn't keep a secret—he would have to tell someone—so I couldn't risk it this time. Although I liked smoking occasionally, it made me slightly nauseous, so I couldn't even think about smoking when I was pregnant. I was already feeling sick enough.

He put the tape of *Swan Lake* by Tchaikovsky in the stereo, and turned it up, and went to get me tea.

"Don't leave your room. You've said enough!"

I collapsed on my bed and sobbed. I couldn't have an abortion because as a woman my signature didn't count. I had to get married so I could have an abortion, but my marriage was against the law. Why did a woman at my age, twenty-two, need her father's signature to get married? I asked myself. Why did a woman need a husband's or a parent's signature to have an abortion? It was *my* life—*my* abortion, *my* marriage. Who was I? *I was a woman who had no rights.* I couldn't even begin to imagine raising a child without a father in my country.

What rights did Vafa have in Iran? I also wondered. I remembered Nilufar, a classmate in high school. She was taller than any of our male teachers. She was built like a man, and she had a manly voice. She could not hide her difference. She used to bring the best cigarettes to school, and Roshi and I were lucky enough to be invited to sneak out and smoke with her. She had her own spot on the fire escape. I remembered the mint-flavoured cigarette that she brought once. I loved it. Her father often travelled to Europe for business, and he would bring back cigarettes that we couldn't find in Iran. Nilufar was lucky because her parents were open-minded and accepted her. She was going to America after grade twelve to have what we now call sex reassignment surgery. She was looking forward to it, but she was also sad because she wouldn't be coming back to Iran afterwards.

"My parents accept me, but they feel others won't and that that would be too hurtful. But no one knows me in America so I can have a new start—a life of not being judged!"

Nilufar used to tell us about the girls who were closeted lesbians in our school. She loved Farima, a girl in our class. "Farima is too afraid to show her feelings for me because she'd be in trouble if her parents found out. She told me that she'll come to America too after graduation."

Now, lying down in bed, thinking of Nilufar and the lesbians at school made me feel less sorry for myself. It was true that as a woman my legal rights were half those of a man. But transgendered and homosexual people living in Iran had no rights at all. If they told the truth about their identities they could be jailed and/or killed by the government of their own country, and they would also risk being ostracized by their own families.

Vafa came back into the room. He always knew how to calm me down. As I sipped the tea, the *ghand*, cube sugar, melted slowly in my mouth, bringing sweetness to my belly. He made the best tea.

"Oh Vafa, I can't even get *ghand* in America. Tea will never, ever taste same without *ghand*. There are sugars cube in America but they melt so quickly. It's gross."

"I will send you *ghand* when you are in America."

"It's not the *ghand*." I started sobbing. "I want you and everyone else in America. I have been away before, but I always came back home. After marrying Sia, I can never come back home. Not while this regime is in power."

"Don't marry Sia. Aly still loves you. Marry him. There are so many other men who dream of marrying you. Don't leave. When I was making you tea, I heard Soraya talking to Haji. She was saying, 'Baba, you must let her marry Sia. You know Mehrnaz too well. You know that she is going to live with Sia if you don't sign the marriage certificate. Or they will escape Iran and then get married in Europe or America. Their marriage is not against the law in those countries.'"

This was first time that Soraya stood up against Baba. She didn't know that I was pregnant.

Baba at last agreed, and finally the day came when Sia's parents came to our house for the formal marriage arrangement. Shortly after the tea service, I was asked to leave the room because our parents wanted to talk about the *mehrieh*. Traditionally, the future bride was not supposed to be in the room during the negotiations. In the Baha'i tradition, opposite to the Islamic tradition, the groom's family gave the *mehrieh* to the bride at the time of the wedding.

"Your Baba is not agreeing with the Baha'i way. He is arguing that the Islamic way ensures financial security for the future if, God forbid, divorce happens," my sister in-law Gita told me.

I was sitting in my bedroom, and Gita had to come to get my agreement.

"I only want a rose for *mehrieh*, so it can be the Baha'i way, and they can give it to me at the wedding," I told her.

After a few minutes, Gita came back to my room again. "Your Baba thinks a rose is ridiculous, and Sia's mother is proposing gold coins for your *mehrieh*."

"No, I do not accept money or gold coins."

"Sia's mother is laughing and saying that she had no idea that the bride would be as stubborn as her son the groom. But your Baba is furious with you," Gita reported.

"Well, tell them that I don't believe in this tradition. I also don't believe in this stupid tradition that keeps me from being in the room."

"I won't say that to them. Mehrnaz, we all have *mehrieh*. It's about security." Gita was getting tired of me too.

"Yeah, but it's time to change the tradition. We can't continue this for the sake of keeping our parents happy. What is Sia saying to all of this?"

"He smiles every time I go back and report that you are insisting on a rose."

Baba finally came to my room, his face red with anger. "Daughter, this is a marriage. This is not like joining a communist party and reading revolutionary books. This is a lifetime commitment. You don't know what will happen in the future. I pray that you have a happy life with Sia, but the *mehrieh* will guarantee financial security if something goes wrong. I will not always be here to help out. It brings me more peace for you to have a substantial *mehrieh*."

"Baba, first of all, how many times do I need to tell you that I am not a communist and I have never joined any political parties? Believing that men and women are equal doesn't make me a communist. You must have faith in me. I am a university student. I will be an educated woman and have my own income."

Baba gave up. In the end, I compromised and agreed to receive a few gold coins, equivalent to the value of a gift, but not a *mehrieh* in the traditional sense.

My dream of wearing a wedding dress did not come true. We could not have a celebration. We did not share the news with any relatives; it was too risky. An old minister was bribed to marry us. We had an Islamic and Baha'i wedding ceremony.

We told my parents that we were going for a honeymoon. Nothing could have been further from the truth. We had the abortion. After the abortion, I stayed in Sia's apartment, resting.

26. A Wedding Without a Groom

SIA'S PARENTS HAD A LUXURIOUS HOME in the middle of Tonekabon, and had invited us to visit for a few weeks after our secret wedding and the abortion. Baba and Maman were concerned about me staying at their house. Sia and I enjoyed anonymity walking in the streets of Tehran, but everyone knew who we were in Tonekabon. I hid my hair under a cap and made myself look like a man for the drive. Like most homes, the property had a gate and walls surrounding it, and no one could see inside.

Sia's father loved gardening. When he wasn't seeing patients in his clinic on the property, he was in the garden, nurturing his beautiful flowers. Sia and I enjoyed sitting on the patio surrounded by colourful flowers, reading books while being serenaded by the sound of chirping birds and the creek that ran through the property. In the evenings, we went out with Sia's parents to restaurants outside the town. After dark, people could not identify me in the car.

I was reading a biography of Henri de Toulouse-Lautrec. He is among the best-known painters of the post-impressionist period, a group that includes Cézanne, Van Gogh, and Gauguin. I appreciated the art of that era. I cried as I read about the hardhip that Toulouse-Lautrec had faced: he fell in love with a woman who admired his art, but she rejected his love because of his deformed body. He had developed an adult-sized torso while retaining his child-sized legs. I identified with him and his misshapen body.

We were anxiously waiting to hear from the smugglers who were going to assist Sia in leaving the country. Soon the day arrived when he would be putting his fate in the hands of total strangers and risking his life in order to cross Iran's southern border into Pakistan. We were young and optimistic; we knew that we would join each other soon. Even so, my heart was aching and I was horrified at the thought of Sia escaping Iran this way. This was not the first time that we had been separated, but it was the first time since we had met that we were separated without knowing when we would see each other again.

It took him forty-eight hours to get to Pakistan. Sometimes, he had to hike through the mountains. Sometimes, he was left all alone behind a bush for hours in the middle of nowhere and ordered not to move. He could see border guards' trucks driving by. Then, finally, a truck came for him.

An uncle in America had sent Sia a plane ticket from Pakistan to Spain, and then from Spain to New York. He had been accepted into the U.S. as a Baha'i refugee. The Islamic Republic prohibited people from using banks to send money abroad, nor did they allow people to leave the country with their jewels, To get around this, we decided that Sia would carry my valuable jewellery items, including the emerald jewellery set my parents had given me at our wedding. If he could get through the border safely, then I could have my jewellery back when I joined him. Our future livelihood in the U.S. was unknown, so I felt that if we ever faced financial hardship, we could at the very least sell my jewellery.

Forty-eight hours passed before I heard his voice. He was safe and staying in a hotel in Karachi, Pakistan. After a few days, he phoned me from the hotel before leaving for the airport and said he would call again as soon he got to Spain. I didn't hear from him for three days. We began our hunt for Sia.

The hotel manager in Karachi said he had left in a taxi to go to the airport. We called the airport police and were told that Sia had not arrived at the airport. We called the police in Karachi, but there was no report of any activity regarding my husband.

Shayda, Sia's mother, prayed in front of Bahaullah's photo and assured me that Sia was safe. I was still in Tonekabon, where the telephone service was poor, waiting to hear from Maman, Baba, and Soraya, who were waiting by the phone in Tehran.

"Did Sia call?" I was frantic.

"We will call you as soon as we hear his voice. We have placed candles and the Quran by Sia's photo in your room, and Baba and Maman are sitting and praying for his safety."

Soraya did her best to calm me down. But I was frantic. Every phone call made me jump. I cried and cried, and could not sleep.

"Mehrnaz jan, Sia will be fine. We are all praying. Your Aunt Masi called and told me to let you know that she gave a donation to the poor at the shrine of Shahazadeh Hossein in Qazvin," said Shayda, rubbing my back and trying to calm me.

"I lost my Uncle Dariush," I cried out. "All my prayers didn't save his life. I no longer believe in the power of prayers. I can't imagine my life without Sia."

Finally the phone rang in the middle of the night. "Mehrnaz, our prayers have been answered. Sia is safe. He gave me a phone number for you to contact him in Spain." Soraya sounded happy and relieved. I was grateful that Baba, Maman, and Soraya cared so deeply about Sia's wellbeing.

Sia had been arrested the moment he entered the airport. There were spies in the hotel in Karachi who knew the place was a destination for many escaping Iranians. They also knew that these refugees would be carrying large amounts of cash and jewellery. The spies would identify their victims and then report them to the Pakistani police. It was illegal to cross the border into Pakistan with large amounts of foreign currency or jewellery.

Sia was accused of smuggling. He was not given the right to contact anyone. He was kept in a cell with criminals, scared for his life. After three days, he was told he could go free if he gave all the jewellery to the police and signed an agreement that he would never claim the jewels in future. Sia was carrying one thousand dollars in cash and a plane ticket to Spain. The police took it all, so Sia's uncle bought him another ticket.

I called Sia in Spain. His voice sounded hollow. He had lost his spirit.

"Mehrnaz, I was in the room with heroin smugglers. I sat on a chair for three days with hardly any food or water. The moment I closed my eyes and fell asleep, the interrogators would walk in and wake me up. They kept me awake all this time. They broke my spirit so I would sign their agreement and never reclaim the jewellery."

Sia was crying. "They took all your jewellery."

"But Sia, they did not take my *most* precious gem. You are alive and I can hear your voice."

Shayda loved going to Tonekabon's farmers market every morning. Although I didn't get up early to go with her, she would bring home my favourite fresh fruits. I was usually still in bed when she came back, and she enjoyed coming to my bedroom and checking to see if I was ready for breakfast.

"Moosa brought you yogurt this morning. I made you *masto khyar* for breakfast. Doctor said you must eat eggs in the morning. Would you like me to make you a tomato and egg omelette?"

When Shayda talked about her husband she referred to him as "Doctor." Everyone including me called him *Aghaye Doctor,* Mr. Doctor, and people referred to Shayda as Mrs. Doctor, but Shayda insisted on my calling her Shayda.

"Shayda jan, I really can't eat an omelette. All I want is a big bowl of *masto khyar* for breakfast." *Masto khyar* is a yogurt, cucumber, and mint salad. I could eat the refreshing salad *all day,* especially when it was made with the yogurt Moosa brought. The yogurt was poured into a sack made of lamb's skin, then hung up. Overnight, the water drained out, leaving thick, creamy, delicious yogurt.

Shayda ate her breakfast early, but sat at the table drinking tea while I ate mine. "I didn't want you to abort your baby. I would have taken care of your baby, and you and Sia could have gone to America to continue your education."

I could hardly speak. This was the first time anyone except Sia had mentioned my pregnancy to me. I started crying.

"Why didn't you share this with Sia?" I had aborted my baby, and now I couldn't believe that I was having this conversation. I had thought I had no choice.

"Doctor asked me not to say anything to Sia. He was afraid that if you had the baby, Sia would not be able to go away to study medicine."

"Shayda, I wish you had contacted me. I didn't want to have an abortion, but I didn't have a choice."

Shayda was sorry that she had upset me. I was not upset at Shayda, though. I was shocked at the realization that both of our voices, Shayda's and mine, had been muffled by our men.

When I shared my frustration with Shayda, she tried to change the topic. "Go to TV room and I'll bring us some tea."

She brought tea and their family albums. I chose their wedding album.

"Oh no, Sia has your nose." I gasped when I saw a close-up photo of her cutting their wedding cake.

When Sia and I had talked about having children, he told me that he wanted our children to get my eyes. I hoped they would get his mom's nose. We Iranians are obsessed with small noses. Sia had a noticeably large one and mine was not small either, but Sia's mother's nose was small and beautifully shaped. Sia had never told me that his mother had had plastic surgery after she had married, thanks to a famous surgeon who was a friend of Sia's father.

"Mehrnaz jan, you should go get it done too," Shayda suggested.

"No!" was my answer. Nasal plastic surgery was common in Iran, but after all the other plastic surgeries I had had for my burn scars, I didn't want to go under the knife again.

She was persistent. "Believe me, you won't feel any pain."

When Sia's father got home from the clinic, she said, "Doctor, ask your friend to operate on Mehrnaz's nose."

"I should call him. I didn't even tell him that Sia got married," Aghaye Doctor said. And later he said, "He has offered to do Mehrnaz's nose as a wedding gift."

"Girls get nose jobs to find a husband. You already have a husband. Your nose is fine. Don't do this. What is wrong with your nose?" Baba was overreacting again.

Shayda told me that it was painless, and she was right. I didn't feel any pain, but I could hear the hammering and the filing of the bone. I was not under general anaesthetic, and the doctor and the nurses kept talking to me. They asked about Uncle Dariush's murder. We could be arrested for talking about my uncle's murder publicly. Luckily, the staff in the operating room were all anti-government. The pain medication loosened my tongue, so I explained all the horrific details of my uncle's murder.

"You were calling Khalkhali a few deserved names," a nurse told me. Khalkhali was the man who had ordered my uncle's execution without a trial. "I am so sorry for your uncle's murder," she said, then paused. "We're all done now. Would you like me to bring you anything to drink or eat?"

"No, thanks. Baba brought me some snacks."

Baba stayed with me until it was very late at night.

"Baba, do I look good?" I asked, still half dazed from the drugs they had given me.

"You look as beautiful as always, Mehrnaz jan."

"But how do I look with my new nose?"

"Your nose is under the cast. I can only see the tip."

In the evening, Soraya and Iraj came visiting me. "You look so good, Mehrnaz. The tip of your nose is pointing up. It will take many years before gravity drops it down again," Soraya said laughing.

The next morning, Baba came to take me home and I caught a glimpse of myself. "BABAAAA, why didn't you tell me that I have black eyes? I look scary." I started crying. "Why did Soraya say that I looked good?

"It was not as bruised last night as it is this morning." Baba was speaking calmly, hoping that I would calm down.

I had not seen our servant, Hamid, for the past year, so I was happy he was there when I got home from the hospital. Hamid always entertained me with his stories, and I was desperate to be distracted. The recovery was painful, and I hated the way I looked with the cast on my nose and my black eyes.

Hamid had been our servant for several years before returning to his home in his village Neshta, where our orange grove was also located. He didn't like living in Tehran, but at home he didn't get along with his mother, so our house became a second home for him.

"Hamid, how did you manage to get away from the war zone?" I asked.

"I was shot in my leg so they let me go."

He began showing me photographs.

"Hamid, oh my God, I feel sick to my stomach. How did you manage to get these photos out of the war zone? Please put them away. I can't look at them. Hamid, you are not even eighteen. How did you get into the war?" I asked.

"Many boys as young as fifteen go to war from my village. As long as their parents sign, the boys can go."

"Why would parents want their boys to go to war so young?"

"*Mullahs* preach that when a boy goes to war he becomes a holder of the key to heaven.'"

"Is that why you went?"

"No! I went because I'm in love with a beautiful girl, Sedigh. Her parents said that I could only marry her if I joined the army. They thought I would wait until I was eighteen, but I told my mother that I wanted to go so I can have the key to heaven, and she signed the permission letter. My mother really believes in this stuff."

I thought Hamid was brilliant and funny. His stories always sounded unbelievable. He was not even eighteen, and it seemed like he had lived so many lives already. I quickly glanced at the photographs once again.

"I heard no one is allowed to take photos because the government doesn't want us to see all the casualties."

"I always managed to sneak in my camera. Most of the boys and men in these photos are dead. They were lying in the trenches, shot. I respected them and did not take photos of their faces, only of their bodies. Do you see how many of them have lost limbs? And sometimes their whole stomachs are blown out. I learned quickly that there is no *key to heaven*; the moment I walked into the war, it was *hell*."

"I am so sorry, Hamid, for what you went through. I'm happy that you survived."

Friends and relatives were gradually finding out about my marriage to Sia. So, Shayda proposed that we have a small wedding reception. "Sia is my only child. It was always my dream to have a wedding celebration for him."

"Everyone knows Mr. Massoudi and me," said *Aghaye* Doctor. "He is a Haji and I am a Baha'i. It is dangerous to have a wedding party for Sia and Mehrnaz. We could all get killed because of a one-night celebration. And besides, Sia is not here anymore, so what's the point?"

"My friends are all asking when the wedding is. Most of them are Muslims, and they say it will be fine if we hold a celebration in Tehran," reasoned Shayda.

"The news will be all over Tonekabon. Even if we have the celebration in Tehran the guards can locate us," Sia's father replied, his tone grim.

I listened quietly. I was neutral about a wedding celebration.

"I have a suggestion!" Baba said. "Invite your friends for a women-only dinner party. Just don't call it a *wedding* celebration."

One of the many new laws of the Islamic Republic forbade men and women to be in the same room during gatherings, including wedding celebrations. We also had to inform the local *komiteh*, the office of Revolutionary Guards, about the planned gathering. I had heard stories about guards walking in on wedding celebrations; if liquor was being served, or if men and women were in the same room, they would arrest every single person.

Shayda agreed to the women-only dinner party, and we invited more than fifty of Shayda's friends and my cousins. Sadly, only friends and relatives from Tonekabon were invited, so I couldn't invite Roshi or Sholeh or Fereshteh. Everything was organized quickly because Shayda was concerned that I would leave before she could have her celebration. Shayda hired several cooks to help in the busy kitchen. They worked for days prior to the event.

"How could it even happen without me?" Vafa was really upset.

"Vafa, this doesn't feel like a wedding to me. I would never have a wedding without you. I feel bad for Sia's mother. This means so much to her."

After a few tears, Vafa felt better. "I should dress up as a female dancer. No one would know."

"Vafa, almost every man and woman in Tonekabon knows you." He laughed.

Just before the celebration, Shayda told me excitedly, "I made an appointment with a hairdresser. You'll be there all day."

"Why all day? It won't take her more than two hours to do my hair," I protested.

"Oh no, you are going to be treated like a bride. She is doing facial hair threading, facial mask, makeup, and your hair."

"No way. There is no way I'm doing facial hair threading. I only do that on my legs and it hurts. I can't imagine doing it on my face. I don't have much facial hair anyhow. I always bleach the hair on my upper lip."

"Farideh does an amazing job with bridal makeup. She either uses wax or threads for facial hair removal. She won't do makeup on top of the facial hair," Shayda insisted.

"I'll do my own make-up."

"Farideh would be so insulted," Shayda said disappointedly.

"I will drop you off and pick you up from the hairdresser," Baba said in a quiet voice.

"I can just drive myself."

"But you're the bride."

"I'm just wearing a dress, not a wedding gown. I can drive." I was being stubborn.

"But I want to be a part of it." Baba sounded sad. I finally acquiesced.

Farideh was threading my upper lip. The tears were running down my face. Her hands were moving so fast. "Your face will numb soon, and then it won't hurt as much," she assured me.

Once she started on my chin, I had to stop her. It was hurting so much. I was not crying, but tears were streaming down my cheeks and I could not stop sneezing.

"Sorry, Farideh, I just can't do this. It's too painful."

I put on my dress. It was ivory, and it flowed down to just above my knees. It was the same dress that Sina had made for me to wear to Roshi's brother's wedding.

"Baba's beautiful Mehrnaz jan," Baba said with a big smile.

"Baba, you don't need to bring me inside the house. Only women are there."

"I want to see everyone's reaction when you enter the room. I told Mahin to bring *esphand*, wild rue seeds. Sia's mother told me she does not have any at home."

"Baba, they are Baha'i. They don't believe in the Evil Eye."

"Burning *esphand* and notions of the evil eye originate from Zoroastrian," he told me. "Muslims and Baha'is both celebrate Persian Nowruz, New Year, which is also rooted in the Zoroastrian religion. Having *esphand* there is about tradition and cultural beliefs."

Zoroastrian is one of the world's oldest monotheistic religions. It was founded in Persia by the prophet Zoroaster, approximately 3,500 years ago. Zoroastrians believe that there is one universal god, Ahura Mazda, whom they worship at a fire temple. The temple is called Dar-e-Mehr in Farsi: The Gate to the Sun. They believe that "light" and "fire" are the cleanest phenomena on the earth; therefore, Zoroaster chose them as the symbols of Ahura Mazda. So there is always fire burning in their temples. They believe fire and the smoke of *esphand* cleanse the room of evil. Zoroaster believed in the existence of good, evil, and retribution. Zoroastrian has three principles: Good Thoughts, Good Words, and Good Deeds.

These principles of Good Thoughts, Good Words, and Good Deeds were written in all our textbooks at school, and beautifully framed in stores and offices. Every elementary school child had to memorize these three principles. The religion of Zoroastrian was accepted among Muslims.

Baba and I walked together, arm in arm, into the room. A servant came forward burning the *esphand* and reciting prayers for my wellbeing and prosperity. One of Shayda's friends sang the Persian wedding song and everyone joined in. Shayda held my arms and brought me around the room to introduce me to her friends. Baba left to join Sia's father in his clinic. They were afraid to leave the property in case the Revolutionary Guards invaded. Maman moved around the room, chatting with everyone. She knew most of the women from when we lived in Tonekabon. We danced all night.

Shayda and her helpers filled the large dining room table with Persian foods. The menu included oval platters filled with green herb rice with fava beans, yellow saffron rice, and red tomato-based green-bean rice all shaped in pyramids. There were also large bowls of green herb lamb stew, brown-reddish chicken *fesenjan*, plates of baked whole white fish and salmon, along with many other side dishes as well as overflowing bowls of fresh green herbs.

27. Leaving Tehran

THE ISLAMIC REPUBLIC CONTROLLED IRAN'S borders to prevent the exodus of Iranians during the Iran-Iraq war. Only those with businesses, students, or people with medical permits were allowed to leave the country. One of my uncles had connections in the Ministry of Health.

"Let's see if we can get you a medical permit. However, since your plastic surgery is not an urgent medical procedure, I am doubtful that we will succeed."

After six months of meetings, bribes, and paperwork, I finally obtained a medical permit to leave Iran for further plastic surgery on my scars.

When I went to America before the revolution, it took seven *toman*, Iran's currency, to buy just one U.S. dollar. Now after the revolution and war, one thousand Iranian *toman* was equal to one American dollar. Iranians were only allowed to take one thousand U.S. dollars with them when they left Iran.

I tried to bring clothing with me so I wouldn't need to buy any for the next few years in the States. Our financial situation in the U.S. was uncertain. Sia's uncle in the U.S. was holding money from Sia's father to support us and pay for Sia's tuition at university, but we had been warned that it would not be enough money to support the lifestyle that we were accustomed to in Iran.

Baba and I went fabric shopping. My favourite place was Zartosht Street, which was lined with fabric shops. I was looking for fabric for formal dresses for evening gatherings.

Baba and I were excited to visit Sina. This could be the last time that he would make me a pretty dress.

When Baba had brought me to Sina's shop for the first time, Sina had said that he would make me dresses like Princess Farahnaz, and he kept his promise for many years.

When I entered the room, I choked. "Where are your friends?" There was no smell of Persian spices, no Persian stew on the heater, and no men sitting around chatting, laughing, and crocheting. Even though it was full of colourful dresses, the room seemed deserted and gloomy.

Sina saw the sadness on my face and quickly picked up a dress and started sewing to avoid making eye contact with me.

"Darling, you know that these days it's not safe to have any gatherings. Some of the storeowners in my street who used to hate my friends are now buddies of the Revolutionary Guards. They spy on people. My friends and I could get killed."

I sat on the chair that Saleh used to sit on. Saleh's laughter was so distinct, and he had made the most loving comments when I had modelled my new dresses for him and his friends in the waiting room.

"Sina, could you ask Reza to bring tea for Mehrnaz?" Baba was referring to the young man who used to always serve tea in the shop.

"Oh, he was the first one I had to tell not to come here. The business owner next door always called him names. He hated that Reza wore tight pants and showed off his athletic body."

Baba changed the subject. "Mehrnaz is going to America soon, and she is insisting on bringing new dresses to remind her of her favourite dress maker."

"*Ey Khoda*, oh God, there is an exodus of young people fleeing Iran these days. We are losing our finest. I still remember the first day you came here to my shop with your Baba."

I didn't look at either Baba or Sina. The weight of my heavy heart was pulling down my face. It wasn't just Sina's room—my whole country felt deserted.

As my departure grew closer, I began spending more time with Baba. I was now choosing to leave Iran, and I knew I might never be able to come back. Baba had leukemia, and my heart was breaking thinking of being away from him when he had only a few more years to live.

"Baba, I would love to learn your favourite song, 'Khazan,' before I leave."

Shod Khazan, it became autumn.
Autumn arrived at the garden of lovers.
Once again the flame of separation has been lit.

We sang together until I got it right. I still remember his soft voice and our laughter when I sang out of tune. Then we read Hafiz's poetry together. Baba could recite many of the poems from memory.

One afternoon, we learned that the daughter of Mashdi, the old man who lived in our villa year-round, was staying in a public hospital in Tehran. She was diagnosed with cancer. Her husband and children were at their home in the village of Masuleh and couldn't afford to come to Tehran to visit her. Baba and I decided to visit her, but we could not find the hospital's information desk, so we began going from room to room, opening different doors. Behind one of these doors was a room filled with young men sitting in wheelchairs. There were hundreds of them. Some were missing legs or arms, and some had badly injured faces. I felt sick.

The news from the war was censored. The media reported only the victorious war stories. There was never any talk of the numerous casualties, nor of the severe life-altering injuries.

"Maman, I don't feel good. I feel so nauseous."

"How many times have I told you not to buy kabob from the street vendors?" Maman thought I had food poisoning. "I've made you lemon water to make you feel better."

"This is so sour."

"It's good for food poisoning."

I was found unconscious in my bed with blood pouring out of my mouth and was taken to the hospital. I had a bleeding ulcer. I continued to suffer from severe ulcer pain for several weeks, in spite of the medications I was on.

"You must go to see Dr. Diba. He's the cousin of Shah's wife. A friend of mine had ulcers for years. Finally, he went to Dr. Diba and he is all fine now," one of my aunts told me.

Baba and I went to see Dr. Diba, and after asking many questions and giving me a check-up, he asked Baba to leave the room.

"I am concerned that you are under high stress," he told me. "As a result, your ulcer is not healing. Why are you so stressed at such a young age?"

I started crying. "My Baba has cancer. We were told that he has only a few more years to live. My husband is a Baha'i and he had to leave Iran. I have been away from him for months, but I am joining him soon. I am so sad about leaving everyone, especially Baba. I'm afraid that I will never see him again because of the war." For the first time in my life, I was prescribed a medication to lower my stress. My ulcer pain soon started to go away.

"What dish would you like for your goodbye party?"Maman was organizing the dinner.

"*Fesenjan*, please."

"Vafa and I thought so. He said he wants to make the *fesenjan,* but not the rest of the meal. He wants to have enough time to be with you and dance."

Friends and relatives started arriving. I was busy in my room packing with my aunts and cousins when Vafa entered the room. "Oh my God, Mehrnaz jan. Aly is here," he announced.

Aly's sister and her family were still living in our building and were invited to the party, but I didn't know Aly was coming too.

"Vafa, you must show me this Aly guy. I never met him while Mehrnaz was engaged to him," Fereshteh said. She and Vafa were giggling.

"Fereshteh, I wasn't really engaged to him."

"Oh, he's handsome."

Then Fereshteh changed the subject. "I called my brother Farzad and told him to apply for a Green Card for me, so I can come and join you in America. I won't be staying here long after you leave. I told Farzad to apply as soon as possible. I'm getting out of here."

"I hope you will join me soon, Fereshteh. Do you think Mehdi will come with you to America?"

"I hope so. I hope he asks me to marry him soon. My mother is so hurtful. She keeps saying that men just want me for sex and that they won't marry me. She's my mother—I can't even imagine what other people think about me. People's attitudes really make me angry. They believe sex is dirty unless you are married. They think if I am having sex with my boyfriend then he must be using me. I just want to scream 'Women are not second-class citizens; we have the same sexual desires that men have!'"

Fereshteh, Vafa, and I left my bedroom and joined the party. It was awkward to make eye contact with Aly. Vafa changed the music to Fereshteh's favourite dance song.

I did not have to ask Fereshteh to dance. She began her elegant solo performance without prompting. I watched her dance the dance that always gave me joy, only this time it made me weep for everything that I would soon be leaving behind. She came over to ask me to join her, but when she saw my tears she turned around and grabbed Vafa instead. In this black-and-white society in which girls must be virgins until they get married, men must be the providers and protectors of the family, Vafa and Fereshteh added colour and light to my life.

"Turn the music off. It's time for Aly to sing," Vafa announced, looking at Aly flirtatiously.

I loved Aly's voice! He started singing while looking at me:

Ahn safar kardeh ke sad ghafeleh del hamrahe oost
Har koja hast khodaya besalamat darash.

The traveller whom a caravan of one hundred hearts accompanies
Wherever she goes may her companion be God.

I looked at Aly and silently thanked him for this beautiful closure.

28. Sia and Mehrnaz in America

ILEFT MY BELOVED TEHRAN, my home, wearing a bright red shawl and carrying two big suitcases. Baba bought this shawl for me to take to America and to use as a tablecloth. It was his favourite colour: red, with darker red flowers. Baba was dressing me up in red once again.

When the pilot announced that we had flown over the border of Iran, many women, including myself, removed their shawls. The fanatic Muslims on the flight objected loudly, but they had no power over us now. I had brought my makeup bag with me in the plane, and I started putting on make-up. As I walked to the bathroom, I noticed that many other women were doing the same thing.

I remembered the time I accompanied Soraya to the female-only swimming pool. I was coming from a friend's house and was wearing makeup. I was not going to swim because I was conscious of other women seeing my body, but I decided to sit on the patio and have a drink with Soraya and her friends.

At the entrance of this fancy club, a woman who worked for Basij searched us for makeup. She was rude to me because I was wearing makeup. I was hurt and humiliated but could not say anything, because I could have beem arrested by the Basij. I had to step away from the line and wipe off my makeup in front of everyone. I also had to remove my nail polish with the nail polish remover they provided.

Afterwards I was allowed to enter, but even then she did not stop yelling at me. "You must be grateful to the Islamic Republic and Ayatollah Khomeini for saving you from going to hell when you die. Keep putting on makeup and you will be hung by your hair on the fire when you go to hell."

It made me chuckle now walking down the aisle of the plane. "I guess all the women wearing heavy makeup in this plane will go to hell, including me."

I was travelling to Dubai and would stay for two weeks with my relative, Amir, his wife, and their adorable son. When I arrived, I found out that Amir had just been released from jail. It was a shock.

Amir began to explain. "I was called to a certain hotel for a business meeting, but no one showed up. I sat at a table by the pool for a while and then left. The next day, the police came and arrested me. An American woman had been raped in the hotel and they accused me. I don't even know what she looked like. My lawyer said that I was being set up. He told me that I resemble a certain Sheikh, and that he believed that the Sheikh had raped the woman. Then the Sheikh and his men had arranged for me to go to that meeting so they could prove I was in the hotel that day. It was a conspiracy!"

Amir was upset and terrified. He described the jail in Dubai. It was frightening; they had not allowed him to talk to his wife or his lawyer for twenty-four hours. I was very concerned about him and his family when I left Dubai. Accusing Amir of rape was unbelievable. I had known Amir all my life, and I had seen him making out with the girls around his age, including my cousins, but there was no way he would rape a woman. My heart felt heavy for Amir and his wife.

I made a last stop at the American Embassy for a final interview. Sia had sent them all the documentation for my visa. I was so relieved to receive the visa that would allow me into America to be reunited with my husband.

Sia was attending college, and had to write an exam the night I arrived in New York. He hadn't been able to tell me in advance. He arranged with his uncle to pick me up from the airport, but when the plane landed, my name was announced and no one was there to greet me.

I had been to New York before with Baba, but now I was alone with two big heavy suitcases, frightened and heartbroken. I had left everything I knew and everyone I loved in Iran. How could Sia not be waiting at the gate for me? I had been imagining our reunion for months and couldn't understand why he wasn't there.

Sia's uncle had booked a hotel for me in New York. After a terrifying forty-five minutes, I managed to find a shuttle. The doorman at the hotel made such an impression on me. He was a tall black man with a deep voice who said, "Ma'am, do not open the door if you hear a knock; it's not safe here."

"What irony," I thought. I had heard so many stories and seen so many American movies that portrayed black people as the ones I needed to watch out for, but I felt safe in the company of this strong African-American man. I jammed a chair and my two giant suitcases behind the door. I did not sleep the whole night.

There was one pleasant surprise for me at the airport. All the young women had hair that looked like mine when I hadn't spent hours straightening it: big, curly, long in the back and short on the top! I had brought my haircutting scissors with me. I gave myself a trim, had a shower, and blew my hair dry. I looked like any other young woman in New York with a perm, but my curls were all natural.

As I was too frightened to sleep, I passed the hours entertaining myself in the mirror, acting like an eighties model with my big hair and makeup. But then I would start crying, remembering everything and everyone I had left behind.

The next morning, Sia picked me up at the hotel. He explained what had happened. I quickly forgot how mad I was that he didn't come to meet me at the airport. I held him so tightly. How I had missed being held by him.

"We must go very quickly. We have an interview with the Canadian Embassy in New York. I applied for us to immigrate to Canada. I didn't tell you on the phone because I wanted to see your reaction in person. You always dreamed of moving to Canada." Sia loved surprising me. He liked America, but I liked Canada's foreign policy. Canada was known to us in Iran as a peaceful country.

Sia and I drove through the streets of New York looking for the Canadian Embassy. The traffic, the chaos, and the high rises reminded me of visiting New York with Baba.

Sia and I were walking toward the embassy holding hands when he said, "One has to be very careful about AIDS in America."

I was shocked to hear this from Sia. "Why did you say that? You and I don't need to be worried about AIDS. We don't have AIDS. People can get AIDS if they sleep with someone who has it. You know this better than me. Why did you say that?"

"Don't overreact. I didn't mean you and me."

I didn't say anything else about it, but my thoughts were racing: Why did he bring this up? And why was he worried about contracting AIDS?

Every morning, Sia went to college and didn't come home until the evening. I had nothing to do all day. I wanted to go to the college with Sia, but he said it would be too distracting for him. Our apartment was a few kilometres out of town, so when I went for a walk there were no stores for window shopping and no one was around to talk to.

We had a small black-and-white television, but I didn't understand the shows. My English was not at a level where I could follow the storyline. I wrote letters to my friends and family, and I struggled to cook dinner.

"Mahin, the girls are growing up not knowing how to cook or do any household chores," I remember Baba saying to Maman. "They should be spending some time in the kitchen learning how to cook."

"When they get married, they will spend enough time in the kitchen. For now, they need to study and be free to have fun," Maman had replied with determination.

In the summers in Iran, I used to spend a lot of time reading poems, books, and women's magazines. When each magazine was delivered by the postman, Soraya and I fought over who would get it first. Now I wished that I had learned how to cook from Vafa, instead of reading every word in the women's magazines.

The Persian New Year, Nowruz, was nearing. I was so homesick. I had never spent Nowruz away from Iran and my family.

"I purchased tickets for you and Sia for the Baha'i Nowruz celebration in Philadelphia," Azin said. Sia had lived with his aunt and uncle for a few months before he got his own apartment.

"You must come—it's fun! And don't worry about bringing a dish. I am bringing a pot of lamb, fava beans, dill rice, and *tahchin*."

"I love *tahchin*. It is on my menu list for heaven," I told her. "I miss Vafa and his *tahchin.*"

"Mehrnaz, I have never met anyone like you—so slim and fit, and yet so in love with food," Azin used to say. Azin was slim too, but she always watched her diet.

"Mehrnaz jan, it took me close to an hour to get through on the phone lines," Baba said. People from Iran were all trying to phone abroad on Nowruz to hear the voices of their loved ones, but there were not enough lines for the high demand.

I began to cry while Sia and I were driving to Philadelphia for the Nowruz Baha'i celebration. He was sad too. This was the first time that he was away from his family for Nowruz.

"Could you get the map from the glove compartment?" he asked me while he drove. Inside was a present for me: a bottle of perfume.

"I love the smell of this perfume, and I love you, Sia."

"*Eidet Mobarak, eshghe man,*" Sia said. "Happy New Year, my love!"

I was happy to be with Sia, but my heart was heavy that night without my family. I just wanted to be back at home celebrating Nowruz with my loved ones.

One afternoon while Sia was at college, I looked at some of the photos he had taken over the past six months. "Sia, where was this? Who took this photo?" I asked when he got home that night.

"I went for a weekend getaway and asked someone in the hotel to take this photo of me."

"But you're sitting on the bed in a hotel room. Who would come and take a photo of you in your room?"

"I can't believe you're questioning my loyalty."

I couldn't sleep that night, but I didn't want to say anything more to Sia either. I hadn't forgotten what he cautioned me about AIDS when we were walking on the streets of New York.

When Sia had stayed with his aunt and uncle, he did not get along with his Aunt Azin. Sia had thought that she would cook and do his laundry, but Azin was not a traditional Persian woman. Her life was not just about cooking, cleaning, and taking care of her children.

Azin worked part-time, and, when she did not work, she was busy having fun with her friends. She and her girlfriends frequently drove to Philadelphia. She wanted me to go with them, but they usually came back around suppertime, which did not give me enough time to make dinner for Sia.

"Oh, buy frozen hamburgers and frozen vegetables. Just make the rice and serve it with hamburger and veggies. If he complains then ask *him* to make Persian food," Azin said, rolling her eyes.

I never missed these outings with Azin and her friends; they were all in their forties, independent, humorous, and rich. It was always a lot of fun.

"I was walking in the farmers market in Philadelphia when I heard two Iranian women behind me saying in Farsi, 'Oh look at her, she must be a hooker,'" Azin's friend, Mojgan, said. Mojgan was married with children and she owned a boutique. She had bleached her hair blonde and wore miniskirts with high-heeled shoes because she was short and petite.

Mojgan turned and asked the Iranian women in Farsi, "Excuse me, what did you say?" The Iranian women were shocked and embarrassed.

Mojgan with her chic, ritzy style and sense of humour reminded me of my friend Fereshteh in Iran.

Sia and I began fighting on a regular basis. It didn't make sense to me that I could not hang around the college while he went to class. And why was he coming home so late? Once I left the house after we fought, but it was too cold, so I came back in and heard him talking to a woman on the phone.

"Who is she?" I asked.

"A friend from college."

"Sia, why is there a red lipstick kiss mark on the collar of your shirt?"

"Oh, you are sick with jealousy," Sia said angrily. "It's all in your head."

I knew something was wrong, but I didn't know what to do. I lived for phone calls and letters from family and friends to relieve my boredom and loneliness.

"Mehrnaz, I have a suitor who is very nice and handsome," wrote my friend Sholeh. "He is a lawyer. My family likes him but I'm not ready to say yes. How I wish you were here. I don't see Roshi. I am the only one who is still unmarried and living in Tehran. I am lonely without you and Roshi. I want to know your thoughts about what I should do."

She and I exchanged a few letters about her *khastegar*. They were seeing each other, but Sholeh was not in love with him. I didn't tell her what I was going through with Sia.

"Your *khastegar* sounds nice, and I like that photo of him sitting on the sofa with a cigarette in his hand. He's handsome. As I write this letter from my living room in this small town, I no longer believe that everyone must marry the love of their lives."

I wanted to write about Sia cheating, but I decided not to.

One day, a woman from Sia's English as a Second Language (ESL) class dropped by unannounced at our apartment. "Oh, I came to welcome you to America," she said. Sia was home, but I answered the door. She was talkative, but Sia was extremely quiet, which was unlike him. I invited her inside, but her visit was awkward. Finally, she told Sia that she would like to share some good news. She looked at him and brightly announced, "I'm pregnant!"

There was silence, but then Sia laughed and congratulated her. He was perfectly charming. She went on to say that her husband was older and they could not have children, but that she had still hoped she would get pregnant. She was a Korean woman a few years older than Sia and me. She didn't stay long. I was shaken inside, but I didn't say anything about it. I made an effort to be polite and thanked her for coming.

I couldn't wait for her to leave to ask Sia questions: "How did she know where you live? If she is that close to you that she comes over to welcome me and share her pregnancy news, why didn't you ever talk about her? Sia, did you get her pregnant?"

My questions only irritated Sia, and he started yelling and hitting me, so I didn't persist.

My only wish was to be back home with Baba and Maman. I wanted to be with Sholeh and Roshi and tell them that my dream of marrying Sia had quickly become my worst nightmare.

29. Baba in Canada

OUR APPLICATION TO IMMIGRATE to Canada was finally granted. We moved in August 1983. Almost immediately, I started a course in physics at the University of Guelph in Ontario. I was so glad to be going back to school.

I only went to university twice a week for my one course. Sia did not want me to take any more courses. "I will be a doctor, and you will never need to work. You will just support me now by doing all the house chores, and when I become a doctor I will pay someone to do them and you can just take courses for fun."

"When you met me, I was a full-time university student. You knew that I didn't know how to cook," I responded. "You also knew very well that I was against the subservient female role in Iran. Look at me, Sia. I will never be your servant. What about your Baha'i faith? It recommends equal education for men and women."

I was getting bored staying home and cooking meals. I loved going for long walks, but we started getting snow in late October. One day, Sia asked me to come to campus to have lunch with him. I took the bus to the university; he had the car. When I got off the bus, I saw Sia's car in the parking lot. I went to the university centre where we were supposed to meet, but he wasn't there. After waiting for a long time, I walked to his biophysics lab. He had told me that sometimes his experiments ran late in that lab. I asked his tutor, and he told me that Sia had gone for lunch. I walked back to the parking lot, and saw that his car was not there.

"Sia, why didn't you show up for lunch?" I asked him later.

"Oh, I'm so sorry. My experiment took so long, and by the time I got to the centre you were gone."

"That's too bad. I waited for a long time. Did you eat lunch at the student centre?"

"I just got a snack and ran back to the lab."

"Sia, your car was gone and your tutor told me that you'd left for lunch."

"You're making all this up. You're sick." He started hitting me. I finally chose silence.

I remember "choosing silence" was always Maman's advice to those women who came to our house for emotional and financial support after they had been beaten and bruised by their husbands. I had hated Maman's advice then, but now I had no choice but to follow it.

The last time I had seen Azam, my friend from the compound across from our home in Tehran, was when she came to see us with her son. She was wearing glasses and she looked so old. She had been in the hospital because her husband had beaten her up. She had suffered a brain injury from the beating, and it affected her eyesight. Maman gave Azam her usual speech.

"When he's angry, just stay quiet. He will calm down when you do not say anything."

I remembered the beaten faces and bodies of other women, but this was my friend Azam. She used to hang out with me, come to movies, and giggle when boys were flirting with us. I thought, is this it for her now? When he got mad, he beat her up. Azam was embarrassed to look at me. Her parents were too poor to take her in with a child. "Azam must listen and not provoke her husband," they said.

There were no social services in Iran. No financial assistance for poor people. No place for single, divorced women with low incomes. A woman was better off in the house of her tyrant husband; otherwise, she would be left to beg on the streets. If a woman asked for a divorce, she would not get any financial support from her husband. The divorce law favoured men, even in Shah's regime. *Mehrieh* was useless if the woman requested divorce. It was only useful when the man wanted to divorce his wife; then he would pay her the *mehrieh*.

I left Iran because it wasn't safe for Sia. Now I was living in a peaceful country, but I didn't feel safe in my own small apartment with the man whom I loved so much that I left everyone and everything behind. I didn't choose silence when the regime of the Islamic government murdered my Uncle Dariush, but now I chose silence in this new, free country. I still loved Sia, however, and I wanted to be with him. I thought it was my fault; I believed that my scarred and ugly body made him unfaithful. I did everything I could think of to make him love me like he had before. I had never thought that one day I would stay with a man who would beat me and be unfaithful to me. What had happened to me?

My life in Guelph was far from my vibrant life in Tehran. Even during wartime, during the regime of the Islamic Republic, Pahlavi Street was filled with vendors, and people who would just come out to stroll and socialize. The cafés were filled every day and evening until late. Just a walk in the evenings would lift up my spirit. Guelph was an agricultural city with a university. Sundays were especially depressing because the only shopping mall in the city was closed.

Baba managed to get a medical visa and came to stay with us for a month. Part of me was so happy to see him, but the other part of me didn't want him to find out about what was going on between Sia and me. It would hurt him so much. But Baba kept asking, "Why don't you dance anymore? I miss the sound of your laughter, Mehrnaz jan."

How could I tell Baba about the real Sia, when I had fought against all odds and risked my life to marry him?

"I found the most beautiful Persian rug for you. The border is a pink-reddish colour. The background is dark navy. There are pink-reddish flowers throughout the rug. It is tightly woven. I couldn't bring it over the border, but Amir is going to bring it to you one day. I have a feeling that this will be my last present to you."

Baba's words reminded me of the dream I had had two nights earlier. In my dream, Baba and I were going through the border at Tehran's airport, but the border guards arrested me and threw me in jail because I was married to a Baha'i. Then I saw Baba walking into the jail holding the Quran in his hand. All the guards paid their respects and let him come to my cell and take my hand, and together we walked out of jail.

Although Baba had handed me the Quran to hold while we walked out of the jail, by the time we got outside it had disappeared from my hand. I turned to look at Baba to ask him, "Where is the Quran?" But I couldn't see him anywhere. Then the scene changed. I saw myself walking on a land without life— no plants, no animals, no humans. It was empty but beautiful, and the sun was shining on me. Then I came upon a majestic old tree with no leaves. I stopped under the tree and put my hands on my heart in the prayer position. I said one word, but it was neither Farsi nor Arabic. I felt tranquil.

I didn't share my dream with Baba. I knew what it meant when I looked and Baba was not there, but I didn't know what it meant when the Quran disappeared from my hand and I prayed in front of the tree. Why was I praying to the tree? In Iran, Maman Aterahm had always interpreted my dreams. Now I had no one to help me make sense of it.

Baba had a medical checkup and was admitted for a colonoscopy. After the procedure, the doctor came over to talk to me. He told me that Baba had advanced colon cancer, and he only had a few more months to live. Also his leukemia was at an advanced stage. Baba stayed a couple more weeks with me. The day he left, I said my last goodbye. Holding him in the airport. I couldn't let go. How could I?

"Daughter, may the compassionate God be your companion."

30. Loss of Two Beloved Men

"MAMAN, WHERE IS BABA? I want to hear his voice too." I had called home for Nowruz. It was my second Nowruz away from home and my family; the last year had passed by very quickly. I couldn't wait to tell Baba that I'd bought myself a red silk dress to wear to the celebration.

"We had to take him to hospital. He had severe stomach pain," Maman told me.

"Oh no! I'll phone him at the hospital."

"He's in the ICU. As soon as he is out, we'll phone you."

After hanging up, I told Sia that I didn't want to go to the Nowruz celebration. I was too worried about Baba.

I called home the next day, but no one answered the phone.

At that time, my cousin Pari was living with us. She had immigrated to Canada a couple months earlier. I was desperate for information and I turned to her for help. "Pari, it's so weird that no one is at our house. How did Aunt Masi sound when you talked to her? Did she tell you how Baba is feeling?" But Pari only shook her head to indicate she hadn't heard anything.

Soon Shayda called. After our conversation, Sia got up quickly to leave the house. "Where are you going in such a rush?" I asked.

"I have to make a few copies at the library. I'll be back soon."

I was confused, but when he returned I understood that he had been stalling. "Your father has left."

"When?" I cried.

"A few days ago. He has been buried. My mother asked me to tell you. Your family didn't want to tell you on the phone."

Tears were soaking my face when I heard Uncle Manoocher's

voice. "Mehrnaz jan, everyone in the family was worried about your reaction. We thought you might fly back if we told you when your Baba went into a coma. Now hearing your voice so calm and collected, I think we should have told you earlier."

Sia's applications to medical schools in Canada were rejected. His three years of university in Iran were not recognized as a science degree. According to medical schools' requirements, Sia had to complete a science degree in Canada before he could apply. But he was accepted into an American medical school in the Caribbean.

I encouraged Sia to leave. "I understand if you think it's an awkward time to leave me, but believe me, somehow I feel very strong. I will grieve, but I don't need you."

At the time, I was actually remembering a terrible thing he had said to me just before Baba passed away: "Mehrnaz, you are beautiful, smart, and charming. Men will fall in love with you, but no man will stay for long because of your scarred breasts."

I did not want Sia's pity.

If Jamal loved one person in his life, that person would be Baba. For the first time, I heard vulnerability in my brother's voice. "We're designing Baba's grave stone. It will be installed on his grave on the fortieth day of his passing. Is there anything you want to put on? Let me know soon."

"Baba would love a Hafiz poem on his grave. I trust that it will come to me," I said. "I will call you back soon."

When Baba had stayed in Guelph with me, we had read the poetry of Hafiz daily, and I thought I would pick one of the poems that he liked best.

I thought back to when I had celebrated my last Shabe Yalda, the Winter Solstice, in Iran, before my departure. We were all sitting under a *korsi,* a low table covered with a large cloth; underneath we had a heater to keep our feet warm. All around the *korsi* were ten or twelve cushions for people to sit and lean on. Maman had placed a beautiful Persian cloth over the top of the *korsi.*

At Shabe Yalda, Iranians celebrate the shortest night of the year. Because the days after this get longer and the nights shorter, the Winter Solstice is dedicated to Ahura Mazda, the God of Zoroastrian, to mark the victory of the sun over darkness and goodness over evil.

Aunt Anise was staying with us for a few weeks. Her husband was Abul Hasan Amidi-Nuri. During the Shah's regime, he was a legislature deputy, a prominent attorney, a deputy prime minister, and editor of the newspaper *Dada*. When the Islamic Republic came to power, friends recommended that Amidi-Nuri leave Iran.

He had protested and said, "I am not guilty of any crime. My record is clean. If the Islamic Republic wants to capture me, then I have the best lawyer to defend me: *myself.*"

The Islamic Republic did not adhere to human rights. Abul Hasan Amidi-Nuri was not given a chance to defend himself at a public trial. Just like Baba, he suffered from leukemia, and he passed away in jail in his eighties. We surrounded Aunt Anise with our love, hoping to ease her grief and help her to cope with this tragedy.

Many visitors dropped by and stayed up until late at Shabe Yalda. We sat around the *korsi* table, which was covered with platters of salted, roasted watermelon seeds, pistachios, almonds, and chickpeas. We served seeded pomegranates, sprinkled with a mixture of *golpar*, angelica seed powder, and salt. The delicate and aromatic flavour of *golpar* enhances the pomegranate flavour. When I put the first spoonful of pomegranate seeds with salt and *golpar* in my mouth, I closed my eyes and allowed the flavour to transport me to heaven. We drank tea throughout the evening. It was also tradition to have a watermelon and a Persian sweet trail mix on the table. Baba and Maman always insisted on us eating the watermelon; they believed eating summer fruit would protect us from winter colds. Oranges and tangerines were also in season at this time of year, and Baba always brought a box from our farm for Shabe Yalda. Many visitors dropped by and celebrated the holiday with us.

The other tradition at Shabe Yalda is reading Hafiz poetry all night. We refer to Hafiz poetry for our inner intentions and desires. We close our eyes and talk to Hafiz from the heart by asking him questions; then another person opens the book to a random page and reads the poem that is the answer. We call this *fale Hafiz*. Aunt Anise read a poem by Hafiz for me.

Barghi az manzale Layli bedarkhshid sahar
Vah ke ba kharamane Majnun delafgar che kard.

At dawn, a bolt of light illuminated from Layli's room
Wow, the fire that it lit in Majnun's heart.

In this poem, Hafiz is referring to the characters Layli and Majnun from the anecdotal poem by the Persian poet Nizami Ganjavi.

"Aunt Anise, I love the story of Layli and Majnun. It's so romantic. When I was a teenager I dreamed about falling in love like Layli and Majnun, but not the ending—they both died in this story. This is the love that Sia and I have for each other now," I said that night.

"Mehrnaz jan, the bolt of light that struck Majnun's heart is Divine Love."

At the time, I couldn't imagine any love more profound than my love for Sia.

"Mehrnaz jan, you make sure to take this book of Hafiz with you. It is an essential companion, especially when you have no family or friends around you."

In Canada, my heart aching for what Sia had done, and grieving profoundly for Baba, Hafiz was my only companion.

This poem by Hafiz is on Baba's tombstone.

Baghbana ze khazan bi khabarat mibinam
Ah az an rooz ke baadat gole ranaa bebarad.

Gardener, I see you unaware of the autumn wind.
Sigh of the day the wind takes your beloved flower

Sia left. I was still in love with him.

Our families knew that he had left for medical school in the Caribbean, but they didn't know that he was leaving our marriage as well. We agreed not to say anything about our separation.

How could I tell anyone why he had left me? He was relieved that I had decided not to share the reason.

I only had a few hundred dollars in the bank. I felt that my English was not sufficient to apply for any job, but I learned that I could apply for a student loan if I enrolled in school full-time. I started my first full-time semester with only a student loan supporting me.

I only slept three or four hours a night. I didn't want to sleep; I had nightmares about Baba dying and Sia sleeping with other women. But I managed to pass all my courses. I would record the lectures and then play them over and over until I could write out the notes. Then I would read and re-read entire chapters from my textbooks, spending hours looking up the meaning of the words in the dictionary. There was a huge difference between the time I took pre-dentistry courses at Marywood College and my time at the University of Guelph. The science courses I had taken at Marywood were prerequisites, but I had not studied any science at all during the past six years. My courses were first-year university courses, but I was suffering emotionally and I felt I was not learning as fast as I had before. But I was determined and I studied hard.

"Did you study all night? Mehrnaz, you need to sleep more. Look at your eyes," Pari used to say repeatedly.

I wanted to keep myself busy. Sleep and silence became my enemies. For lunch at the university, I would take a sandwich with one slice of cheese, along with one apple and one orange. The gift shop at the university centre sold a white chocolate bar with crispy rice at the bottom. When Baba had visited, we had both loved that chocolate bar. But now I only treated myself to it after all my final exams were done. I wore my smart clothes and leather shoes, and I carried the leather purses that I had brought from Iran. No one could tell that I was suffering financially.

Sia phoned me every day, collect, from the Caribbean. Although it had been his decision to leave me, now that we were separated he was lonely and he missed me. As for me, I never stopped loving him. He came back at the end of his semester, and we filed for Baha'i divorce. According to Baha'i law, the divorce would be issued after one year of separation. But we couldn't apply for

Islamic divorce because the Iranian embassy in Iran required valid Iranian passports along with our immigration papers. Sia didn't have a passport, and our immigration papers stated that we were refugees.

Sia continued making collect calls. Being together was a habit that we both had a hard time quitting. I knew that as long as I kept hearing his voice, I would not have the strength to heal and to get over him. I began to ask Pari to tell him that I was not home.

Soon, the phone company began calling, asking me to pay over three thousand dollars for the collect calls from the Caribbean. The phone was in Sia's name. It was disconnected.

Pari and I moved to a new apartment. We got a new phone number under Pari's legal name from her birth certificate. Sia didn't know Pari by this name. I didn't want him to find me.

We now had a large two-bedroom apartment. We got another roommate, an Iranian woman named Sepideh. She shared the bedroom with me so my rent was cut by half. Sepideh became a source of happy energy for me. She made me laugh and dance again. She had been living in the university dorms, sharing a room with a Canadian girl, before she moved in with us.

"My roommate always brought different guys home from the bar, so I would put cotton wool in my ears and pray all night. I was so afraid because they were always both drunk. They made out while I was in the room."

Sepideh was traumatized by her wild roommate, and she made us laugh by sharing stories about her and her various men.

One morning, Sepideh's roommate—while she and one of the men she had entertained in their room were dressing—asked her to explain what she was doing. Sebideh told her she was praying. "Why do you cover yourself with that?" the roommate asked. "You look like a ghost. You could use that thing for a Halloween costume." That *thing* was a white patterned *chador* that Sepideh had brought from Iran. She did not wear a *hijab*, but Muslim women must cover their hair for daily prayer.

A young Arabic man, Abu, a Sunni Muslim, became my chemistry lab partner. "My brother is also here studying engineering," he told me. "My father told me and my brothers that we must obtain engineering degrees, and then we can become part owners of his company." But Abu did poorly in science courses. He loved philosophy and poetry. We spent hours reading poetry together. He gave me the book *Rubaiyat* by Omar Khayyam, a Persian poet. He never asked me out, but once he told me that he liked me. I did not tell him that I was married and currently separated. I was only twenty-four years old, and I needed a fresh start. And, I didn't want anyone to know the painful story of my husband's betrayal.

During the Christmas holiday, the phone rang; it was Sia. He had returned to Guelph and contacted the people who knew me and subsequently found me. He claimed to be hurt that he had not been able to reach me for the last few months. Then he said he wanted to see me for a few minutes and promptly came over.

When he arrived, he held me close and said, "I never stopped loving you." I was happy to hear these words. And I welcomed him back into my life with open arms.

Sia stayed with me for two weeks. After he left, he called me regularly from the Caribbean, collect again.

I was still healing from the loss of Baba, but now that Sia was back in my life I was happier and wanted to do more fun things. I was excited when I found out that there was a skating rink at the university. In Tehran we had only one such place; it was called the "Ice Palace." It was a chic place: an ice rink surrounded by a number of restaurants and cafés. We would put on our best clothes to go to the Ice Palace. Most people came to socialize.

I'd bought a cheap pair of skates for public skating. Pari did not want to skate; she just came along to watch me. "Pari, do I look good?" I asked her as I paraded around the room in a big sweater and matching leg warmers. She laughed at me, glad to see that I was finally happier.

When we arrived at the rink, however, I was shocked and disappointed. "Oh my God, Pari, what is this place?" There were no cafés or restaurants around the ice rink, just dismal bleachers and empty grey walls. I was expecting something like Tehran's Ice Palace. There also didn't seem to be anyone around.

I walked onto the ice, and, to my surprise, I could not stand up straight. I began slipping. I held the wall and tried my best, but I kept falling. Pari was holding her face, looking down and laughing. She tried to get me to look in the direction of some hockey players she had spotted who were watching me and laughing.

"Did you get your skates sharpened?"

Two hockey players came from the change room to help me.

"What do you mean *sharpened*? I just bought them new from a store."

"Do you see my blades? They've been sharpened. Yours are dull. You can't skate with them. Would you like us to help you?"

"Sure!" I had fun with them as they took turns holding onto my arms and skating with me around the rink. Pari had her head down laughing. She had gone to school in England for a few years when her family lived in Basildon, and she was more familiar with the culture of Canada than I was.

"Those guys were hitting on you," she said.

"Oh, I didn't notice that. They looked really weird in their uniforms," I said. The most popular sport in Iran is soccer; male soccer players are like celebrities. I didn't find the hockey players attractive—it was hard to see them in that way.

After the Christmas holidays, Sia's phone calls became more frequent. "Mehrnaz, I cannot imagine living without you. Give our marriage one more chance. I am looking for a beautiful place for us to rent. Please come. You will love this place. There are mango trees everywhere. You can eat mangos every day."

I still loved Sia, and I loved mangos! So, I decided to give our love another chance. I didn't register for more classes, and I rented out my room for the summer. Sia was to fly in and stay with me for a couple of weeks before we went back to the Caribbean together.

Abu and I continued our friendship; we spend a lot of time drinking tea and reading poetry. We weren't dating—we only saw each other at university—but we liked each other, and it was hard for me to tell Abu that I was going away with Sia, but I did.

"I was married, but we separated. Now my husband is asking

me to give our marriage another chance. I'm so sorry for not sharing this with you before."

He didn't say much. He was sad. I was attracted to Abu, but our relationship was platonic. We were friends and it was what I needed at the time.

Sia finally arrived for our grand reunion. I ran over to hug him and immediately spotted a big hickey on his neck. I sat on the floor and wept. The marriage was over.

I had no money for the summer. The next day, I applied for a student loan. This was now my fourth full-time semester in a row. I was worried that most of the summer jobs were probably taken by then, and that no one would hire me. I had a heavy accent and no job experience. Abu, I noticed, was avoiding the university cafeteria. I knew he didn't want to run into me, but one day our paths crossed by accident.

"What happened to your wrist?" he asked, about the dark-red burn mark I had gotten from the steam of a tea kettle. He had not spoken to me for a couple of months, but he was concerned when he saw the burn. I explained to him what had happened with Sia, and after that, we met occasionally for tea, but we never spent time together like we had before.

I recently found Abu's name listed as one of the top five hundred most influential Muslims leaders in the world, and now he is one of the running candidates for presidential election in his country. He became an engineer, and then he had continued studying theology, and later entered the political arena. His moderate poetic approach to Islam had earned my respect. I don't believe Abu understood back then, when we were so young, why I didn't tell him right away that I was married and separated. I hope he understands now.

31. Here Comes Naz

"SORRY, DEAR, I'M HAVING A HARD TIME understanding your accent," said the sales clerk who was helping me at a clothing store. I wanted to buy a top, but they didn't have my size. I was trying to tell her that I wanted her to order the top in my size from another store.

"May I have your name and address?" she asked.

It had taken so long to communicate with her about the top that I no longer had the energy or patience to spell my name. "Nahz is my first name!" I told her.

"Oh dear, what a beautiful name."

No one in Canada had ever said that Mehrnaz was a beautiful name. People didn't even try to pronounce it. A few days later, the phone rang. "Hello, may I speak with Naz?"

"Okay," I thought. "One less barrier to blending into Canadian culture. From now on my name is Naz."

I was pleased about my decision. "Nahz" is the ending of female names in Iran, but no one was *called* Nahz or Naz in Iran.

Everyone I talked to about working in Canada said that I needed to find a volunteer job since I had no job experience or referrals. So, I was very excited when I was offered a volunteer job in a virology lab. My job was to make a virus concoction and feed it to tiny bugs; then the next day, I would count the dead bugs. I volunteered on Friday evenings and Saturday afternoons for the whole winter semester. I achieved my goal: I landed a summer job in a food microbiology lab.

My roommates loved my summer job. Every Monday, I went to the university where they processed beef and pig carcasses. I had to add friendly bacteria to the ground mixture and watch the butcher make the sausages. Several butchers did the cutting up and prepping of the meat. I never did like the smell of uncooked meat, and all my life I had avoided touching the raw flesh. Now I was spending half a day in a room filled with hanging carcasses being ground up. I was there to make sure that the butcher added the measured amount of friendly bacteria into the sausages. He would also make sausages without bacteria for the control study.

He gave me the extra ones without bacteria to bring home. I didn't eat any, but my roommates were happy to have them.

Every day, I blended a few raw sausages with a solution. Then I put a pipette in my mouth to suck up a small amount of the mix and pipette it out onto petri dishes. I left the petri dishes in an incubator overnight to see how many bacteria would grow. The aim of the research was to extend the shelf life of sausages by adding friendly bacteria. I didn't complain about my job for the whole summer. I was grateful to have a well-paid science job in Canada. I used to like food microbiology, but after that experience, I was no longer interested in food microbiology—my stomach couldn't handle another project like that sausage one.

Sia was back in Canada, studying for the American Board exam and taking a couple of science courses. I had three roommates, so he couldn't live with me, but he stayed at my apartment for a couple of weeks before renting his own place. I didn't trust him, but when I was with him I only saw the Sia whom I loved and had married. And inevitably, we would end up in bed together.

"Let's go to a movie after I take a shower. If the phone rings, just don't answer," Sia said as he left the bed.

"Why can't I answer the phone?" I asked. I was still lying in bed, my legs tangled up in the sheets.

"Can we talk after I have a shower?"

Later, he suggested we go to a restaurant rather than a movie. "I need to talk to you, Mehrnaz," he said. We had just ordered our meals when he began. "I had a girlfriend when I asked you to come and live with me in the Caribbean. After my father died, I didn't receive money from Iran for a few months. My girlfriend at the time, Ashley, told me that I could move in with her. She covered my living expenses, and I love her."

I couldn't believe what I was hearing. "If you had such a nice girlfriend and you were living with her, why did you call every day?"

"I still missed you," Sia said. "And everything feels different when we are together. Maybe because we have such a long history together. But what I wanted to tell you is: Ashley and I are engaged!"

"But you just slept with me!"

"I am sorry, Mehrnaz."

"Were you phoning me from this woman's place?"

"Yes."

"Did I hear you right? Did you say you are engaged to this woman? I have to leave."

"Mehrnaz, I love you. I am so sorry," he called after me. I stormed out just as our meals were being served.

"Hi. May I speak with Ashley? My name is Mehrnaz. I am Sia's ex-wife." I had to call her. Her phone number was displayed on my phone bills, but I had thought it was a public phone that Sia used to call me collect.

"I don't believe you." Ashley was shocked. "Sia told me that he married you out of pity, but he couldn't have sex with you because your body is covered with burn scars." I was crushed. In retrospect, however, I should have known better; he had made comments about my scars before. Why had I forgotten how hurtful he could be?

Sia was furious that I had called his fiancée.

"Mehrnaz, I will hire Chinese gang members to kill you! You have destroyed my life. Ashley is helping me financially. Her father is a university professor and she is modeling while she is at medical school. She is gorgeous. Look at yourself. Why would I want to be with you?"

He began showing up at my apartment unexpectedly. I started phoning my roommates before I took the bus home from university to ask if it was safe for me to come home.

Once I buzzed from the main door to get in and my roommate

told me, "Run away! He's waiting in the hall outside our door. He's very angry. He thinks we lied to him about you not being home."

One Friday night, after my volunteer job, I had just climbed onto the bus when Sia jumped on and sat behind me. "Mehrnaz, I am going to beat you up and scar the rest of your body." His voice was menacing and I was afraid.

At the next stop, I got off and ran into a shopping mall. I didn't want to continue home because the bus stop close to my building was dark and quiet. I ran into a store, picked up a dress from the rack and pretended that I was talking about the dress to the sales person.

"Could you please call the police?" I asked her. "The man who is standing in front of the store is threatening me."

"I called the security guards. They're outside the store. If he does anything to you, then they can protect you, but otherwise they can't do anything because he's just standing there. Go for a walk in the mall. They will be right behind him."

Sia was calling me names in Farsi and asking me to stop so he could talk to me. When I didn't stop, he grabbed my backpack so hard that the handle ripped. The two security guards pushed him against the wall.

"You're not allowed to do anything to me. She is my wife!" he yelled.

"I'm his ex-wife. He has a fiancée," I told them.

The police arrived and suggested that either I go to the station with them to file a case against Sia, or they put me on the bus and keep him from getting on. I chose to get on the bus.

The next time he phoned, I threatened him. "Sia, if you come around one more time, I will file a case against you. If you get charged, your medical career will be jeopardized."

I was stuck with a phone bill of a few thousand dollars from the collect calls that Sia had made from his fiancée's phone. I had to make payment arrangements and eventually paid the bill off over the next few years. Another price to pay for loving Sia!

A few weeks later, I was sitting in a campus restaurant when I spotted a striking couple getting out of a car. Sia was walking across the campus hand in hand with his fiancée.

32. James and Maman

I WAS READING THE INSTRUCTIONS for the new ultracentrifuge machine in the virology lab when a tall blue-eyed man with sandy blond hair approached me. "Would you like me to show you how to use it?" he asked. His name was James. The next day, while walking in the hallway of the virology department, I heard James's voice call from behind.

"Nahz! I was just wondering why you put your name down in the logbook as *Naz*. You pronounced it as *Nahz* (or *Na-az*). I'm going for coffee. Would you like to join me?" he asked as I turned around to face him.

James was not my type. I liked men who were fashionable, soft spoken, and polite. He wore jeans with holes—they were definitely not fashionable at the time—and he tucked his jeans inside what looked like construction boots. He smoked and he chewed bubble gum, and he liked to blow bubbles at work and in public. Maman raised me to believe that blowing bubbles in public was disrespectful.

Nevertheless, I agreed to go for coffee with him.

"I've been listening to the news about Iran. I was listening to Hashemi Rafsanjani's speech. It seems there is no end to the war. It must be very difficult for you."

Hashemi Rafsanjani was the commander-in-chief of the Iranian military during the Iran-Iraq war.

I was struck by his knowledge. It was the first time a young Canadian knew what was going on in Iran. Mostly, people only said things to me like, "You must be so happy that you are here and not in Iran. We see horrible things in the news about Iran."

James continued. "There was a guy in my class from Iran. His name was Sia. He was a Baha'i. He had horrific stories about escaping from Iran and being arrested in Pakistan. He had to give all his wife's jewellery to the corrupt police. He is not here now. Do you know him?"

"Yes, I know of him."

A few days later, I ran into James again. "Naz, I just saw Sia. He said that he knows you. He's back in Guelph taking some courses."

James told me this after Sia had physically attacked me in the mall. Sia and I were no longer talking to each other. I was relieved that Sia didn't tell James that I was his ex-wife.

I was too emotionally drained to handle James's energy, so I avoided him as much as possible. After a couple of months, my roommate Sepideh said that the baseball team from our department was playing against another university team. She asked me to go with her to watch the game. James was playing. He looked so athletic in his t-shirt and shorts. He made a home run, and when he was at the base he climbed the net to show off how fast he was running.

I was finally recovering from my relationship with Sia, and I no longer had any doubts: I knew I would never go back to him. I wanted someone in my life who could make me laugh. James suddenly seemed an interesting possibility and I began paying attention to him.

James loved to go for drinks at the pub in the university centre. I saw him there one evening and I bought him a birthday drink. We sat together at the bar and chatted about the wedding he had recently attended.

"I was my buddy's best man. I'm so happy for Lisa and Angelo—they're a great couple—but I don't believe in marriage. How about you? Do you believe in marriage?" James asked.

"Well, I have mixed feelings about it since I have been divorced recently."

"What? You never said a word about being married."

"I choose not to talk about it."

"Was your ex Iranian?"

"Yeah," I paused. James was looking at me intensely.

"It was Sia!" I abruptly confessed.

James was shocked. "But ... you both lied to me. Did you ask him not to tell me?"

"No. During that time, Sia and I were not talking." I didn't tell him then about the harassment and abuse, nor about his unfaithfulness.

My relationship with James was like my other Iranian relationships. We didn't kiss or have sex. We spent most of our time at the pub or dancing. As a result, I started drinking beer and coffee thinking it would make me "cool."

The first time I went to James's apartment for dinner, I smelled Aunt Banafsheh's cooking. My eyes filled with tears. The aroma of green herbs and garlic made me ache for home. James noticed and asked, "Does the smell of garlic bother you?"

He was making Italian pesto: a paste of basil with garlic and pine nuts. I loved the pesto sauce; it was similar to the paste that my Aunt Banafsheh made with a mixture of herbs, walnuts, and garlic.

"You will love Toronto," James said. "It's a multicultural city. I grew up in the Italian area. I would love for you to come with me one weekend. I could take you to the Italian neighbourhood. Most of my friends' parents are Italian immigrants."

I agreed to go, and then I regretted it. We would be staying with two of James's friends, and I was very nervous about staying with three men in one place. I had no idea what kind of men James's friends were. I didn't even know James that well.

But I was also excited to experience the metropolitan life of Toronto.

Alex and David's apartment was in a popular neighbourhood called The Annex. There were many cafés, restaurants, stores, and flower and fruit stands lining the street. To my relief, David and Alex were very nice.

"Hey guys, I knew Naz's ex-husband before I met her," James told them. He continued telling them about how I had initially kept my marriage to Sia a secret. I smiled sheepishly but let him finish his story about how we met.

"Let's go for a walk in the Italian neighbourhood." James was excited to introduce his Toronto to me. He was born and raised in Toronto and had lived in the Italian area for many years. I loved seeing people sitting on their front porches and enjoying the evening.

In one of the gardens, I was amazed to discover a fig tree. "We have fig trees in Iran," I said. "I didn't know that they grew here as well."

"Italians grow fig trees," James explained. "They bury them with leaves in winter time, then dig them out in spring," James explained. "Here, let's drop by to say hello to Mr. and Mrs. Ricci. And be prepared if they ask you if you want to eat. They will feed you even if you say no."

They brought so much food to the table. I didn't want to leave Mr. and Mrs. Ricci's porch. I had not felt this kind of warmth and hospitality since leaving Iran.

Mrs. Ricci could hardly speak English so she pointed at the food and with a big smile said, "*Mangia, mangia!*"

"I was raised by a single mom. She worked two jobs to support me. I spent much of my life at my Italian friends' homes. I love the Italian culture and food," James told me.

"David's sister Paula will be here tonight. You'll be sharing David's bed with her," James informed me. I had completely forgotten how nervous I was about coming to Toronto. James's friends were lovely.

Then James told me excitedly that we were all going to the "hippest" place in Toronto: the Horseshoe Tavern. I didn't like the place. It looked rustic. A band was playing that I had never heard before: Blue Rodeo. I liked dancing to pop and to the top 40, but this music was very different and not to my taste.

In the morning, we all had coffee in the kitchen, and everyone grabbed a section of the newspaper. I didn't know what to do. I didn't read the newspaper in Canada. It would take me hours to read one article. There was one section left on the table, so I grabbed it and pretended to read it. Months later, I found out that the section that I was pretend-reading was the classified ads.

I was horrified at the thought of James seeing my burn scars. What if he thought they were horrid and told everyone in our department? There were a couple of other guys in this circle who had asked me out. I was enjoying all the attention and flirtation, but I didn't want to share my body with any man. After we had dated for a few months, James and I finally made love.

"Naz, you're beautiful. Sia is an asshole. If I see him again, I will punch that jerk. Your body is no reason for any man to leave you." But James's opinion of my body could not erase Sia's words from my heart, nor could it change my own beliefs about the scars that covered my chest and legs.

I was still taking classes and needed to earn more money. I started reading the classified sections in a variety of papers to look for a job. I spotted an ad in one of the papers—an Afghan restaurant was looking for a server.

"Do you speak Farsi?" Jacob the owner of the restaurant asked over the phone.

"Yes."

"*Salam, hale shoma khoobeh? Kay mitoonid shoroo konid?* Hi, how are you? When can you start?"

"Pari, Pari, I just got a waitressing job!"

She couldn't believe it.

I never thought speaking Farsi would be an asset for me in Canada. The kitchen staff were all relatives of Jacob's. They spoke Dari, an Afghan Persian. The cook and a few of the other kitchen staff could hardly speak English. They played Iranian music in the kitchen, which I enjoyed immensely. Iranian pop music was banned by the Islamic Republic, so I hadn't been able to bring my tapes across the border.

This restaurant was like heaven to me, with its jewel rice with almonds, raisins, and carrots; and meatballs served with spinach stew, with a side dish of mint chutney. The desserts were baklava and rice pudding; it was just like the Persian rice pudding that was served in our home at Ramadan—rice, milk, butter, cardamom, with ground pistachios on top.

The owner's wife was French Canadian. Before the guests arrived, she would pour herself a glass of wine and ask me to serve myself a drink too. Instead of a drink, I would have a bowl of rice pudding. It was a small bowl, and I would eat as slowly as I could while she sipped her wine. The flavour of butter, cardamom, and pistachios made me dream of our kitchen in Tehran. I could picture Vafa standing at the stove, stirring the pudding. I missed my loved ones in Iran, but I also missed Persian food. Every smell brought back the faces of my loved ones.

It wasn't long after I started the new job that Soraya phoned from Iran. "We just got a letter telling us that Maman successfully passed the last step of the immigration process. We're getting her a ticket. She's coming."

I could not utter a word. Tears were pouring down my face.

"Mehrnaz, this is the start of a happy time. Your suffering is behind you now," Soraya said.

James was so happy for me. "I could drive you to the airport. I can't wait to meet your mom," he said.

"Oh thanks, but no. Give my mom a week before I break the news to her: 'Hahaha, Maman, I have a Canadian boyfriend.' I don't think so, James."

Maman arrived in late August. She was in a wheelchair. She had aged so much since I had last seen her. She kept talking about the war. Iraq was bombing Tehran.

"Once, a bomb hit close to Jamal's condo. We had to go and live at Maman Aterahm's for a while because Tehran was under attack. There is a shortage of essentials like toothbrushes, toothpastes, medications. People who don't have much money are suffering from the inflation. Iranian currency has dropped so low in the world market."

"Maman, tell me about Baba. How did it happen so quickly?"

"We thought he had a bad cold; then his fever went up, and by the time we got him to the hospital, he was in a coma. We were told that he died from meningitis that was brought on by complications from the cancer. Dr. Hushang was by his bed. Everyone took turns staying overnight with Hedayat. One night, Dr. Hushang stayed by himself and sent everyone home to rest. The next morning, your Baba passed away."

"I love Dr. Hushang. I sent him a card when Aunt Anise passed. Maman, how was Farid? I can't even imagine how sad he must have been to lose Baba. They had been inseparable since childhood."

"Farid was at the hospital daily. But the hardest part was when your Baba was buried. Farid dropped himself on his grave and said that he was not ready to part with your Baba. Your uncles sat beside him while he grieved; then they carried him away."

"I thought about phoning Farid to let him know that I was thinking of him after Baba passed, but I was worried that if I heard Farid's voice I wouldn't be able to speak. I still imagine him sewing his *termeh*; he must feel Baba's presence beside him."

A few days later, I said, "Maman, my friend James is coming to meet you. He is studying in the same department as me."

"What's he studying?"

"He's doing his masters in science."

"Have you met his parents? Are they nice people? What do they do?" It was Maman's way of conducting a background check on James.

James came over for dinner. He brought a beautiful bouquet of flowers and a nice bottle of wine. I made the Afghani jewelled rice with spinach stew.

"Why do you say 'Afghani?'" Maman asked. "This is Persian food. You just have to add more lemon to the stew, and there is not enough saffron in the rice, but otherwise it's just like Persian food."

"Tell your mom about the time I made you rice and you wouldn't eat it," said James.

"James, I'm sure she'll understand. You made me brown sticky rice with no flavour!"

"You don't add flavour to rice." James fancied himself an expert in the kitchen.

"Oh, yes, you do. You must always cook your rice with a pinch of salt to enhance the flavour. We also eat only good quality Basmati rice—when you cook it, every grain grows longer and the grains separate from each other rather than stick together. I don't need to translate this. I know she agrees with me. You can't fool around with Persian tea and rice."

The evening went well, but James could not stay overnight. Maman needed a few more weeks before I could introduce the concept of James and I sleeping together.

"Mehrnaz, be careful. American men are not the marrying type. I heard that the divorce rate is very high here."

"Maman, this is Canada. You don't call them American. And if women in Iran had financial independence, then the divorce rate would be as high as here. There is so much pressure on women in Iran to stay married."

"What was wrong with Sia? He was such a nice boy from a good family. Why don't you go back to him? Shayda was so upset when she found out you two had separated."

Shayda cried whenever we talked on the phone. "Mehrnaz jan, please tell me why you and Sia separated. I am heartbroken. Sia is not telling me why."

After a few phone calls, I knew that Shayda would not give up, so I told her that Sia had left me because of my burn scars. It was the hardest thing for me to do. Sia's leaving me was hurtful, but sharing the truth with other people was even harder. I had hidden my body and emotions for too long! I never told Shayda about her son's unfaithfulness; I still firmly believed Sia was unfaithful to me because of my scarred and ugly body.

"That's not a reason for divorce. He knew about your scars when he married you." Shayda was disappointed with her son. She thought if she phoned me often enough she could convince me to go back to him. She had no idea that the divorce had been her son's decision.

A few weeks into Maman's visit, I began occasionally staying the night at James's place, but it took a while before James would stay overnight at my place.

James had offered to prepare Thanksgiving dinner in my apartment and he had cooked us a small feast. We were about to sit down to eat when the phone rang—it was Sia. I had not given him my phone number. He had somehow found me again.

"Mehrnaz, my mother told me that your Maman is with you. I would love to see her. I'm doing my residency in America so I am here now."

Sia said he wanted to hear Maman's voice, so I passed him the phone.

"Sia jan," Maman said. Then she started crying. She'd felt so much sadness since the last time she had spoken with Sia—the divorce and the deaths of both Baba and Sia's father.

Poor James had been so excited about roasting turkey with all the trimmings and baking apple pie from scratch for Maman's first Thanksgiving dinner but Sia's phone call had made Maman sad. For the rest of the evening we weren't able to cheer her up.

"You must tell her what a jerk Sia is," James insisted. "He used to beat you and destroyed your confidence about your body. How can you let her still love and respect Sia? I can't believe that you invited him over for dinner."

"I want you to come to dinner, too, James." I had agreed to allow Sia to visit with Maman and had suggested an evening later in the week.

"Oh no! I told you before. If I see him, I'm going to punch him. And it's not because I'm jealous. It makes me so angry that he hurt you so much. He's still after your ass! And you're behaving like he's a decent guy."

Maman was delighted to see Sia. The two of them had tea and chatted about what was happening at home. The Revolutionary Guards had expropriated Sia's family home and his father's clinic because they were Baha'i.

"Sia jan, the people of Tonekabon were angry about the guards taking your family home," Maman explained. "Your father was highly respected in Tonekabon. But no one could say anything, because they would have put their own lives in danger."

Maman was very disappointed when she heard James's name in my conversation with Sia. She didn't want Sia to know about James. She was still hoping for Sia and me to get back together.

But I had decided to tell Sia about him. "Do you remember the guy in your science class? The one who you said was really interesting and informed about world affairs?"

"James?"

"I'm dating him."

"He's a nice guy," Sia said, nodding pleasantly.

"So where is your fiancée now?"

"We broke up. I wasn't serious about her. She found out that I was seeing someone else and she freaked out."

"Same old Sia," I thought.

James and I were enjoying some of the food that Maman had been allowed to bring into Canada. "I have never eaten pistachios like these, so fresh and creamy inside, crispy outside, and so flavourful." James loved his food.

"*Pesteh Irani ahli.*" He was trying to learn Farsi, but he was really only interested in learning more about our food. Maman sat and patiently taught James the names of several typical Persian foods, but they needed me to help translate. "*Pesteh Irani ahli* means 'Iranian pistachios are the best.'"

When she wasn't talking to James, Maman complained about being bored. "This town is like a ghost town. It's so quiet. No one seems to visit and enjoy these beautiful parks."

In Tehran, there's not enough green space. The few parks that we have are always packed with people walking or picnicking on the lawns with tea and snacks. Young people play volleyball or soccer and young lovers chat for hours under the trees.

I was sad to learn that soon nothing would be left of us in Iran. Our apartment building in Tehran, our villa, and the orange groves were all being sold. The war was still going on. Soraya and her husband, and Jamal with his wife and two children, all wanted to immigrate to Canada.

33. Everyone in Canada

ONE AFTERNOON, THE MANAGER of my apartment building said, "When your mother sees me in the lobby she always says 'squeeze me.'" He had stopped me as I was walking to the elevator. "I just wanted to let you know, so you can remind her to put on a jacket when she sits in the lobby. It seems that she's always cold."

Maman did not enjoy being alone in the apartment when I was at the university, often there all day attending classes. "I sit in the lobby watching people going in and out. Most of them try not to look in my direction even though I am sitting right in front of them."

"Maman, what do you say to the manager when you see him?"

"I apologize to him for sitting in the lobby."

"So, are you trying to say 'excuse me'?"

"Yes, he understands me. He always gives me a kind hug."

"Maman, that's because what you are actually saying is: *squeeze me*." She looked up at me wide-eyed and we both chuckled.

Maman was being treated with new medication for her rheumatoid arthritis. Her pain was lessening, and she was becoming more mobile. That pleased her.

"I'm getting excellent medical treatment here," she told Soraya on the phone. "I can go into the street without a *hijab*, and there is no fear of bombs coming down. But I don't speak the language of these people. I am alone here."

Maman was very homesick for her life in Iran. To me she said, "You're so busy with school. But there are so many hours in a day that I crave connection with people."

Maman was not interested in watching television or going to the mall. She missed being with people. "You don't know any neighbours in this building. When visitors come in Iran, we do our best to connect with them and make them feel welcome, even when we don't speak their language. In the elevator in this building, people look down so they don't have to make eye contact."

There was little I could to help her. In order to maintain her immigration status, Maman had to be in Canada for six months of the year. The day she fulfilled her six-month requirement, she flew back home.

"Your mom will be back in six months." James held me at the airport. I was crying.

"I hugged Baba here, and then I never saw him again. I hate saying goodbye in the airport."

Once again, I was being left alone in Canada. I was envious of my university friends who would talk about going home to see their parents. "After my last exam, I am going home," they would say. "I can't wait. I miss my mom's cooking. It's so good to be home." I was twenty-three when I lost my home in Iran. Now my only home was my apartment in Guelph. I could not pack up and go home.

I kept myself busy studying and spending time with James. Over the last year, most of my courses were in molecular biology. I found DNA cloning fascinating, and I spent long hours in the lab. James was busy working on his master's thesis. I hoped to graduate with a high average so I would also be accepted into a master's program. I needed a lot more time to study, considering that English was my second language. James loved the party life—smoking and drinking—but I didn't like partying anymore. I didn't care to join him to go to bars as much as I had when I met him. And something was happening with my breathing; I was developing asthma-like symptoms, that were aggravated during parties and in bars where people smoked.

During my fourth year at university, I was offered a full-time job in the molecular biology lab learning techniques like DNA cloning. I went to school part-time and worked full-time. James finished his master's degree and was hired by the government as a forensic scientist in Toronto. He asked his friends to join him at the pub to celebrate his new job but I had an exam the next day so I didn't go.

I was at home studying when one of the cute guys from my biochemistry class, Nathan, called and invited me to go to the opera *The Tales of Hoffmann* in Toronto. He had two tickets from his father. How could I resist? Nathan had a crush on me and had asked me out a couple of times, but he knew that I was seeing James. We were classmates and he was sweet, and funny, and cute. I agreed to go, but it was understood that we were going just as friends.

I had only ever listened to opera on the radio. I had never been to a live performance. I was so glad I went. It was beautiful beyond anything I had imagined. When Nathan dropped me at James's place after the opera, James was furious.

I was also spending time with Adam, a professor from my department. He was an Australian in his early forties. He was an avid sailor, and he took me sailing a few times. I was very attracted to him.

"Naz, James is not your type. He drinks a lot," Adam said one night.

"You're just jealous of James. He's the perfect man for me!"

"If he's so perfect for you, why do you spend so much time with me?"

Mostly Adam and I went to restaurants for dinner or sailing on his sailboat, but he did ask me to go to his house once. I had seen his house from the outside, but I hadn't been inside before. There were beautiful old brick homes on his street, and his was one of them. Once inside, I wasn't surprised to discover it was equally beautiful—he had decorated it with antique furniture.

In his living room, I had noticed an original painting on the wall and moved closer to examine it. He was standing beside me, telling me about the painting, when suddenly I turned around to face him. In that moment, I knew I wanted to kiss him and to make love to him. The only thing that held me back was my body; I didn't want Adam to see my scars. He worshipped me, but I was afraid he wouldn't if he saw what I really looked like.

Something was stirring inside me. I couldn't put my finger on it, but I think I wanted to experience life more fully somehow. That year with James had been exciting, and exploring a new culture with him was fun—beer, pubs, and music, Saturday night hockey games, season passes to Blue Jays' baseball games, Sunday afternoon football—but I wasn't really connecting with James's love of sports and watching every game of his favourite teams on television. And I could not keep up with his partying. James spent a lot of time hanging out in pubs and partying with his own group of male and female friends. It was during those times that I would see Adam. And I realized I was craving passion and a romantic life of ballet, art galleries, and sitting in cafés with friends talking about books and music.

After my experience with Sia, it was hard for me to trust men, but I trusted James. I didn't feel the romantic love for him that I'd felt for Sia, but I was afraid to look for love again.

I was imprisoned by my own perceptions of what my body looked like to others.

Finally, there was a ceasefire between Iran and Iraq. The war had lasted eight years, and approximately one million soldiers and civilians had been killed. An accurate number is not available, since both governments announced themselves victorious and denied the actual number of casualties. This was what we were afraid of when, at the start of the war, we found out that the U.S. was supporting Saddam Hussein and his army. Iran and Iraq had a long history of border disputes, but there had never been a war that had caused a million deaths and casualties.

So when Maman said, "Soraya and Jamal's immigration applications have been accepted. They're getting their tickets to come," I was happy.

Finally, they arrived in Canada. When I had left Iran, I didn't have many war stories to share because the war zone had been mainly near the Iraqi border. Now the stories that Jamal and Soraya were sharing were all about the war, how many nights they had to spend in a small shelter that they had made in the basement of their condo building. My beautiful niece, Jamal's daughter who was five, would shake with fear whenever she heard a loud noise, thinking that it was a bomb.

One evening while we were all sitting around and drinking tea, Jamal said, "It was really sad when Mottee died. She suffered toward the end. She had cancer, but she refused treatment. She died at home."

"I know. Maman told me. It was so sad. I want to send a card to Fereshteh. I feel so bad for her—her boyfriend Mehdi left her, and then her mother passed away. She must be heartbroken."

"You don't need to send a card to Fereshteh," Jamal muttered. His eyes were fixed on his teacup.

"Why not?"

"It happened a month ago, but Maman thought it would be better not to share the news until we got here."

"What news?"

"Fereshteh ... Fereshteh committed suicide," he stammered.

"It happened all of a sudden," Jamal said. Tears were coursing down my cheeks; I couldn't utter a word. He continued. "She fell into a deep depression. The men she was seeing were all using her. They had sex with her and then married someone else. We tried to talk to her, but she told us that we didn't understand her. She said that you were the only one who understood her."

My heart was pounding. I couldn't breathe. Finally I spoke with such rage. "She had boyfriends. She didn't sleep with random men." I always hated it when I heard people judging Fereshteh. "How did this happen?"

"She threw herself out the window of her bedroom on the fourth floor."

"Did she die right away or did she suffer?"

"She was taken to the hospital, but all the way there, she kept saying 'let me die.' She died from internal bleeding when she got to the hospital."

Memories of my friend began flooding my mind. It was my birthday and Fereshteh was dropping by to give me a present, a very stylish shirt. "Fereshteh, this is from the Ghasemi boutique! I've never bought anything there." It was one of the most expensive shops in Tehran, and Fereshteh loved shopping there.

"If I had more money I would buy you more things. Everything they have in that boutique would look beautiful on you, Mehrnaz.

I never had a sister. You are the best little sister I could ask for."

I would never have imagined that after her last dance at my goodbye party, I would never see her dance again. My beautiful Fereshteh had become the victim of the Iranian social norms that guaranteed male superiority. Men slept with as many women as they wished, and they were still highly respected in Iran, while women were judged very harshly. I never imagined my feisty, fun, smart, beautiful Fereshteh would lose her battle to this double standard.

Dance became a shield for Vafa, Fereshteh, and for me—a shield from judgment, a shield from sexism, sexual repression, and Islamic law. And we had all loved expressing ourselves through dance. And, well, Fereshteh, was the most graceful, the most expressive of dancers.

In the silence, I heard Fereshteh's voice: "Let nothing take your dance away."

34. James and Iraj

A FTER I GRADUATED FROM UNIVERSITY, I was offered a job in a research lab at Mount Sinai Hospital in Toronto. A friend of mine was moving out of her place, and she thought her old room would be perfect for me. Now I was sharing the second and third floor of a Victorian home in the Annex with two roommates and numerous cockroaches. My new roommates, Eliana and Maya, were Jewish Canadians, and Eliana was a lesbian. Maya was studying fine arts and Eliana had a degree in English Literature. We made an interesting and enriched trio with our different backgrounds.

"I am introducing Naz to Leonard Cohen," my roommate Eliana told her friends with such enthusiasm. Eliana had a turntable with a collection of Leonard Cohen albums. I fell in love with "Take this Waltz." I played it over and over and waltzed all by myself in our living room on the old hardwood floor. "Fereshteh would've loved this song."

James lived close by. He and his friend Alex bought a house in the Italian neighbourhood in Toronto. Their backyard had a big space for a vegetable garden, but James and Alex wanted to cover it with grass. They did not want the hassle of a vegetable garden.

"I *dream* of having a vegetable garden. Please don't cover it with grass," I pleaded with James. He knew that I wouldn't give up.

"We don't want to do any weeding or planting or anything. It'll be your garden," James and Alex announced.

I had never grown a vegetable garden before. Alex's father, Mr. Joe, was retired and he became my helper. I loved his company,

Mehrnaz's graduation from the University of Guelph, 1988.

and soon we had planted a beautiful vegetable garden. I loved watching my herbs, beans, and tomatoes grow. I blasted music while I worked in the garden.

"Shame on you boys, sitting and watching Naz working so hard in the garden," Mr. Joe would say to James and Alex as they sat outside, drinking beer and watching me work.

"It's okay, Mr. Joe. I like it this way. The boys' place is in the kitchen, and my place is in the garden. They do the cooking and dish washing."

Mr. Joe made me laugh. "I don't understand why these boys," he was pointing at James and his son Alex, "watch football. It's like watching field wrestling."

"James, Alex, guess what! I bought a plane ticket to Greece and

Turkey!" I announced. My job at Mount Sinai was not starting for another month, so I decided to give myself the best thirtieth birthday gift: a trip to Greece and Turkey on my own.

"What about your vegetable garden? Are you going to let it die?" James and Alex were laughing. I frowned at both of them, but I had already taken care of this. Mr. Joe took the subway every day from his house to come tend to the garden while I was away.

Travelling alone was challenging, especially in Turkey, but I was used to the way men there treated women; it was similar to Iran. I wore a wedding band, and whenever a man hit on me I showed it to him. He would immediately back off. I still remembered how to speak German from the few months I had spent in Germany ten years earlier. My German became handy in Greece because there were so many German visitors. A few of the Germans that I hung out with told me to go to the Island of Ikaria. It was less touristy than the other islands. I arrived at Armenistis in Ikaria. Then I was told that if I walked about five kilometres, I would get to Nas beach. There was only one motel and one store there. The motel was on a cliff, which I had to climb down to get down to the pristine beach with rock caves. It was such a synchronicity to be at Nas beach for my thirtieth birthday.

I was sitting on the balcony off my room inhaling the night air of the Aegean Sea when I heard the song "Fast Car" by Tracy Chapman. It reminded me of the evenings sitting in James's backyard in Toronto watching my vegetables grow. I walked around, trying to figure out where the music was coming from. A young Greek woman at the motel's office desk was playing a tape. We sat and chatted about life in Canada, and then feasted on some strawberries that she had picked from her garden.

Strawberries are not a native fruit to Iran. The translation into Farsi is "foreign berry." On rare occasions when I was a child, we would see a vendor selling strawberries. They were very expensive. I loved them—I always savoured the delicious foreign flavour. When I was much younger, I had purchased a colouring book with strawberries on every page. It made my mouth water while I was colouring. At the time, many children in Iran did not know how strawberries tasted. I always wondered how could they could crave something they had never eaten before.

Later, I wondered what my life would have been like if I had married Kyan and had never left Iran. I thought I might have been like the children in Iran who had never tasted a strawberry. Living in Canada was like tasting a strawberry, and now a song by Tracey Chapman made me think of my garden at James's place and feel homesick for my life in Canada.

For the past six years, my heart had been aching for the life I'd left behind in Iran, and now that I was so close to my home country, hearing this one song had transported me back to Canada. Would I be happy moving back and living in Iran? I wondered. I had been dreaming about my life there, but would I be homesick for my life in Canada?

Aunt Masi and her family were still living in Turkey while I was there. They had moved to Turkey so that they could apply for immigration to Canada. Pari applied to sponsor them in Canada, but her application had been rejected. They were stuck in Turkey for ten years before they were finally accepted into Canada. I stayed with them in Istanbul. I walked around the city during the day with my cousin, and at night we stayed up late, talking about Canada and their dream of immigrating, and our relatives in Iran and all over the world.

As I lay in bed at night I wondered why I was living a life of exile. Why couldn't I go home to Iran? Turkey and Iran shared a border. I could get on a bus and be back in Iran in a few hours.

According to my Iranian birth certificate, I was still married to Sia. Our marriage was documented on my birth certificate. Sia and I had to send our passports and birth certificates to the Iranian Embassy to receive an official divorce. But Sia was a Baha'i and had been smuggled across the border, and he didn't have a valid Iranian passport. My soul was thirsty for Iran, especially now that I was so close to home. But going to Iran meant risking my life as I was still married to a Baha'i man.

The magnificent architecture of the Blue Mosque in Istanbul took me back to the Shah Mosque in Isfahan, Iran. The Shah Mosque is covered with Persian mosaic tiles—a vibrant blue—and beautiful calligraphy. The two tall minarets at the entrance are also decorated with blue mosaic tiles. When I was a child, we had made a family trip to Isfahan. I wanted to look at all the artistic decorations on the dome and the slender minarets, but my neck would get tired, they were so high up. *How had they managed to build such tall buildings*, I wondered at the time.

Isfahan is located in the lush land of the Zayanderud River, in the foothills of the Zagros Mountain Range. It's just over three hundred kilometres south of Tehran. Isfahan was the capital of Persia in the sixteenth century. It's famous for its Islamic architecture, with many beautiful boulevards, covered bridges, palaces, mosques, and minarets. My favourite site in Isfahan is the Monar Jonban, which means "Shaking Towers." It was built in the fourteenth century. There are many stairs inside to climb to the top of the tower. People walk up the stairs, and when they get to the top, they push the tower from side to side to make the other tower move. I was too scared to try it, but I loved watching it from the ground.

When I returned from my trip to Turkey and Greece, James asked me to move in with him. I wanted to get married, but he continued to insist that he didn't believe in marriage. Maman was not happy about us moving in together.

"What about our Iranian friends and family? What would they think?" Maman's usual concern. We compromised. Maman lied to our Iranian friends and family. She told them that we got married at City Hall. But we also agreed to have eighty Persian and Canadian guests for a dinner celebration.

"What will you be wearing?" Pari asked.

I had no idea what I would wear. "I guess this is it. I have to accept that I'll never wear a wedding dress," I said.

James and I were walking to my house one night. It was garbage night. Under the lamppost, I noticed a yellow dress with beadwork on the collar sitting on top of a neighbour's garbage bin. I brought it home. It was dirty, but the fabric, the dress, and the yellow colour were beautiful. I sent it for dry cleaning, and it came back just like new. I decided to wear it for our pretend wedding celebration.

"I love this dress. The 1950s style looks beautiful on you. It goes so perfectly with your long, dark, curly hair," Maya, my roommate, said.

"I used to have dresses like this. Beaded dresses were fashionable at the time. But don't tell people that you found it in a garbage bin," Maman said.

Soraya and her friends prepared a Persian meal for eighty people. Many of our Canadian friends had never had Persian food before, and Soraya's many dishes inspired them to begin love affairs with Persian food.

"I am at peace now that Mehrnaz and James have decided to settle down," Maman said.

Shortly after this conversation between Maman and a friend, Soraya showed up at my work and announced that she was leaving Iraj. Soraya had left Iraj once before, after they had moved to Canada. She had stayed with me for a week, but then she went back to him. Now a year later, she was determined to file for divorce.

"I was a CEO at a company in Tehran making a good salary. I can't find a job. I have an MBA from an American university, but I am told that since I don't have Canadian job experience, I'm not eligible to work here. So I'm being paid minimum wage and I work as a telemarketer. People hate it when I phone them at their home. I'm just doing my job, but they're so rude to me. I want to go back home, but Soraya doesn't want to."

Iraj was frustrated and he blamed Soraya for wanting to immigrate to Canada in the first place. He was in a rage. "Iranian women—as soon as they get here, they want a divorce. The divorce rate is so high here; women leave their husbands for no reason. Marriage for these people has no value. As soon as they have an argument they leave each other."

Iraj was so different from when I had last seen him in Iran. He had become angry and controlling. "Iraj, that's not true," I protested. I was trying to defend Soraya, but she signalled me to keep my mouth closed.

Later, she said, "Iraj calls you a hooker because you're living with James and Alex."

I knew that Iraj was angry with Soraya on the night of our moving-in party because her dress was too revealing—it *was* revealing—but I had no idea that he was disgusted by my living with James and Alex.

Soraya and Iraj had been married for fifteen years, and Iraj treated Soraya like he owned her; she was his possession. "He is always angry and suspicious of any man around me. He doesn't want me to come and visit you because he's suspicious of Alex."

Soraya did not use to share much about her life with Iraj but now she was opening up. "When I left Iran, I put all my jewellery in a box and left it with Iraj's sister, Farimah. I was very close to her," Soraya continued. "After we split up, I told Aunt Roohi to get my jewellery, but Farimah told her, 'if Soraya wants her jewellery then she must go back to Iraj.'"

Soraya wanted her freedom, not her jewellery.

Iraj continued harassing Soraya; in his mind he thought by harassing her he could get her back, but Soraya persisted and they eventually divorced.

35. Laila and Roya

JAMES FOUND HIS JOB as a forensic scientist depressing. He simply no longer wanted to know about all the crimes that were happening. He decided to make a career change. He was accepted into the Faculty of Education for teachers at the University of British Columbia (UBC) in Vancouver. My asthma was becoming worse and I assumed it was due to the pollution in Toronto. So we quit our jobs, packed our few belongings—mostly camping gear—left Toronto, and drove west.

We camped for a month as we travelled across the country. It was a beautiful way to see the Canadian landscape. The unlimited blue skies and golden hills of the prairies, the Rocky Mountains of the west, the majestic lush green mountains of British Columbia, and the infinite view across the Pacific Ocean.

I started working in a lab at UBC, and James became a full-time student with my income supporting the two of us. I was pleasantly surprised in February to see cherry blossoms blooming on the trees lining the streets of Vancouver. We were expecting a baby in May. We had planned for this and we were delighted with the thought of meeting our baby in a few months.

"I am not going back to Ontario!" I officially announced to James. I couldn't imagine another long winter in Ontario after experiencing the sweet, moderate temperatures of Vancouver in winter. However, we did get a lot of rain and my asthma was worsening. When I consulted a doctor, she told me that I might be allergic to the mould in Vancouver. It was often rainy and humid.

James and I started having arguments. I was tired of working full-time and being pregnant, and I wished for a more relaxing lifestyle. James wasn't working, and we were living on one income—*mine*. It was hard to continue living the way we did when we both had jobs. This was a challenge for James. He still liked eating out, partying, drinking, smoking, going to pubs, and his new hobby—betting at the horse racing tracks.

As my baby grew inside me, I felt myself growing farther away from her father. I became in tune with the sacred life inside me. I started not recognizing Naz, who watched hockey and baseball, and who partied and drank with her partner. I had changed so much to be accepted and loved by James and the community around me that I no longer recognized myself.

Every time we had an argument, James threatened to leave me. The thought of him leaving made me anxious and reminded me of when Sia left me. Each time, I talked myself into changing and accepting James the way he was, so he wouldn't leave.

Our baby girl, Laila, was born. We were in love with our precious baby. Because I didn't have nipples, I couldn't breast feed. James and I took turns waking up at night to bottle feed her. I was grateful for the nights that I could sleep in, and James would get up. He said that the quiet of the night was his favourite time to bond with Laila, with no sound except that of our daughter drinking milk from the bottle. James was not my ideal partner, but he definitely was a precious father to our baby.

Laila was the light keeper of my heart.

"Look, Laila jan, he dances like Uncle Vafa," Maman pointed at an Iranian dance teacher on television. When Laila was two, I bought a video of Mohammad Khordadian who taught Persian dancing in America. Laila loved dancing along.

"Laila is learning to dance by watching Mohammad Khordadian's video," I told Vafa over the phone. "Maman thinks he dances just like you."

"I've seen his dance videos. He is famous in Iran. Of course his videos are illegal in Iran, but still people have them. People tell me that he dances like me. If I lived in America, I would be a dance teacher too," Vafa said laughing.

Vafa had to have heart surgery and I began to phone him more often after I found out he was sick.

James started working as a teacher and I was still working full-time and Laila was in day care when I got pregnant with our second baby. The fear and anxiety of James leaving me was growing stronger, as was my resentment of him for partying, drinking, and us digging deeper into debt. Somehow, either naively or optimistically, I felt that he would eventually get tired of the lifestyle he was choosing, that he would eventually change. I kept reminding myself of his positive qualities: he was a great dad; he was loving toward Maman who lived with us most of the time; and he loved cooking for us.

We had another girl: Roya. Her name means "dream," and Laila means "night." They are *the dreams of my nights*!

James and I decided that I should be a stay-at-home mom. We were making around the same income and although James would have loved to be a stay-at-home dad, the potential for financial growth was greater at his job. I was so glad to wake up every morning knowing that my daughters could sleep as much they needed to. We no longer needed to rush them to daycare. I loved the small things: taking them to the library and coming home with books, visiting the park, and savouring our tea and story times in the afternoons.

My asthma was worsening and I began to suffer from frequent fevers. I was sick for a year before being diagnosed with chronic lung disease. The lung specialist told me I would have this illness for the rest of my life. When the infection was under control, I had more energy, but the fever was completely unpredictable.

My doctor also told me that I wouldn't be able to go back to work, and that in fact, working with chemicals, as you do in a science lab, would be harmful to me.

I had been suffering for a while but I had never expected to hear this. Did this mean that my science degree and my experience in research labs would never be useful again in my life? I was shocked and saddened by this news. I was only thirty-five.

The treatment the doctor prescribed involved antibiotics and steroids. I was on the steroids for a couple of months. My face became puffy and round, and I felt nervous and irritated. Every few months, I developed a fever and again, bronchitis, and would have to take another round of antibiotics and steroids.

James had become passionate about the stock market and had been following a diamond mine closely. He took out a two-thousand-dollar loan and invested in this stock. He was convincing and I trusted him to make the investment. He wanted to invest even more because he was certain that this particular stock would go up soon. I had my jewellery that I never wore, so we considered selling it.

The day before I left Iran, my aunt and I had opened the hems on two of my skirts to hide my jewellery. Although I sent a few sets of my jewellery with Sia that were confiscated by the police of Pakistan, I still had some valuable jewellery at home. I remember the fear on Baba's face when he found out what my aunt and I were doing. "As long as I am alive, I won't allow you to do this. Revolutionary Guards will find out and arrest you at the border. But I do promise you that I will get your jewellery to you one day."

Because of the war, the government wouldn't allow Iranians to take their assets out of the country. But people were coming up with different ways to smuggle what they could. Before my flight, Baba checked every item in my suitcase to make sure I was not smuggling my jewellery through the border. As it turned out, Baba saved my life once again. The border guard *did* check my suitcases thoroughly and specifically touched the hems of my skirts. When Baba came to visit me in Canada, *he* hid my jewellery and brought it to me, risking his own life.

Baba sewed small thin cotton bags to hold my jewellery. Then he took fabric off the back of his *termeh* and carefully sewed a few small bags on to the back of them. Then he sewed the fabric he had removed once again to the back of the *termeh*. He made sure not to put too many pieces of jewellery in the same bag so the *termeh* would stay flat. He brought me many of his *termeh*.

"'Haji, you are bringing so many *termeh* to Canada!' The border guard told me," Baba had said when he arrived, delighted to share his success story. "'Yes, my daughter just got married and moved to Canada. I have put prayer beads and prayer rocks inside each *termeh*. I pray that one day when she has children, they will not forget their roots and their religion. These are for my future grandchildren to pray on, and for my daughter.' The border guard put aside all the *termeh* and searched the rest of my suitcase instead."

I was laughing when Baba told me what he had done. "Baba, you are a Haji. You are not supposed to lie."

"I am a Muslim and I am a Haji. All I did was bring my daughter's jewellery to her—there is no sin in doing that."

As I walked into a jewellery shop in Vancouver with all my precious gold, silver, rubies, emeralds, and *brilliant* diamonds that Baba had risked his life to bring from Iran, I could hear Baba's voice in my head. I remembered what he had said when Sia's parents had come over to discuss wedding arrangements: "You don't know what will happen in the future. I pray that you have a happy life with Sia, but the *mehrieh* will guarantee financial security if something goes wrong. I will not always be here to help out. It brings me more peace for you to have a substantial *mehrieh*."

I watched the jeweller place my jewellery on a scale.

Afterwards, I sat in the car with a four-thousand-dollar cheque in my hand and tears streaming down my face. "Baba, I was so young when you left this world. You always believed in me. And now I am a mother of my two beautiful daughters but I have no faith in myself. I feel so lost, Baba. Who am I, Baba? This is not the life that I dreamed of."

"Here, James." I presented him with the cheque when I got home. He invested the money in the diamond stock; *my* diamonds to invest in *his* diamonds. After one year, all the money was lost.

James had not forced me to sell my jewellery; I did it because I was tired of being broke. I was buying clothes for my little girls from the thrift stores. All we had was the furniture that I'd owned when I was in university, and a bank loan that kept getting larger and larger.

36. Breast Cancer and a Broken Heart

JAMES AND I DECIDED TO MOVE our family to a small town in the interior of British Columbia on the recommendation of my doctor. The damp weather and mould in Vancouver had become the enemies of my lungs.

"You need to live at a higher elevation with a dryer climate," my respirologist had said.

James became the vice principal at the high school. From our house, we could see bluebirds blending in with purple wild flowers. There were lakes, mountains, and nature trails. We were delighted with our new life in this beautiful small town.

The dry climate was helping, though I was still getting bronchitis often, so my respirologist recommended that I take a low-dose steroid every other day, indefinitely. The steroids helped my breathing and made me feel more energized, but I was terrified by the side effects as it was considered an immune-suppressant drug.

We took the girls on nature hikes, but I was nervous. I had heard that a child had been mauled by a cougar the year before we moved there. The cougar then killed the mother who had rushed to rescue her son. I never went hiking without carrying pepper spray.

"Stop clapping your hands," James barked at me. "You're scaring the wildlife away. I want to see them."

"I am terrified of running into a cougar or a grizzly bear," I said.

"Cougars are shy. They won't come close to us. I go for hikes by myself all the time and I've never seen one. Stop constantly clapping your hands—it's so annoying."

I wasn't convinced, but I tried to acquiesce.

One morning, I dropped Roya at her preschool and went for a walk around the high school where James worked. I felt comfortable walking by myself because there was a small neighbourhood of houses in that area, and I was within city limits and not out in the woods.

I glimpsed an animal moving in the ditch. At first, I thought it was a deer—there were many in the area—but when it raised its head and turned towards me, I realized it was a cougar.

I couldn't breathe or move. I just kept staring at it. I didn't have my pepper spray. It eyed me directly for a few seconds, and then turned and walked away. I still couldn't move. I was terrified that any movement would attract its attention and that it would come running back.

James thought I was lucky, but that wasn't how I felt.

"That's so unfair," he exclaimed. "I go into the wilderness *hoping* to see a cougar and I never have. Then you go out for a stroll behind my school and see one!"

There was not much going on in this small town. There was no indoor pool or community centre that offered activities for children. The town promoted shopping in local businesses, but there were hardly any shops at all. We had to drive to the next city for shopping. Thankfully, there was a small hospital, but it was mainly used for emergency cases.

I joined every club in town: the cross-country ski club, the tennis club, and the book club. The same small group of people belonged to all these clubs, so it was an easy way to make friends.

I was excited for the girls to take dance and piano lessons. There was only one dance studio: the School of Highland Dance, so my Persian-Canadian daughters started Highland dancing. I loved every second of it. I think they did too. Their teacher taught Irish step-dancing too, just like in the movie *River Dance*. When I watched the older dancers performing, I was filled with joy, hoping that one day I would be watching my girls doing those steps. It was such a gracious dance.

James's salary was much higher as a vice principal than his previous position as a teacher. We were able to invest in a beautiful piano for the girls. I can still see my daughters' little fingers playing on that piano.

Laila's ankle began hurting a few months after she began her dance lessons. Our doctor thought it could be a dance injury, but soon most of her joints were inflamed. She was diagnosed with juvenile rheumatoid arthritis. She was only nine years old.

I discovered a new meaning for having a "broken heart."

All my life, I had witnessed Maman suffer from rheumatoid arthritis.

Shortly after hearing Laila's diagnosis, I received bad news about Maman who was still living in Vancouver. A pinched nerve in one of her neck vertebrae had suddenly paralyzed her. She couldn't move her hands or legs. Most weekends I made the three-hour drive to Vancouver to visit Maman.

It was a Sunday night, after driving back home from visiting Maman, that I felt a lump in my right breast.

"James, I hope this is not what I think it is."

I had a biopsy and waited for the result. The tumour was cancerous.

I had never done breast self-examination. I had no family history of breast cancer. I was slim, active, a non-smoker, a non-drinker, and we ate mainly whole foods, so I was at a low risk for breast cancer. What I didn't consider was that stress also causes cancer. Also, over the past few years, I had often been on antibiotics and taking steroids for my chronic lung disease—could they be the cause?

I was devastated. Baba had been seventeen when he lost his mother. He always talked about the sadness of not having his mother in his life as he grew up. I couldn't imagine dying so soon. I was only forty-one years old. Laila was in grade four and Roya was in grade one. My only wish was to be here to watch them grow up.

I chose to have a bilateral mastectomy: the removal of both breasts. My surgeon told me that the lump was small and I did not need chemotherapy.

The rheumatoid arthritis medications were all immune-suppressant so Laila became susceptible to cold and flu viruses— she kept getting sick. We decided to homeschool her. Now Roya did not want to leave me either and she, too, wanted to be home-schooled.

Three weeks after my cancer surgery, I started home-schooling both girls.

My family physician sent me to an oncologist who prescribed Tamoxifen for the prevention of breast cancer recurrence. I read the side effects and didn't like what I read. I requested a second opinion. I was referred to a cancer clinic at a bigger centre. This was the first day in six weeks that I could drive. The bilateral mastectomy had left a deep scar across my chest and it was very painful to move my upper arms.

Even so, I was excited to spend a day in Kelowna, a bigger centre, with Laila and Roya. We planned to go shopping and have lunch in a nice restaurant. Laila, who was old enough to sit alone, sat in the waiting room reading, while I took Roya with me into the doctor's office.

The oncologist said that the cancer had spread to one of my lymph nodes. With this new finding, she recommended I start chemotherapy as soon as possible. Inside, I began to shake, but my little Roya was in the office with me, so I kept calm while listening to the doctor's terrible news.

Roya liked to draw two circles with dots for eyes, a smile, big black long curly hair, and two straight lines for legs and underneath, "Mom."

"Is my mom going to lose all her hair?" Roya asked the oncologist.

I wanted to sob. I was so sorry that my little girl was in the doctor's office with me. I had no idea that I would hear this bad news. I had merely wanted a second opinion about taking Tamoxifen. If I had anticipated getting bad news, I would have come with James.

Didn't the doctor know how difficult it is for a cancer patient to be told that they must have chemotherapy? Could the doctor at least have told me not to bring my little daughter into her office?

The following week I went for my first chemo treatment. I had read all about it. Short hair was recommended to make it less physically and emotionally painful when hair starts falling out. So I had made an appointment with a hairdresser across the street from the cancer clinic to have my hair cut short. Once there, I told the hairdresser that immediately afterwards I was going to have my first chemotherapy treatment.

The hairdresser had tears in his eyes.

The other women in the hair salon made these sweet comments. "Oh dear, you have beautiful hair. Are you sure you want to cut it that short? You are going to regret it. Oh, how I wish I could have thick long hair like yours."

I smiled and thanked the women for their compliments.

Even though my hair was short, it was still emotionally painful when it began falling out. There were traces of my shed hair all over the house. My bed looked terrible with hair all over it.

One day I asked James to take the girls out so I could shave my head. When I was done, I covered it with a scarf and sobbed.

What irony: I hadn't liked the possible side effects of taking Tamoxifen and now I was on chemotherapy to kill every growing cell in my body!

I used both traditional and alternative medicine and was under the care of a naturopath and an oncologist. The naturopathic doctor complemented my chemo treatments with supplements and a wheat- and dairy-free diet.

I became extremely fatigued while I was on the chemo. I was weak. I lost all my hair. I was emotionally drained and impatient with the girls. We hired someone to help me with home schooling in the mornings. I was so appreciative of this lovely woman, Terry, who was with us during this difficult time.

During my dark nights of the soul, when I paused I found there were many stars that shone so brightly in my life. Some days, when Terry saw how drained and tired I was, she would take the girls to pick up her daughter, Kyla, from high school and then back to her home where they all baked cookies together. My girls adored Kyla.

There were many disadvantages to living in a small community. James and I drove for hours to get to my chemotherapy appointments, and he had to stay in a hotel when I had my surgeries. We had thought we would have to bring the girls with us when I had my surgeries and my chemo treatments. But one of the advantages of living in a small community is that although we had only lived there for four years, we had made many friends. Many of those friends took Laila and Roya so that they didn't have to come with us to my chemo treatments. Friends and neighbours also brought us meals. And one special friend, Lisa, stayed with the girls when I had my surgeries! Lisa was there for us anytime we needed her. Many days she picked up the girls and took them hiking for a couple of hours so that I could rest and recover. Lisa was a brilliant star who shone brightly during my dark nights.

There was another shiny bright star: Breezy, the dog. Our neighbour Bev and her husband had gotten a new puppy, a golden retriever. The girls were in love with Breezy. When Bev was at work, Lisa and the girls took Breezy for walks. They were supposed to also train Breezy during these walks. The girls and Lisa made a report card to record Breezy's progress and when they came home, they couldn't stop talking about how well Breezy behaved on their walks. But the truth was that when I watched them from our kitchen window, one of the girls would be holding Breezy's leash tightly—he was on a lead and leaping way ahead of them—while the three of them ran hastily behind him. And all I could hear was, "BREEZY, STOP!"

Friends would say, "Naz, you look amazing. Naz, you are so strong, you can beat this."

When I looked in the mirror, I could see that I looked ill. My skin was a dull, sickly colour. I had lost most of my thick eyebrows. My eyelashes were falling out. I wore hats and scarves to cover my bald head. I didn't see myself as beautiful and I wanted to share that with friends. I wanted them to hear how sad it had been when the hairdresser was cutting my hair short. I wanted to tell them about the day I had finally decided to shave my head. I wanted to tell my friends about the sadness in my daughters' eyes when they saw me bald. I was breaking up inside with the anxiety of wondering, "What if I die? What if I never see my daughters grow up?" I imagined my own funeral many times and pictured my two daughters there. These thoughts were real.

Every card I received urged me to think positive. I felt guilty. I worried that all these negative thoughts would bring the cancer back. Meanwhile, I would hear from friends that when there was a suspicious lump in their breasts, they couldn't sleep until they heard it was not breast cancer. They were afraid of cancer. They were afraid of my cancer. So when they said to me, "Think positive thoughts," they meant well, but I could sense that their positivity was not authentic. They were as afraid for my life as I was.

As a result of everyone trying to be positive around me, I ended up not sharing how weak and fragile I felt inside. Since then, I have never treated cancer patients as though they are athletes in a race. Believe me, it doesn't feel like any race. It doesn't feel like, "Go, girl, you can beat this."

A friend offered me a weekly Reiki treatment. I loved receiving healing energy from her in silence. She coached me how to do breath work and how to let go of the tension in my body. Another friend sent me a relaxation and guided visualization CD. I listened to the CD a couple of times a day and every time it helped me breathe and feel calm.

My relationship with James, which had always been rocky, was failing terribly during this time. Ours was not a loving relationship, and it could not weather such a stressful time. He still talked about leaving me, but he never did, and I couldn't imagine what I would do on my own with my poor health and no career.

Laila and Roya began attending public school that fall. Maman was finally back in her home again—she had been hospitalized and in rehabilitation for five months. Christmas was coming, and I was happy that I was healthy. I began anticipating a joyous holiday with my girls. Although I didn't grow up with Christmas, I loved celebrating it with the girls. James loved to prepare meals for Christmas. We did it all: presents under the tree and letters to Santa. And Maman always came and stayed with us to celebrate.

"Maman Mahin, open your eyes and see what Santa brought for me." Laila and Roya made sure their Maman Mahin saw every single present they received.

Maman had never been a morning person. She would lie on the sofa falling asleep while the girls opened their presents. "I hear in some traditions, presents are opened after midnight mass. You guys should do that too. This makes children too tired."

While I continued to prepare for a joyous Christmas, my doctors found a lump in one of my ovaries. I had a total hysterectomy. The lump in my ovary turned out to be benign.

Within one year, I'd had a bilateral mastectomy, chemotherapy, and a total hysterectomy. I had lost all of my female organs!

As I lay in bed in the hospital, I heard a choir walking along the hallway singing. Laila and Roya were at home with James and I was in the hospital by myself. Walking was very difficult with the fresh hysterectomy scar, but I got myself out of bed and stood at the door of my hospital room watching the Christmas carollers. Tears rolled down my face. I just wanted to be home with Laila and Roya.

Two years after my breast cancer, James packed his belongings. We had been together for seventeen years.

"I am leaving before anyone else gets sick," he said.

At first, James had wanted me to move out. A few years earlier, we had bought a house with a big yard. "You are too sick to take care of the house, the yard, and the girls, and I want half-time parenting."

I was sick, but I also felt an incredible strength within me and I was determined to be there for my daughters.

"Dad, today is Mom's birthday," the girls told their father as they watched him pack his belongings.

"Oh, shit! Do you want me to leave tomorrow? You know how I am with birthdays. I never remember birthdays."

My birthday became the official date of our separation.

37. Prayers and Ramadan

AFTER ALL THOSE YEARS, the first time I sat on my prayer rug and held the prayer beads in my hand, I felt as though I had arrived home. The many *termeh* that Baba had hid my jewellery in were left in my trunk for over twenty years. Now I took a couple of them out of the trunk and used them as prayer rugs. I closed my eyes and started saying the prayer that began with, "In the name of the compassionate God."

This prayer transported me to the time when Baba hugged me at the airport and said, "Daughter, may the compassionate God be your companion." That was the last time I saw Baba.

And now I remembered the dream I'd had when Baba was visiting me in Guelph. I had dreamt that I was in jail because I was married to a Baha'i. And Baba had gotten me out and had handed me a Quran. But when I walked out of the jail and looked back, there was no Baba and the Quran was no longer in my hand. I saw myself under a tree with my hands placed over my heart in prayer position. I felt safe, calm, and tranquil.

The dream finally made sense. I was in jail and Baba's soul was saving me once again. I had ignored and forgotten the power of prayers.

During my years of studying at the University of Guelph, I had dissociated myself from my culture and my spiritual practice in order to be accepted into my new life. When people asked me if I was Muslim, I responded, "I was raised Muslim. But I am not a practising Muslim anymore."

That was my standard reply. It sounded empowering to me in those years when my English was thick with a Persian accent.

Denying my Muslim heritage was my passport for integrating into Canada, especially when many misinformed people equated Islam with terrorism.

When I was in Iran, I didn't pray daily. But prior to the Islamic Republic, there had been periods of the year—like the holy month of Ramadan—when I had gravitated toward praying and fasting. Ramadan for Muslims comprises one month of fasting from sunrise to sunset. Ramadan is not a set month every year; the period is based on the lunar calendar.

Baba always fasted in Ramadan, but Maman could not because of her illness. Maman didn't encourage me to fast, but I loved the rituals, so I insisted on fasting from the age of seven. Baba and those servants who were fasting would get up before sunrise. They would turn on the Samovar to make tea and heat up any leftover dinner. The radio played the most beautiful special sunrise prayer for Ramadan. As a child, I didn't know the meaning of the sunrise prayer, but I loved how it sounded: it was mesmerizing.

Some mornings when I woke up, I would find out that I had missed the sunrise prayer and meal, and I would cry. But the mornings after the nights that we had *fesenjan*, my favourite Iranian stew, Baba would make sure to wake me up before the sunrise—he knew I wouldn't want to miss the leftovers. The base is made with sautéed onions and ground walnuts in pomegranate paste. The meat is prepared separately, and then added to this base to simmer for a couple of hours. Different meats were used in *fesenjan;* my favourite was small lamb meatballs. Like many leftovers, the stew always tasted better the next day.

When I lived in Iran, during the month of Ramadan, special foods were prepared all day long for the sunset meal called *eftar*. Different varieties of rice puddings were made throughout Ramadan. Mainly they were flavoured with cardamom, saffron, and rose water. They were prepared in the mornings and poured into small bowls to become cool for dessert. Stews and rice were made for the sunset meal as well.

I only fasted when Ramadan was in the fall or the winter. On those shorter, colder days, it was easier to go without food and water from sunrise to sunset. In the summer, it was too hot to go without water. When I would get home from school, the puddings

223

would be sitting in our guest-receiving room cooling down. We did not heat the guest-receiving room during winter unless there was a special gathering. The smell of saffron, cardamom, and rosewater always made my mouth water.

The temptation to eat was so strong some days I would break my fast at lunchtime, with Maman's encouragement. She helped me sew pieces of fabric together for each day that I broke my fast at lunch and then, at the end of Ramadan, I counted each piece as a half day of fasting. At the end of the Ramadan, I was proud to look at my little quilt.

What precious moments those were, sitting quietly and tallying up the days I had fasted. During the Shah's regime, we were not forced to fast during Ramadan; the restaurants served meals during the day. But when the Islamic Republic came into power, people were not allowed to drink or eat in public or in work places. Eating during fast time became an underground activity, except for children, pregnant women, the elderly, and the sick.

I stopped fasting during the reign of the Islamic Republic. The practice had lost its spirituality for me.

Ramadan also has a significant economic message: less food is purchased during the month of fasting. At the end of Ramadan, Muslims are encouraged to donate the money saved on food to the poor. There is a compassionate message as well: observe the hunger but don't feed the hunger; stay with the hunger. This encourages people to have empathy for those who do not have the luxury of satisfying their hunger.

There was always excitement in our house when we celebrated the *Eide Fetr*, the feast to break the fast, which takes place at the end of Ramadan. Baba, Maman, and all the servants would be busy bringing abundant supplies of rice, oil, beans, and many more other food items to the families suffering financial hardship.

Now after breast cancer and divorce, I was emotionally broken, physically ill, and struggling financially. When James and I separated, we had agreed on everything except one issue: spousal support. I had been a stay-at-home for ten years; James was legally obliged to pay spousal support, but he refused. It took four years until he agreed to pay some support. I felt just like I did in my dream, when I was sitting in jail. But, in my dream,

Baba walked to me holding a Quran in his hand and saved me from jail. Now I understand why the Quran disappeared from my hand—I had lost my faith for almost twenty years, but now realized that nothing could take away the seed of spirituality that had been planted in me many years earlier.

I closed my eyes and whispered, "Baba, please guide me out of this jail."

The Arabic words of Islamic prayers no longer resonated in my heart. Daily, I sat on the prayer rug and prayed. I created my own prayers in my own simple words—in English and Farsi.

"Catalyst"

Do not despair.
When you are in the midst of suffering,
Become an alchemist.

Every day add a pinch of a catalyst to your suffering
And let it simmer.

Love is my catalyst.
What is yours?

38. Paddling and Meditation

ONE DAY, SOON AFTER James left, the girls and I were driving to Penticton to spend a day on the beach when I spotted a tall man on the side of the road. He was wearing long, terra-cotta-coloured robe, and hitchhiking. I picked him up. His name was Leon.

I had heard about "Leon the Monk" a Buddhist monk who lived in a cave near Hedley. He was open to receiving visitors and sharing his guidance. I had wanted to see him for a long time, but I hadn't made the time. And then, suddenly, Leon showed up in my life when I was at my most vulnerable. I had been driving that same road for the past seven years but had never seen him before. Seeing him that day made me believe that I had guardian angels.

I asked him many questions. "I am so angry but I don't want to be angry. How do I stop worrying about my financial situation? How do I stop my racing thoughts? How do I lessen my anxiety of cancer coming back?"

When he answered, I felt as though he was pouring water over the fire. Leon asked me and the girls to visit him in his cave. A couple of weeks later, we went to visit him and we brought friends along with us too. It was a long hike—it was up hill and over three bridges. The last bridge, which was wooden and very narrow, was tricky to cross with just a thin cable to hold onto.

I was nervous. I didn't know much about Buddhism. What would I say to him? It turned out that I didn't need to say anything. He conversed easily and amiably with the children and with the adults. He made me feel so much at ease that I didn't feel the need to say anything.

His cave was designed beautifully on the inside. He had a devised a pulley system to hang his duvet and mattress up on the ceiling during the day. He had woollen curtains around his meditation cushions, so that when he was meditating he could pull the curtains all around to keep himself warm. He had turned another space in the cave into a kitchen.

When we arrived, there was a sign at the entrance to the cave letting us know that he was eating his meal. He only ate one meal a day. A young couple ahead of us were also waiting to see him. The couple visited for close to an hour with Leon before I had my opportunity.

"Where do I start, Leon?" I asked after Leon and I had chatted for awhile.

"Start a daily meditation ritual. There will always be ups and downs in life. The more you meditate, the less you will react emotionally to these ups and downs." Leon also spoke about creating a balance in my life independent of my children, a spouse, or material things. Later on I understood that Leon was teaching me about *detachment*—one of Buddhism's central concepts.

The girls and I decided to move to Penticton. I had no friends there, but we drove there on a regular basis to shop and spend time on the beach in the summer. I had always admired the beauty of Penticton, with its two shimmering blue lakes, the fruit orchards and vineyards, and the surrounding mountains.

I applied for many jobs. It did not help that I had been a stay-at-home mom for the past ten years. I was hired part-time at a local health food stores selling supplements, and earned close to minimum wage.

Laila and Roya were excited to show our new home to their Maman Mahin. James and I had sold our house, and I had bought a modest town home in Penticton. They had not seen Maman for a few months: she had been visiting Iran and had recently returned.

When the girls were in bed, I asked Maman to tell me about everyone back home. "Look at this photo of your Naneh JiJi. She still wears your red robe every day."

When I had visited London at the age of twelve, I had bought myself a beautiful red quilted housecoat. It only went to my knees so I grew out of it quickly, and I gave it to Naneh JiJi. Naneh JiJi and I were growing in opposite directions; I was getting taller and she was getting shorter. She had started bending from what I now know was osteoporosis. Naneh JiJi wore my red housecoat every day, all year round. The material was a hundred percent polyester. She washed it by hand and hung it to dry. The last image I have of my sweet sad Naneh JiJi before I left Iran is of her bent over in that red housecoat, a thin white scarf on her head. An elastic attached to her round black glasses kept them from slipping down those precious chubby cheeks while she washed clothes by hand all day. She spent almost all her time in the quiet of the laundry room in the courtyard of Baba Jafar and Maman Aterahm's house.

"Naneh JiJi said to tell you that, 'Mehrnaz jan, your coat keeps my bones warm. I will always pray for you,'" Maman said.

"I brought three folk costumes for the girls to share," Maman continued. "These are representatives of three regions in Iran: Baluchistan, Gilan, and Kurdistan." Maman had filled one big suitcase with these outfits and brought them from Iran for Laila and Roya.

"I remember this one. Maman, how old was I when we went to Kurdistan?"

"You must have been eight or nine years old." Maman started laughing. "I still remember the night you came home and began to cry because you wanted a particular Kurdish outfit."

"Maman, I remember it. It was the colour of this blue one."

"You loved your Aunt Munir's stories from Kurdistan. You asked her to teach you Kurdish dancing."

"Speaking of Kurdistan, did your brothers and sister manage to visit Uncle Dariush's grave in Kurdistan?"

"After months of no one being able to visit Dariush's grave, Vida, Dariush's fiancé, could not take it any longer. So she risked her life and went to the place where Dariush was buried, only to find out that he had been buried in a mass grave with the Kurdish freedom fighters. Vida organized the removal of his body and succeeded in reburying him. Your aunt managed to go to Dariush's new grave site a few years ago."

I remembered the anger, sadness, and frustration I had felt

when Uncle Dariush was murdered by the Islamic Republic. I remembered that at that age I had wanted the whole world to know about his murder. Now, I only wished to have the love and the courage he had had.

After we moved to Penticton, I stopped praying daily—I was too busy and distracted. I was overwhelmed living as a single mother in a new city with no network of friends or family. I desired balance in my life, and I knew that in order to achieve a peaceful and emotionally balanced life, I must practise meditation as Leon had suggested. But I couldn't sit and meditate by myself. It was anything but calming and relaxing. I would sit and what seemed like twenty minutes would only be three minutes, and the whole time I would be fighting to slow down my racing thoughts, trying not to think them.

I found a meditation group in Penticton that I could join. I was very nervous at that first gathering, *satsang*. The group meditation began. I closed my eyes, but after a couple of minutes, I wondered if everyone else's eyes were open, and worried that I would look ridiculous." So I opened my eyes and surreptitiously peered around the room. To my relief, I found that everyone's eyes were closed.

People were sitting either on their meditation cushions on the floor or on chairs. I had never sat in the lotus position before. I sat on the sofa cross-legged. My back started killing me. Every muscle in my body began aching. I don't know why I sat cross-legged. I never sat cross-legged at home. I wondered, how long the meditation was going to last.

I was so relieved when I heard the singing bowl to end the meditation. I opened my eyes. People were still sitting with their eyes closed. "Haven't they had enough?" I wondered.

I knew that I needed to bring myself to the present moment and slow down my thoughts, but even that was more triggering than calming—being in the now!

I decided to attend a day retreat facilitated by Moni Vangolen, a student of Eckhart Tolle. Her teaching was about being in the *now*. In the beginning, I huddled in the periphery during these gatherings. I did not know much and I was just a beginner.

During the question and answer periods, I generally stayed quiet, not wanting to attract attention, but this time I couldn't.

It was challenging to stay in the present moment with everything that was going in my life. Laila had been hospitalized for two weeks and we'd had to celebrate her birthday in the hospital room. I had decorated the room and brought Persian meals and cake to the hospital and we sang happy birthday in English and Farsi. I wanted to sob in that hospital room but I needed to show strength for my girls. Laila had to see me standing!

She had an infection in her hipbone—a side effect from the medication she was taking for her juvenile rheumatoid arthritis. My daughter was in so much pain. I sat by her bed, and talked about what we were going to do in the summer, our first summer in Penticton. We now lived two minutes away from the beach. She and I imagined all the things we would do in summer. She dreamed of floating along the channel, and she wanted me to get Roya and her their own big floaties. She also dreamt of packed lunches and picnics, and playing on the beach and in the water until sunset.

I asked Moni Vangolen, "How can I be in the *present moment,* when the present situation is too hard to endure?" I told Moni about sitting in the hospital with Laila, while she was in so much pain, and trying to distract her from her suffering by imagining with her a pleasant future, where she wouldn't be in pain and where instead she would be able to do the things that she enjoyed.

Moni looked at me with compassion and said, "Just keep doing what you've been doing." Moni did not take her eyes off mine. She nodded and let me know that she was feeling my pain. I had been a warrior all my life. My daughter's chronic illness was another battle for me. Moni's compassion made me cry. I don't know how long I cried. There were many people in the room—I had no thought about them. I just returned Moni's gaze and cried in complete silence.

I knew I was healing but it was such a slow journey and it felt I was *crawling* towards a distant light.

I later also joined the local breast cancer survivors' dragon boat team. It was healing to be on the water, and in the company of women who have been on the same journey. Sitting in the boat reminded me of my childhood at our villa. Jamal had a rowing boat—it was big enough for my cousins and us. He paddled us far from the shore and then we all jumped into the deep blue pristine water of the Caspian Sea. It was not easy to daydream at the dragon boat practices; we had to watch the paddlers ahead of us for timing and so we could be all in sync. We lost members to breast cancer recurrence; we attended their celebration of life together with our pink team shirt. Our team trained hard for races. I couldn't participate in the out-of-town races—it was costly—but I didn't want to let the team down so I joined them for one out-of-town race per summer. I took Laila and Roya along. A carnation ceremony was held at the end of the breast cancer race in memory of those who lost their lives to breast cancer. I would watch the faces of my daughters waving pink carnations on the shore and I sobbed with the thought of losing my life to breast cancer and not being around for them. The anxiety of cancer coming back was so real. The rate of cancer recurrence was high in the first five years of the diagnosis—I had a few months to go. I was told by my oncologist that with all the treatments that I had, lateral mastectomy, chemotherapy, and taking Tamoxifen, I have a sixty-five percent chance of surviving. Of course, I immediately calculated that thirty-five out of one hundred women would not survive.

I read every book that I could get my hands on, and listened to every audiobook and podcast available to learn techniques to bring calm into my life. I was also doing my best to prevent a breast cancer recurrence. My girls and I ate vegetarian foods, I meditated, I practiced Ashtanga yoga, and I did my best to be in the now when I could.

If I had the wisdom that I have now, I would've asked my doctor to give me the diagnosis but not the prognosis.

39. Unannounced Romance

AFTER MY SEPARATION FROM JAMES, I stayed single for almost seven years. Men asked me out, but I had created a long list of qualities that my ideal man must have. Without knowing it, I had built a wall around myself to protect me from being hurt again. I also no longer had the courage to share my body with anyone. I had too many scars and no breasts. Well, it wasn't just that; now, I was a woman without female organs—no breasts, no ovaries, and no uterus. I was afraid of the person I became when I was in a relationship. I had the tendency to stay in a relationship no matter how unhappy and abusive it became. I realized now it was my struggle with self-worth, but then I could not fathom why I had let myself become a victim in my relationship with both Sia and James. And I was afraid I would continue to make the same mistakes.

I abused myself by hating my body. I attracted abusive relationships because that's what I felt I deserved.

Seven years of no dating and no romance came to an end when I dropped by to see my friend at her art gallery. Her friend, Ethan, was also visiting her. But Ethan was with a woman so I assumed they were a couple. He and I chatted for a long time. His blue eyes, and the way he spoke to me—never taking his eyes away from mine—charmed me. As he spoke, his hands moved ever so gently in the air like strokes of a paint brush on canvas. The woman who was with him, an attractive woman in her thirties, was much younger than he was. He followed me right to the door and wouldn't stop talking to me.

Later, I was surprised and pleased when Ethan sent a friend

request on Facebook. I could not tell from his profile if he was single, but we started chatting on Facebook. I learned that Ethan was two years older than me and that he had retired early, and had chosen to live somewhere sunny and warm to avoid Canada's cold winters. However, he always came back for the summer.

One day, just as I was logging off my computer and getting ready to go for a walk along the beach at sunset, his name popped up on chat. I told him that I was going for a walk and asked him if he wanted to join me on the beach.

We met at the Japanese Garden behind our local art gallery, a place I loved. It was by Okanagan Lake and it had a beautiful view of the mountains and the lake. The garden was also delightfully designed with shrubs, trees, and a large pond with lilies.

When I got there, I just reminded myself that this could potentially be my first date after seven years. I was still not sure if Ethan was even available.

There was a definite chemistry between us and right away we started talking about our lives. The young woman I had seen him with was his ex-fiancée. Their relationship had ended the previous year.

"My problem is that I fall in love too quickly." He looked at me when he said that. He was not attempting to flirt with me; he was trying to justify him being married and divorced three times, as well as his recent relationship with his ex-fiancée. "I don't fool around or cheat though," he explained. "I grow out of love, and then I leave."

Normally, that would have frightened me. Normally, I would have walked away and never seen him again. But I was pulled towards him by forces that were beyond logic.

He asked me to go for a motorcycle ride the next day. "Have you seen the White Lake? We can stop at the lake and then go for lunch at a lovely rustic winery down the road from the lake."

I told him that I didn't know that lake and that I had not been on a motorcycle since I had been in a motorcycle accident at the age of nineteen.

"I've been on one most of my life. I haven't had any accidents. You'll be fine."

What was happening to me? I didn't know. I was fifty-one and I agreed to go on a motorcycle ride with him. I didn't give a second thought to the fact that since my breast cancer treatment, I had developed osteoporosis. I had chosen not to take any medication for it and I had been advised against activities like motorcycle riding. I decided quickly that Ethan did not need to hear that I had osteoporosis. After all, he'd already heard that I had breast cancer. Did I really need to list all my illnesses? Thankfully, it was a good summer for my lungs, so he didn't have to hear me coughing non-stop.

Ethan took a windy back road. He was going over a hundred kilometres per hour. I was terrified.

He stopped the motorcycle. "Are you okay? You are holding onto me so tight."

"I am really scared. You are going too fast," I gasped. He slowed down and I was less afraid then. I didn't tell him that the scene of my motor accident in Iran kept coming to my mind.

We stopped at White Lake. The rolling golden hills and the quiet of the lake calmed my mind. I wanted to reach out to him and hold him. I hadn't felt this desire for many years. But I didn't allow myself to do that. We got back on the motorcycle; the road was windy and downhill but he was going slow and I was loving it. Finally we reached a gem of a winery with a stunning view of the valley, and the lake. I was feeling what I had been missing for so long: sitting across from a man, looking into his eyes, the gravity of attraction pulling me toward him. I can't remember what I ate for lunch in that beautiful winery, under a sunny blue sky and the protective shade of a tree, but I do remember Ethan's blue eyes. We spent the whole day together. After lunch, we went for a walk above the beach on a cliff and then lay on the grass under an old tree. He closed his eyes and took a nap, but I kept my eyes open and savoured the moments of togetherness.

"Can we have dinner together?" Ethan said.

I invited him for dinner at my place—a light dinner—it was a hot September day. I made a Greek salad and served it with baguette. Then we had some dark chocolate with Persian tea for dessert. It was getting late and we were both tired, but I still did not want him to go. He finally got up to leave. He grabbed his helmet and leaned over to kiss my cheek good night. I turned my face and kissed him on the lips. Hello, courage!

I wanted to make love with him and share my "imperfect body" with him. I didn't want to contemplate for days how I would tell him about my body, or worry about what his reaction would be. Or, after how many dates I would have to tell him about my body. No, I didn't want to do this anymore.

He was kissing my neck and my chest when I said, "I am keeping my bra on. These are prosthetics; I have no breasts."

"Do what makes you comfortable; either way is fine with me. All I know is I'm making love to a gorgeous woman."

We both just wanted to be together. Everything flowed and nothing felt rigid. One day he got me a present, *Portraits* by Steve McCurry, a book of his photographs of people from around the world. "If the photographer saw your eyes, your portrait would be in this book, too," Ethan said. We had tea and looked at the portraits for a couple of hours together. Ethan was entering my heart and I felt no fear.

We were together every day, until one morning, when Ethan brought tea to bed for me. I looked him in the eyes and told him, "We are done!" At first he thought I was joking, but I wasn't.

It was a whisper that got loud and clear—a soul whisper! The same energy that had pulled me to him was now pulling me away from him, without loving him any less. I understood that falling in love for some people was an addiction—it was the best rush. I wouldn't be any different from his three ex-wives and his ex-fiancée. He would "grow out of love" for me too.

Ethan was a good man and he never had anything negative to say about the previous women in his lives, "It was just me growing out of love; it had nothing to do with them."

Ethan was shocked and sad when I asked him to leave.

The first day after we broke up, I was fine, but it hit me hard afterwards. Even though I was hurting, I was grateful that Ethan had been in my life. I had denied myself love and passion for too long. He broke down the gate to my heart and entered so suddenly and I had once again tasted the nectar of life—love.

I thought having a soul mate meant when two people love each other and stay together forever. After being with Ethan I tossed out the old definition of soul mate and wrote a new one: we are on a journey and this journey leads us to many paths and on each path there is a place and the time that a soul mate might show up and guide us to the next path. This meeting of a soul mate could be dreamy and filled with love, or it could rock our ship. Either way, our soul mates show up to guide us closer to our own essence. Ethan showed up at the right time. He showed me that soul mates see each other beyond their mind and body, and that love is beyond our physical being.

If I hold you in my heart, you'll wither;
Become a thorn if I hold you in my eyes.
No, I'll make a place for you within my soul instead
So you'll be my love in lives beyond this life.
—Rumi

I did not hear from Ethan for a few months and I missed him. Then one day he messaged me. He wanted us to get back together, but he was away at the time. Nevertheless, we started chatting again.

I had just finished reading a book, *If the Buddha Dated: A Handbook for Finding Love on a Spiritual Path* by Charlotte Kasl. I felt encouraged to go out and look for love again after reading this book, so I signed up for online dating. I had been working on a list of qualities that I hoped to find in a man for seven years prior to meeting Ethan. Ethan didn't meet all of my criteria. But drawing up the list made it easy for me to answer the questions about the kind of man I was looking for. I signed up for three months. I found online dating very time consuming, however. It seemed that men who contacted me hadn't taken the time to read my profile and see what I was looking for on my dates. I was getting requests from twenty-year-olds to eighty-year-old men. I only went on a couple of dinner dates with one man, but I never felt any connection to him.

Just when my online dating subscription was running out, I met Neil. He had many qualities that I was looking for in a man: he meditated, he practised yoga, he had been vegan for twenty years, he loved nature, and he was athletic. I admired his calm nature. When we were together, we did yoga, meditated, read books, hiked, and paddled.

Some time later, Ethan messaged that he was back in town and wanted to see me. He knew I was seeing Neil; I had posted enough photos of Neil and me on Facebook so that Ethan would see that Neil was real. Did I really post those photos for Ethan to see or was it for me? Had I needed to assure myself that I was with Neil and had moved on from Ethan?

Ethan and I decided to meet at our usual spot behind the art gallery and go for a walk along the Kettle Valley Railroad trail. It was a beautiful autumn day. He messaged again and suggested we meet earlier and visit the exhibition at the art gallery, the *Griffin & Sabine Trilogy*, before going on our walk.

Neil lived in White Rock, a four or five hour drive from Penticton. He knew about Ethan, and I had told him that I was meeting him.

The exhibition was beautiful and romantic. I realized I was still in love with Ethan. I was happy with Neil, but not in love.

"Have you read the *Griffin & Sabine Trilogy*?"

I shook my head.

"I've read all three. It's such a romantic story. Why don't you sit and let me read one of the books to you? These are just letters. It won't take long."

I sat on a bench beside Ethan, surrounded by the paintings from the *Griffin & Sabine Trilogy,* and listened to him read from the book to me.

After saying goodbye to Ethan that day, I knew that I could no longer be with Neil, even though we had been for a year. I wanted to be with a man who insisted on me sitting down so he could read me a romantic book!

40. Amir

IRECEIVED A DIPLOMA IN ACCOUNTING, and was teaching accounting at the Continuing Studies Department at our local college. I was also doing bookkeeping from home.

I was gradually finding a new balance as a single mom, in my life. I had started paddling with Outrigger Canoe Club. Paddling Dragon Boat with survivors made me realize that I loved paddling and I especially loved long-distance paddling. Dragon Boat paddling was more like a sprint—the aim of practise was to train for five hundred metre races; outrigger canoes were used for long-distance paddles.

I also continued my Ashtanga yoga practise, but daily meditation was still a challenge. I now owned two beautiful meditation cushions and I had learned to sit in a lotus position. I also had a beautiful altar with a statue of Tara—a female Buddha—in the middle, but I had no luck harnessing my racing thoughts. Training my body physically and creating a beautiful altar had both been easy, but stilling my mind continued to be a challenge.

One afternoon, a Buddhist teacher, Philip Starkman, whose silent retreats I had attended, was having tea with me at my house. Looking back, whenever I was given the chance to be around a monk or a Buddhist teacher, I see that I craved answers. It was like sitting beside natural spring water when you're very thirsty. I didn't want just to drink the water from the spring, I wanted every cell of my body to soak it up. I wanted to be immersed in it.

"Philip, I've have been meditating for a few years now. I'm meditating on creating equanimity and balance in my life. But it's not working. I trained my body and I can sit in lotus position, but why is it still so hard for me to go deeper in my meditation practise?"

"Join a *Satsang*. The collective energy of the group will assist you in staying on your spiritual path." *Satsang* is a Sanskrit word that means a community that practices together for the purpose of cultivating awareness, and truth.

"But there is no meditation group here." The one I had joined earlier had dissolved.

Philip looked around my living room where we were sitting having tea. "This is a good place for a *Satsang*. You can start a group meditation in your house."

I used many excuses to explain why holding group meditations in my home was not a good idea. But, mainly, I was not confident that I could actually host a group meditation because I was so new to meditation myself. There were many other people in town who had been going for years to ashrams in India or retreats around the world. They knew many gurus and spiritual teachers. So, my instinct was to put it off; but then I gathered all my courage and started hosting a meditation group.

To my surprise, many people attended, from brand new beginners to people who had been meditating for a long time. I looked forward to our gatherings, the collective energy, and our chats over tea after.

Maman's eightieth birthday was approaching. She wasn't physically able to live independently, anymore, so she moved to an assisted living facility in my town.

I had planned a small gathering for her birthday and insisted that Amir, who had moved with his family from Dubai to Canada, come join us. Maman was glowing at her birthday party; she was so happy that Amir was there. I never thought that Maman, who had been so sick most of her life, would make it to the age of eighty. She never gave up. She had always fought hard to be with us, and when she was around Laila and Roya, I could see in her eyes that she felt her fight had been worth it, in spite of all the physical pain. For Maman's birthday present, Laila and Roya framed the photo of Maman with the Shah. It had been taken when she had approached him to request funding for the Qazvin orphanage.

The girls were happy to spend time with Amir. Laila and Roya didn't have many relatives from their father's side, and my big family had spread all over the world after the Iranian revolution. They had only met a small number of my relatives, but they were close to Amir and his family. He was planning to stay with us for a few days, so Maman stayed overnight after her birthday party at my house. She did not want to miss a moment of being with Amir.

I was making breakfast in the morning and Maman was sitting in the living room. Amir went to the basement to wake up Laila. She was nineteen and was working at the local nightclub. I was nervous about her working there at such a young age, but Laila was independent and made her own decisions. I almost wanted to ask Amir not to wake her up because she had worked until late, but today was the last day Amir would have with her before she went off to stay with her boyfriend in another town. I thought he would not want to miss spending more time with Laila. We all had breakfast together but then Laila left the house immediately without saying anything.

"Mom, something bad happened and Dad is telling me not to tell you. I won't be coming home," Laila announced on the phone.

I phoned James. "Is Laila okay? What's happened?"

"She is fine, but something has happened and she doesn't want to share it with you right now," James said.

Amir and Maman kept telling me not to worry; that everything would be fine.

I heard noises in the house around five in the morning, and I thought it was Laila coming home. I'd hardly slept that night, but now that I knew Laila was home I could relax and sleep for a few more hours. When I got up in the morning, her bed was empty. I went downstairs and saw a note on the kitchen table.

"I am so disappointed about how your daughters turned out." The note was from Amir. "They took me to a house to buy marijuana for them. My camera is missing. I am ashamed of the way they turned out. I suffer from depression...."

Then Amir phoned me from the airport. He repeated what he had written in the letter, then he told me his money was missing. Amir had changed his flight and left two days early.

I phoned James right away. "Amir sexually abused Laila," he said.

When Amir had gone down to the basement, he had started massaging Laila and inappropriately touched her underwear. At first, Laila was asleep, but she woke up to his touch and then heard the clicking sound of a camera and then a flash. By then, he was lying on top of her. She pushed him away and ran upstairs. Later, she checked his camera and found many photos of her and Roya.

"Smile ... look this way ... turn that way," he would tell them again and again. He took so many photos of them and I had thought, "How sweet of him, he wants to show the girls' photos to his family." But he was only taking photos of their bodies, without their faces. Laila took a photo of one of the shots with her cell phone and texted it to her boyfriend. Then she deleted all the photos from Amir's camera. Her boyfriend told her to leave. She also phoned James, "Take the camera with you. Maybe the police can retrieve the photos."

By the time I found out what had happened, Amir had left the province. We reported the sexual abuse to the police. They investigated, but did not charge him. We were told that if we wanted to go further with the case, we would have to hire a lawyer.

All my life, I had done everything I could to prevent my daughters from being harmed, and now Laila had been sexually abused by a member of my family.

I sobbed for an entire week. Amir was a Massoudi. He was a part of many of my memories from Iran. I couldn't talk to anyone.

"James, please keep Laila for a few days. I don't want her to see me in this shape. I was of no help to her." Roya was shocked and felt betrayed, but she kept her feelings to herself.

I sat to meditate. I needed to breathe but I couldn't. The group meditation was scheduled in a week. I kept thinking I should cancel the session, but somehow I didn't. Later, sitting with the group in silence allowed me to breathe.

After the group meditation, I had the strength to call Aunt Masi and tell her what had happened.

I remember that I had been frightened for Amir when I was in Dubai and he had been accused of raping a woman. Now, I felt rage and betrayal. He was sixty years old. How many women had been the victims of his sexual abuse?

The following year, I gathered all my energy to celebrate Maman's eighty-first birthday, but it was tainted by the horrible event of the year before. After her party, on the anniversary of Amir's crime, I sent him an email and informed him that I would be contacting every relative and mutual friend in Iran and abroad, to tell them what he had done. This was my first contact with him after he'd phoned me from the airport a year earlier.

The response from the Massoudi family and other relatives was heartbreaking. Many of my very close cousins phoned and wrote back to say that they were disappointed that I'd shared the news with everyone.

"The Massoudi family is highly respected in the community. You must not do this to the Massoudi family. We don't want our husbands to know about this. Our husbands are honoured to have married into the Massoudi family."

I remembered that when Vafa and I were still living at home, I would walk out of my bedroom and find him sitting around with women and gossiping. I would scold him, "Vafa, you are gossiping again."

I did not like gossips.

"*Ghaybat nist haghyghate;* it's not gossip; it is truth," he would say, rolling his eyes at me and continuing to gossip.

Now I phoned him and told him, "Vafa, please tell everyone about what Amir did. I want everyone to know he is a sick man, so no one will get hurt by him again."

Amir was a sick man, but the silence of the people around him gave him the power to hurt more innocent people.

When Vafa tried to spread the news, most of my female cousins silenced him, "Mehrnaz jan, they told me to be quiet and not to mention a word to anyone! Don't upset yourself with them.

You must think about your health. Your voice worries me. You're coughing so much."

I practised meditating daily, even though most of it was spent thinking horrifying thoughts about what Amir had done. Why had I trusted him with my daughters? Why hadn't I stopped him going downstairs to wake Laila up? Why?

I wondered what the purpose was of Phillip showing up only a few weeks before this incident and suggesting that I hold group meditations at my home. Was it a mere coincidence that he had showed up that particular day? It was because of Phillip that I was offering the group meditations in my home throughout this difficult time. And it was only during these group meditations that I could calm down and not be at war with myself or with Amir.

During my free time, I listened to Tara Brach's podcasts. She was an American psychologist and a Buddhist teacher. I listened to more than hundreds of her podcasts. Her dharma talks and guided meditations also helped me tremendously.

41. Sexual Abuse

"I AM SHOCKED! I can't believe Amir would sexually abuse Laila. I am not going to share this with my husband. Something like this has never happened in the Massoudi family."

I was listening to a cousin on the phone.

"What do you mean?" I asked. "How about those Massoudi men who were found having sex with the servants? I remember many of those cases, don't you?"

"Yes, I do remember, but that was different. They were servants!"

My cousin's comment ignited something in me that I had never been aware of before: Iranian men who had servants treated them like slaves in plantations. I'd read so many books and watched many movies of the lives of African slaves, but I didn't remember the servants in Iran being treated like that. This opened my eyes to a sad era in Iranian history that I had witnessed, but that I hadn't understood at the time.

I walked back and forth, pacing the floor, until it was seven in the morning Iran time. I didn't want to call earlier and wake up Vafa. "Please tell me, Vafa. Did Baba sexually abuse or rape any of the servants?"

"Haji was an angel. But I know that many men in your relatives didn't stay away from the servants. Amir was dirty, but never in a million years would I have imagined that he would touch Laila." Vafa was crying. "Mehrnaz jan, you're coughing. Since the abuse, every time you talk on the phone with me, you keep coughing. I'm so worried for you."

When we lived in Tonekabon, our gardener, who was living

at our orange grove with his wife and children, had started helping out with the school superintendent's yard work. The superintendent and his wife were friends of my parents. When their teenage servant became pregnant, the superintendent and his wife demanded our gardener marry her, even though he was already married. Muslim men were allowed to marry four wives. Our gardener was a sleazy man, but he claimed that he had only fooled around with the servant and that he didn't have sex with her. "The master is having sex with her," the gardener had said to my parents. When the baby was born, a blood test showed that the baby was the child of the superintendent.

"What happened to the servant and her baby?" I asked Maman. Maman knew of many sexual abuse cases but she did not want to talk about them now.

"She was sent back to the village."

I remembered that many of the wives would blame the servant when they found their husbands were having sex with her. And then the servant would be sent back to her village. I remembered so many similar stories. I had heard of one young servant who had been raped by her employer. In that case, the wife had told her husband that it was *their* responsibility to take care of the girl, since no one would marry her now that she was no longer a virgin. So the servant stayed and served her rapist, his wife, and his children. I went to this house many times and this servant cooked the meals and cleaned my dishes. I knew her story. How could I have been so insensitive?

Now, as a mother of two daughters, it breaks my heart to think about the mothers who sent their daughters and sons off to be servants so they could have a better future, only for them to be sexually abused and raped by the men of the house.

My eyes had been opened and I couldn't stop looking for evidence of abuse in my family. I found out that a cousin had been sexually abused by Amir when she was eight years old and Amir was in his thirties. When that cousin heard my daughter's story, she cried and shared her own story with her mother for the first time. My cousin was in her late thirties then and she had never told anyone else before. I have no doubt that there were more children and women in our extended family who were sexually abused by Amir, who chose not to come forward because they knew that they would be condemned by their parents, husbands, and relatives.

Vafa and a few other relatives began admitting that there had been other instances of sexual abuses in our extended family. The victims were not only the servants. I learned, for example, that a beautiful little girl, who I loved so much, was sexually abused by her stepfather, and about another young teenager who was sexually abused by her uncle. There were so many that had fallen victim to sexual abuse and, to this day, those men, the perpetrators, are respected and living without shame.

This behaviour is not in any way unique to the Massoudi and my extended family. Iran is a male-dominated society and follows Islamic law to this day. The voice of a woman is not equal to that of a man. If a woman witnesses a crime, her testimony counts for only half of that of a male witness. It requires two female witnesses to equal the testimony of one male witness. So many women choose to stay silent in the face of evil because their voices will not be heard.

I grew up hearing, "Men have greater sexual needs and desires than women." In Iran, men can have four wives, and they can also have *sigheh* or temporary marriage, which allows them to have sex with a woman for a period of time without having to marry her. The men go to a *mullah* or a Muslim minister and ask them to marry them temporarily, for a few minutes, or months, or years. This is especially encouraged for men who travel, so when they do not have the convenience of having sex with their wives, their needs can still be met.

Muslim men must not look at a woman's body or her face. It is a sin if they look at a female body or a face, even if the woman is covered. Practising Muslims walk with their heads down. The purpose of the *hijab* is to cover the women's hair and the curve of the bodies, which are considered sexual temptations for men. In Islam, only the face and the hands of women can be uncovered. But men can wear pants and shirts without needing a robe to cover their bodies.

Child brides are still legal in Iran. The minimum age of marriage for girls in Iran is thirteen. Of this, I am appalled.

42. Never Without Love

I WAS WALKING DOWN THE HALLWAY at the old age home, visiting Maman one afternoon. She had been transferred from assisted living to a nursing home. There was a photo of each resident on the wall beside their door. This helped residents with dementia to find their rooms. It was only Maman's body that was failing, not her mind. I stopped and looked at her photo. Her long white hair was braided, her smile was beautiful, and her eyes.... Well, the expression in one's eyes doesn't change with age.

I couldn't walk away from Maman's door. I was drawn to her photo. Now in her eighties, I saw love in the purest form in Maman's eyes when she looked at Laila and Roya. I was grateful that in spite of all the pain and suffering that she had endured, she had lived long enough for Laila and Roya to receive their Maman Mahin's unconditional love.

Roya was sixteen when she began insisting on getting a tattoo. I felt she was too young for it.

"Maman Mahin, what is your favourite phrase? I want to tattoo your favourite phrase on my arm," Roya asked Maman.

I thought Maman would tell her not to tattoo her skin. But instead she said, "*Bedoone eshgh hargez.*"

Never without love.

I gasped! I thought this was Baba's favourite phrase, not Maman's.

Ethan was coming home for summer; we were meeting at our usual spot—the Japanese Garden behind the art gallery. It happened that on that same day, in the morning, I was attending the celebration of life of a friend of mine. The celebration was taking place on a lovely property overlooking Okanagan Lake. There were many people, most of whom I didn't know. I was gazing out at the view and thinking of my friend who'd passed, when her sister, Liz, joined me with a friend of hers.

"Do you remember, Daniel?"

I looked at her puzzled. I hadn't met him before. Then she refreshed my memory: he was a physician who was interested in alternative health and, yes, Liz had talked to me about him before. Liz left and we kept chatting. He could not hide the crush he had for me. He had heard from Liz that I had breast cancer and was interested in my approach to living healthy. We chatted about how medicine was failing those who fell in the grey area—patients with chronic disease. Daniel was an orthopaedic surgeon, a Harvard graduate. He bought a property near here to get away. His primary residence was in Seattle. He said that he was interested in attending meditation at my place; I gave him my phone number.

That afternoon, I went for a long paddle on my paddleboard and wondered if the universe had conspired to have me meet Daniel on the same day that I was going to see Ethan. A long solo paddle was what I needed to clear my mind.

I showed up at the garden and Ethan was there already. We hugged, he held me, and I melted in his arms. People were walking by but I claimed that moment of togetherness without any apology. We did not kiss on the lips. We had not kissed on the lips since the day he brought me tea in bed and I told him it was finished between us. Ethan and I walked for a while and then sat and talked on the beach until long past midnight.

The next morning, I got up early and joined the Sunday paddle with the Outrigger Canoe Club. We paddled more than twenty kilometres—a great cure for racing thoughts. After the paddle there were two voicemails: one from Daniel, the other from Ethan. They both asked me to go for dinner that night.

Now fast forward to the next year. "Naz, you've been seeing Daniel for a while. Are you planning on getting married?" Ethan asked. He was back in town.

"You are the only person who still calls me Naz."

"I can tell that you are not in love with Daniel. Mehrnaz, listen to your heart! Did I pronounce it right? 'Mehrnaz'?"

He could see right through me. He knew I was still in love with him. In that moment, I felt pain—the pain that I could never be with Ethan, but for a millisecond I imagined, 'What if...? Would I marry him?'

"Ethan, maybe one day I will marry you."

"When? In this life time?"

"Three years today." No idea why I chose three.

"Let's get that promise tattooed. What's the date, today? September 9th?" He pulled me by the arm and walked me toward the tattoo parlour and the tattoo artist gave Ethan an appointment.

Ethan wanted to tattoo the date on his shoulder. I told him about Maman's favourite phrase, "*bedoone eshgh hargaz*—never without love." Roya didn't tattoo it. Her dad changed her mind; he didn't like the two negatives in "never without love." Instead, she had tattooed the words, "Always With Love," in English.

"How can we get 'never without love' in Farsi script?"

"Ethan, you know that we will never..."

He interrupted me and said, "I know! Just promise me: 'never without love.'"

Maman's friend in Vancouver, Nariman, who does beautiful Farsi calligraphy, wrote it for us. Daniel saw the writing and he thought I should frame it. "It says, 'Never Without Love, Ethan.' It's for his shoulder, not for my wall." Daniel didn't ask why Ethan was getting this tattoo. When Daniel and I started dating, he had told me that for him it was love at first sight, but knew that I didn't feel the same way.

I stood by Ethan holding his hand while he was getting the tattoo. The Farsi phrase looked like it *belonged* on Ethan's shoulder.

"What date did you say you wanted to put on?" the tattoo artist asked.

"Ethan, let's not tattoo the date."

"Are you sure?" He was still lying down on the table.

"Yes! No date."

43. This Precious Moment

MY ALARM WENT OFF. It was five in the morning. I boiled water for green jasmine tea, grabbed a wool shawl, and headed to the rooftop of the hotel. I'd been staying in Whistler B.C., and was planning to join the sunrise meditation led by Davidji. This was my morning routine during the five-day Chopra's Seduction of Spirit retreat. I was there to learn from Deepak who believes, "*You Are the Universe*. Each of us is a co-creator of reality extending to the vastest reaches of time and space." When Deepak was asked about his spiritual teacher, he answered that he read Rumi every day.

> *You are not a drop in the ocean.*
> *You are the entire ocean in a drop.*
> —Rumi

It was in that moment that I understood the true meaning of what Great Aunt Anise had said to me when I was leaving Iran. "Mehrnaz jan, you make sure to take this book of Hafiz with you. It is an essential companion, especially in the land of no family and friends." Rumi and Hafiz are Persian mystical poets from the thirteenth and fourteenth centuries. Aunt Anise sent me off with a book by her spiritual teacher, Hafiz. Such a long journey!

> *I wish I could show you*
> *When you are lonely or in darkness*
> *The astonishing light of your own being.*
> —Hafiz

Sitting in silence, I visualized myself as the entire ocean. I was not merely riding the waves—I was the waves. Then I saw my four-year-old self, engulfed in flames, burning. She'd been waiting for me, all these years, to dip her in this ocean. I dipped her in the ocean then I looked at her and said, "For so long, I saw you as a beauty only with clothes on; without clothes, I saw you as a beast. I am sorry. I love you. Please forgive me."

In this lifetime, there is only one person we must forgive and that is oneself!

I was visiting Maman, when a staff member entered the room and said, "Mahin, this afternoon is the service at the chapel. Would you like to go?"

When Maman had moved to the old age home, I was called to attend a meeting because there was some confusion. "I am told that your mother is Muslim, but she attends the services at the chapel," the chaplain said at the meeting.

"Tell the chaplain that there is only one God, and the God in the chapel is the same God in the mosques of Muslims," Maman replied.

"Could you ask your mother if she wishes me to sit by her when she leaves this life?" the chaplain then asked.

I did. And Maman nodded. "Yes, I would appreciate that," she said.

"There is a community of Muslims here," the chaplain continued. "Does she wish me to connect her with them?"

"No!" Maman was adamant. "I do not need to connect with a religious community. I just need to be around people when they pray. I love the energy of the room when everyone is praying. I say my own Islamic prayers when I am in the chapel. I don't have to be in a mosque to pray."

A year later, I sat holding Maman's hand for three days while she was in transition. The nursing home staff set up a cot in Maman's room that I slept on for two nights, but on the third night I slept beside Maman in her narrow electrical bed holding her, knowing that I would always miss her. "Maman, I am so grateful that you are granting me this chance to see you in such peace, feeling no pain in these last days of your life," I whispered in her ears.

The chaplain came by daily and sat by Maman's bed. He read Maman her favourite prayers and sang "Amazing Grace." I had no idea that Maman had favourite prayers. Did she understand what the prayers meant or did she simply like listening to the sound of the prayers? And she liked "Amazing Grace"? This was new to me. The chaplain told that me that Maman loved it when he sang "Amazing Grace" to her in his own language.

He was Creole. He was born in Haiti but had been adopted and raised in Canada. Initially I felt a wall between me and the chaplain, but slowly I looked forward to him coming to sit beside Maman. He didn't speak much to me, but every time he left Maman's bedside, he put his hand on my shoulder, and that gesture made tears stream down my face and onto Maman's hand.

I had felt resentment towards Maman for distracting herself with her social life and not being emotionally available to us, her children. But, in recent years, as I heard *her story,* I let go of my resentment. And now, sitting on the cot next to Maman's bed, listening to the sound of her breathing and witnessing her transition to the other realm, was a precious moment. Saying goodbye was sad, and I cried like a small child whose mother had suddenly been taken away from her. But in that moment, I also felt the perfection of her spirit aligning with my soul and, then, there was nothing but Love.

"This Perfection"

When I was young,
The burn scars on my body terrified me.
No one told me
When I got older,
Every scar would have a story to tell in the garden of love.

When I was young,
How I searched for the groom of my dream.
No one told me
When I got older,
I would be a "bride married to amazement."

When I was young,
How I longed for perfection.

No one told me,
When I got older,
The only perfection would be in that moment
When I looked at a flower in bloom,
When I heard the call of an owl,
When I let the waves carry me on my board.

And when, in that perfect moment,
In that beautiful spot on the lake,
I scattered my mother's ashes.
Oh, would I see a fish nibble on her ashes?
That was her wish.
Oh, this perfection.

Acknowledgements

It takes a soul tribe to publish a book.

To Cathryn Matthes, my coach editor: I literally couldn't have done it without you. Thank you for helping me to weave this Persian tapestry of *Never Without Love*.

To Nina Shoroplova, my fabulous editor of earlier versions of this memoir, thank you for making everything go smoothly.

Gratitude to the team at Inanna Publications and especially Luciana Ricciutelli, Editor in Chief, for seeing the beauty and the power of my story, and especially for her skilfull editing of the final version of this book.

To Laila and Roya, my love for you gave me the courage to rise, roar, and write.

Mehrnaz Massoudi was born in Iran and immigrated to Canada in 1983 after the Iranian revolution and in the midst of the Iran-Iraq war. She obtained her Bachelor of Science degree from the University of Guelph, Ontario, and worked as a molecular biologist at Mount Sinai Hospital in Toronto and the University of British Columbia in Vancouver. She integrates her science background with her knowledge of meditation to guide seekers toward new levels of self-love, courage, and inner tranquility.